# MASGAGE

## *a career* at *your fingertips*

## FIFTH EDITION

The Complete Guide To Becoming A Bodywork Professional

# MARTIN ASHLEY

## ENTERPRISE PUBLISHING

*Bound.*

Published by Enterprise Publishing
P.O. Box 530 / 3 Londonderry Lane
Somers, New York 10589
(914) 248-0325

courtesy of Bancroft School of Massage Therapy, Worcester, MA
All other illustrations by Lorrie Klosterman
Cover design by Renée Skuba, New York, NY
Typesetting by PDS Associates, Allenhurst, NJ

Publisher's Cataloging-in-Publication Data

Ashley, Martin
  Massage: a career at your fingertips : Martin Ashley. — 5th ed.
  p. cm.
  Includes index.
  ISBN 0-9644662-5-2


  1. Massage—Vocational guidance. 2. Massage—Practice. I. Title.

RA780.5.A75 2006 615.8'22'023

10 9 8 7 6 5 4 3 2 1

# Contents

## III: Sex, Gender and Touch

## IV: Business, Practical and Legal Information for the Practitioner

Why buy insurance; kinds of insurance available to the professional bodyworker: professional liability, business liability, business insurance, disability insurance, medical insurance

## VI: Bodywork Organizations and Trainings

## VII: How to Choose a Massage School

This book is dedicated to my parents,
Sam and Sarah Ashley,
who gave me the luxury of a good education and plenty of slack;
to my wife Deborah who puts up with me every day
whether she likes it or not
and to my children Joshua and Rachel,
two remarkable individuals beginning to create their lives.

# Acknowledgments

I want to thank Doug Brodeff, who gave me the idea to write this book. I am also grateful to Pete Whitridge, who took the time to read the original manuscript and give me many helpful criticisms and suggestions.

This Fifth Edition was prepared with the assistance of Lynn Zephryna, a teacher at Twin Lakes College school of massage in Santa Cruz, California.

In addition, the following massage and bodywork practitioners all contributed to the writing of this book by allowing me to interview them, or by furnishing useful information or reference material. Thank you all.

Paul D. Arneson
Lauren S. Bain
Kathleen Bennett
Ann W. Bertland
Wes Boyce
Gordon E. Bradford
Alberto Breccia
Iris Brown
William T. Bunting
Sharon Callahan
Robert Calvert
Norman Cohen
Karen E. Craig
Paul Davenport
Jo Anne Davies
Patrick Dempsey
Doug Deyers
Bob Fasic
Adeha Feustel
Andre Fountain
A. Ann Gill
J. Joy Gottus
Roy Gottus
Ruth R. Haefer
Susanne Setuh Hesse
Pamela Hodgson
Stuart Holland
Sita Hood
Shirley Hooker
Jeff Hopkins
Jeffrey Kates
Deborah A. Kimmet
Bob King
Apara Kohls

Shivam Kohls
Scott Lamp
Mae Leone
Glenn Lloyd
Jerrine F. Manders
Danila Mansfield
Charles Mardel
Massage Magazine
Maureen A. Miller
Artie Mosgofian
Ginann Olmstead
Grieg A. Osmundson
David Palmer
Cindy Patterson
Laura Perna
Anna Pekar
Chad Porter
Cate I. Rainey
Deeta Rasmussen
Kay E. Richey
Dennis Simpson
Timothy Starbright
Christiana Stefanoff
Bruce Stephens
Kathy Tanny
Debbie Thomas
Jack Thomas
John "Shane" Watson
Dana S. Whitfield
Sherri Williamson
Carl S. Yamasaki
Etelka M. Zsiros

# Introduction
## Who This Book Is Written For

When I was embarking on a massage career in 1982, there was no source to turn to for information about the field, educational programs, or equipment. There has been an incredible amount of change in the field since then.

My idea in creating this book was to provide you with everything you need to know in order to consider, plan and execute a career in massage or bodywork. This book will not only help you decide whether to get into the field, but will help you make all the plans and choices that bring you a rewarding career. No other source contains the information you can find in this volume.

### For the novice:

For someone contemplating a massage or bodywork career, this is truly one-stop-shopping for all the essential information you will need. First you will find an over-view of a career in massage or bodywork Next you will be guided through choosing a career path, acquiring a clientele, and opening an office. Business skills, bookkeeping, record-keeping, filing income taxes, receiving insurance reimbursement, massage laws nationwide, and even saving for retirement are all covered. Finally, there is a reference section that includes over one hundred equipment manufacturers and distributors, 62 forms of bodywork, and a guide to searching out and finding the best massage school to suit your particular needs.

### For the massage student:

If you are already enrolled in a massage school, this book will expand on your school's courses in business, ethics, marketing and legal issues, or you may be using it as the textbook for your Business and Professionalism course.

The practical information about career strategies, bodywork modalities, marketing your services, opening a massage office, ethics and boundaries, billing insurance companies, legal issues, taxes, professional associations, professional politics, and sample forms, will be useful to you for years to come.

### For the practitioner:

If you are already a trained and practicing massage therapist or bodyworker, you will still find much of value in this book to help you expand your practice and be more successful. The chapters on marketing, ethics, opening a private office, working with abuse survivors, insurance reimbursement, scientific evidence for massage and income tax may give you information you do not have. You may also be interested in bodywork modalities, schools teaching different modalities, and requirements for practice in states you might move to.

You may also want to have this book in your library for the time when an aspiring massage therapist asks you how to get started in the field. It could save you a lot of time!

Browse the table of contents and see if you aren't interested in learning more. And whether you are investigating a new career, already in massage school, or already in practice, I hope you find much in this book that you value and enjoy.

# Introduction to the Fifth Edition

In 1992, when the original edition of this book was published, massage was still seen as being on the fringe of society, not part of the mainstream. Each new edition since then has reflected the remarkable growth in the industry and in the American public's acceptance of massage.

There were 190 massage schools when the original edition was published in 1992. Now there are well over 1,000 schools. In addition, there are these recent advances in the profession:

- Many schools now offer an associate's degree in massage.

- Scientific research documenting the health benefits of massage has grown exponentially in recent years, largely due to the efforts of the Touch Research Institute. (Chapter 20)

- Thirty-five states and the District of Columbia now regulate the practice of massage, and others have legislative activity in the works. (pages 143–151)

- Chair massage has grown into a tremendously popular modality that has gone into the workplace, storefronts, street fairs, airports, health expos, and many other locations. (pages 30–31)

- The spa industry is experiencing a great surge in popularity.

- A specialized medical massage credential is now available. (page 130)

Massage has come out of the shadows and onto Main Street. In large and small cities, in neighborhoods, in small towns, and even on rural roads, signs advertising massage businesses are in abundance. Few places in America lack access to an establishment publicly offering professional massage.

With all of the growth that has already taken place, a hundred million Americans have yet to experience their first professional massage. Massage is still an expanding field with room for a great variety of practitioners. This book will help you understand the field, find your place in it, and create a successful career. I wish you a wonderful journey . . .

# I

# An Overview
# of the Profession
# &
# What It Takes
# to Succeed in It

# 1 Is a Career in Massage for You?

Massage can be a delightful career. Your clients regard you as the person who gives them relaxation, helps relieve their pain, and assists them in improving their health. You have freedom to set your own schedule, and can earn a good living with a clear conscience.

Massage can also be a frustrating career. You have great skills and desire to help, but clients are not calling, bills are piling up, and a client has asked you for sex at the end of a massage. You may wonder whether the whole thing is worth the effort.

If you are considering pursuing a career in massage or bodywork, it is worth your while to spend a little time now examining what lies ahead and whether it is what you want. You will find information throughout this book that will help you get a fuller picture of what it is like to be a massage professional. However, certain pros and cons should be set out at the start.

## First item: Money.

Many people are lured to the idea of a massage career by some simple arithmetic. The local massage therapist is charging $60.00 per hour. Eight hours a day times $60.00 per hour comes to $480.00 per day, or $2,400.00 per week. Eureka! How can I get into this!?

It is true that there are *a few* massage therapists whose economic picture is like the one in the last paragraph, but they are the exception and not the rule. The vast majority of massage professionals have a very different story to tell.

A recent AMTA member survey revealed that 57% of full-time practitioners earned less than $30,000.00 per year. A similar survey by ABMP found that the overall average for practitioners was $23,194.00 and the average first-year income was $7,700.00.

Although some massage therapists do quite well financially, it has been my experience that those who enter the field *for the purpose* of making a lot of money are not happy in the field. They either do not succeed in massage, or become so absorbed by their desire to succeed financially that they are basically unfulfilled human beings even though they earn large amounts of money.

The people in the field who are financially successful *and happy* are those who got into the field out of a sincere desire to help other people, who have good skills and who have the determination necessary to achieve success.

Those who keep at it and succeed in establishing massage careers report an extremely high rate of career satisfaction regardless of their income – the same AMTA member survey quoted above found that more than 50% of respondents were "extremely satisfied" with their careers.

## Second item: Drive and motivation.

What massage has in common with other professions—such as law, medicine and accounting—is that the professional has to attract a following, a clientele, in order to earn a living.

True, there are jobs available in which you can work for an hourly wage or on commission, but these situations are usually regarded as "entry-level" positions, or situations in which you can gain experience before you are truly established in the field. Jobs where some person or institution brings you a clientele are seldom well-paid jobs; your employer might take up to 70% of the amount paid for your services.

Therefore, to succeed in the long run, you will need to establish yourself as an independent professional with a substantial client base. Every client is an individual who could choose any massage practitioner, but chooses you because of what you have to offer. To be worth choosing and to be well-known and respected take time, dedication, and organization. Know before you begin that this is the path you are choosing for the long run when you choose a career as a massage therapist.

## Third item: Commitment.

From reading this far, you are getting the idea that massage is not a field you just drift into and easily start making money. Getting started will be easier if you have substantial experience in a related hands-on therapy field or a solid reputation in your community. Otherwise, you can expect that during your first year or two after massage school you will have a limited income from massage, and will be spending a fair amount of time promoting yourself in an attempt to become established.

Therefore, make a commitment to your massage career. If you approach the field in a mature way, it will be a rewarding choice for you. However, if you approach it with a half-hearted commitment, you are likely to abandon your attempt to create a practice before you reap the rewards of the marketing and promotion you do.

Making a commitment to your career means making some commitment to a place. That is not to say you must settle down in the first place you practice massage, but ultimately you should make a pledge to yourself to spend at least three years in a location as a massage therapist. If you don't take that step, you don't do justice to your chances to have a successful career in the field.

### Still interested?

If none of this scares you off, you probably have a good chance of making it as a massage therapist. Other chapters will provide you with strategies and techniques that will enable you to minimize your frustration and maximize your success as a professional. If you are making the decision to undertake a career as a massage professional, may I extend a warm welcome to you, and a wish that you enjoy all the ups and downs and in-betweens that await you...

# 2 The Massage and Bodywork Field
## Its Time Has Come

Massage is an ancient art that has been having a renaissance during the last 50 years in the United States. Many types of massage have been developed, and many types of closely and not-so-closely related therapies have evolved in recent times. In an attempt to clarify this sometimes confusing picture, I offer the following discussion of massage and definitions of various terms.

## What is massage, anyway?

In one sense, the term "massage" deserves to be many words, because one word cannot be stretched enough to include the various therapeutic techniques practiced by people who call themselves massage therapists. Consider these categories:

- **Wellness massage,** for preventative general health;

- **Relaxation massage,** to remove the results of stresses of daily life, including "on-site" or chair massage;

- **Pampering (or beautification) massage,** to provide a sensuous, pleasurable indulgence or as an adjunct to beauty services. Spa massage is the fastest growing segment of the massage industry today.

- **Sports massage,** for training, preparation and recovery from exertion during sporting events;

- **On-Site or Chair massage,** brief clothed massage done in a wide variety of settings, such as fairs, airports, business offices and conventions;

- **Pain relief,** to relieve muscle soreness, minor injury pain, headaches, or the like;

- **Rehabilitative massage,** for recovery after physical injury such as -broken bones and stroke;

- **Medical massage,** as an adjunct to medical treatment for illness, such as depression, cancer and AIDS;

- **Chiropractic adjunct,** to enhance the effectiveness of chiropractic adjustments;

- **Personal transformation massage,** to explore emotional or psychological issues or to produce shifts in consciousness.

## "Bodywork" and massage

Confusing the matter still further, many people also include "bodywork" in the term massage. Such hands-on therapies as shiatsu, Trager, Rolfing, polarity, and at least 60 other forms of bodywork now available are sometimes referred to under the umbrella term "massage," especially in the Western United States.

In order to make the information in this book easier to organize and use, I have drawn a distinction between "traditional" massage, and other newly-formed kinds of hands-on therapies. With apologies to those who prefer a definition of "massage" that includes a broad spectrum of bodywork styles, I have settled on the other, perhaps more conservative definition.

In this book, the term "massage" is used to mean traditional "Swedish" massage, or systems very much like it. Swedish massage is characterized by the five strokes effleurage, petrissage, friction, vibration and tapotement. Other systems that work with the body are called "bodywork." The following definitions are offered for clarification.

## *Definitions*

*Please note: There are no "official" or widely accepted definitions of the terms "massage" and "bodywork." These definitions are offered to clarify the meanings of these terms as used in this book.*

*Massage.* The application of touch by one person to another, using manual techniques of rubbing, stroking, kneading or compression (effleurage, petrissage, vibration, friction or tapotement), when done to produce relaxation, pain relief, injury rehabilitation, athletic preparedness or recovery, health improvement, increased awareness, or pleasure.

*Bodywork.* The application of touch by one person to another, to produce relaxation, pain relief, injury rehabilitation, health improvement, increased awareness, neuromuscular re-education, or pleasure, using any techniques other than those used in massage (see definition of massage, above). Bodywork does not include chiropractic, osteopathy, or any other system which has an organized licensing structure and grants the title "doctor" to its practitioners. (See the Bodywork Organizations and Trainings Directory starting on page 221.)

*Massage Practitioner.* Any person who publicly offers massage in return for money.

*Massage Therapist.* A massage practitioner who has received training in the theory and practice of massage, and is competent to use massage as a means of promoting pain relief, injury rehabilitation or health improvement.

*Bodyworker.* Any person who publicly offers bodywork in return for money. The following definitions clarify the meaning of several words used in the above definitions:

"Compression" does not include static pressure applied to one spot (as in shiatsu and trigger point therapy), but does include pressure that increases and decreases or moves along the body, such as tapotement and friction.

"Health improvement" includes mental, psychological, emotional and spiritual health, as well as the health of the body's immune system, or any other system of the body.

"Pleasure" means the enjoyment of the sensations in the body, but does not include sexual arousal or stimulation of sexual organs.

## Recent growth of massage—factors involved

In 1960, the average American had one of two associations for the word "massage." It was thought of either as a prelude to sex or a health club rub-down, heavy on the "karate chops." These images still remain for some people, especially older people whose personal experience of massage has been one or the other of these types. However, the last fifty years have seen phenomenal growth of legitimate, therapeutic and scientific massage. Today, for the first time in American society, massage is considered a conventional treatment for stress reduction, pain relief, treatment of medical conditions and emotional and physical well-being.

Several societal trends have facilitated the rediscovery of the ancient art of massage. The hippie movement in the 1960s, and related consciousness-raising activities, opened doors for massage as a tool for self-exploration and personal transformation. The explosion in fitness activities during the 1970s and 1980s brought acceptance for massage as both a wellness modality and a sports training aid.

In the 1990s, the widespread promotion of chair massage, (also called on-site or seated massage) introduced massage to huge numbers of people who would not have been comfortable undressing to experience massage. Chair massage went into workplaces, shopping malls, storefronts, airports, street fairs, health fairs, and many more locations. It played, and continues to play, a major role in making the general public aware of the benefits of massage, and making it more attractive to a mass market.

The medical community's view of massage has begun to shift as well. Early on, massage was considered an "alternative" treatment – something a patient might choose *instead* of medical treatment. More recently it has been referred to primarily as a "complementary" therapy – meaning one that adds to or supports other medical practices. The trend now is toward "integrative" medical clinics, which include massage and other modalities with conventional medicine under one roof. Many universities now have such integrative clinics, and hundreds of private integrative clinics have opened across the United States.

As a result of all this growth, massage schools have proliferated (one person described it as an "algae bloom"), the membership of massage organizations has skyrocketed, and massage has evolved from a service for the wealthy to a service accessible to and used by the general public.

The change has been taking place at a different pace in different places. In some parts of the West coast, massage has been popular for so long that there exists a surplus of massage therapists. In contrast, many remote or rural locations still have very little activity in the massage field. However, in most of North America, large numbers of people either have recently become aware of massage, or are ready to be shown for the first time how wonderful and therapeutic massage can be. Most areas are continuing to experience a steady, even dramatic rise in the popularity and availability of massage.

# What does the future hold?

People have been doing massage for many thousands of years. Massage was something people were doing before surgery was ever performed, before medicines were prescribed, before science was even conceived, before almost any other human activity you can name. It has lasted these thousands of years because it is good. Much like gold has been the investment of choice throughout much of history because of its inherent value, massage is a part of human culture that has stood the test of time because it has real value for people.

Because massage is a service with inherent value for people, it does not need to have a market created for it in order to be in demand. Instead, massage is naturally in demand as soon as people release the artificial barriers they have against using massage services.

## *People's barriers to massage*

These barriers are 1) anxiety about nudity and about one's own body, 2) fear of making contact with another person or oneself, 3) a belief that spending money on oneself is indulgent or wasteful, and 4) fear of the unknown.

These are significant barriers, but they are the sort of things people tend to outgrow. The more sophisticated our society becomes, the more irrelevant these barriers will seem to the general population. The general societal and scientific acceptance of massage will help these barriers continue to come down in the years to come.

Another issue is affordability. The 1980s saw an increase in income for many, and facilitated the growth of massage in part by creating a larger group of people who could afford it. Price is a factor for many people. The economy experienced a downturn immediately after the World Trade Center tragedy, but most massage therapists felt little or no effect on their practices. Even so, the economy will necessarily play a role in how much massage continues to grow in popularity, and the profession can aid the growth of massage by not pricing itself out of reach of most people.

Finally, the payment for massage services by insurance companies, if widely available, would open a whole new market for massage services. A certain number of potential massage clients will receive massage only if it is covered by their medical insurance policy. Currently, insurance reimbursement plays a minor role in the overall picture of massage therapy, but that factor might be poised to increase sharply. Whether that will change in the near future is one of the topics touched on in the next chapter.

# 3 Current Professional and Political Issues

This is a very lively time in the life of the massage and bodywork profession. If you liken the massage field in the U.S. to a growing person, it has passed through its youth, survived its adolescence, and in poised to face the world as a young adult.

The 1960s saw the birth, (or re-birth) of massage as a sophisticated profession worthy of widespread acceptance in society. The '70s, '80s, '90s were a time of phenomenal growth, and a time when the profession as a whole went in many different directions looking for a sense of identity, or for its personality. Massage expanded into many different contexts, and related forms of bodywork grew up by the dozens.

Now the profession has taken root in many venues; massage therapists are commonplace in chiropractic offices, health clubs, spas, corporations, and stand-alone private offices. State regulation of massage exists in 35 states, and in many towns, cities, and counties. The National Certification Exam has been in existence for over a decade, and most of the states that regulate massage require or accept it as their written licensing exam, facilitating therapists moving from state to state.

Mainstream America has realized that professional massage is not sex, and that it is a scientifically-proven health modality. Related forms of bodywork have evolved and blossomed into a rich tapestry of touch therapies that present almost unlimited choices for the practitioner and for consumers. The profession is firmly entrenched on the American scene.

The purpose of this chapter is to set out the main political and professional issues currently confronting the industry. Understanding this information may not be essential to your career as a massage or bodywork practitioner, but you might find it helpful to have a broad understanding of the political issues in your chosen field. Some of this information may help you decide which school or schools to attend, and which association or associations to join. An awareness of the political process in your chosen profession may also help you avoid unpleasant surprises in the future.

## What is at Stake in Political Issues?

The following scenarios are drawn from real-life experiences. While you may not experience the problems indicated by these examples, they are meant to alert you to some of the real-life situations that provide motivation for governmental regulation of massage and bodywork:

- You have a successful private massage practice. One day, your mail carrier delivers a certified letter from the State Board of Physical Therapy, ordering you to cease and desist practicing massage unless you can prove that you have a license to practice physical therapy or chiropractic.

- You want to move to a new state, but on investigation, you learn that your educational training is considered inadequate under that state's licensing law, and you must attend school at a massage school in the new state from start to finish, and then take that state's licensing exam.

- You are working with a car-crash victim who could benefit from massage therapy. She asks you "are your services covered by my medical insurance?"

- You are attempting to establish a referral relationship with a physician and when you say you do "medical massage" she says she has never heard of that and asks what credential you have that allows you to practice.

This chapter will give you an overview of the current political situation and some of the conflicting views that are being advanced, and will suggest some directions for progress in the future.

## Governmental Regulation of Massage

Massage is the newest member of the group of regulated professions. Dentists, doctors, psychologists, nurses, lawyers, physical therapists, and chiropractors, among many others, have all gone through the process of establishing procedures to regulate who can and can't practice the profession. That regulation process has begun in the massage and bodywork field, but is not complete.

At present, 35 states and the District of Columbia have laws regulating massage. The requirements differ from state to state. Texas, for example, requires 300 hours of educational training. Many states require 500 hours. New Hampshire requires 750 and New York and Nebraska 1,000. Most use the National Certification Exam as their written test, a few do not.

The 15 states without regulatory laws require *zero* hours, and do not restrict the practice of massage. Although some municipalities and counties in those states regulate massage, most practitioners in those 15 states do not have to answer to anyone.

### *Why regulate the practice of massage and bodywork?*

Why not just let people do what they want, and let the free marketplace take care of who succeeds and who fails? Many in the profession believe that's the best approach and for that reason oppose governmental regulation of massage in those states where it has not yet been enacted.

Proponents of governmental regulation put forth several arguments in favor of governmental regulation of massage:

First, the public deserves protection. When a state agency regulates the practice of massage, they maintain a hearings board or grievance board to consider complaints by members of the public about how they were treated by a practitioner. In this way, the profession gives the public a quick and easy remedy against a practitioner who is incompetent or unethical. This inspires trust and confidence on the part of the public and enhances the respect of the entire profession. If there is no agency regulating massage in a state, it is much harder for an injured party to get satisfaction from the practitioner who injured her. The only remedy available is to hire a lawyer and pursue a lawsuit, which is usually a very lengthy, traumatic and expensive undertaking.

Second, state licensing protects the massage profession from other professions that claim *they* are the only ones with the right to do massage. Physical therapists in Maryland battled for many years to for the right to control the practice of massage in that state. They instituted legal proceedings against massage therapists, charging them with practicing physical therapy without a license. These conflicts finally ended with the enactment of a massage licensing law in Maryland. Similar challenges have taken place in Oregon and the District of Columbia. State regulation of massage prevents this kind of headache—the state, by regulating the field, ensures the right of massage practitioners to practice.

Third, governmental regulation of massage helps in getting rid of those who offer sexual gratification as part of a massage. Where massage is regulated by the government, there is a quick and easy process for suspending the license or registration of one who is unethical. However, where massage is not governmentally regulated, the only remedy against unethical practitioners is the criminal justice system, which is notoriously slow and inefficient. Therefore, in areas where massage is not regulated by the government, it is harder to stop those who offer sexual massage.

Finally, some believe that state regulation of massage encourages mainstream society and the medical profession to take massage practitioners seriously. The desire for acceptance as a mainstream health care provider has been an undercurrent in the licensing and certification debate for a number of years.

### *Why Some Oppose Attempts to Create State Regulation*

Some people are against governmental regulation on principle—they are suspicious of government and don't want any outside authority taking control over their lives.

Others oppose regulation because the situation in their location does not need improvement. Perhaps the profession is well-established, unlicensed practitioners are able to receive insurance reimbursement, and there is no lack of respect and acceptance for massage and massage practitioners. Governmental regulation adds expense, burdens and restrictions. If there is no problem to be solved by regulation, then regulation is unnecessary.

For the last ten years, I have subscribed to an internet discussion group for massage and bodywork practitioners. Governmental regulation of massage has been the most frequently debated topic on the list, and has evoked the most heated debate. Most of the members of the internet discussion group who express an opinion on the subject favor not regulating massage. The main issues seem to be 1) freedom to choose the amount and kind of education one wants, and 2) the desire for freedom from the tests, rules, restrictions and expenses that inevitably come with governmental regulation.

Another area of controversy in the debate, however, concerns not whether licensing is a good idea in principle, but *the way* in which the attempts to enact licensing laws are sometimes made.

Specifically, some groups within the massage profession attempt to create new licensing laws by keeping their legislative proposals secret, submitting legislation to state governments without consulting the majority of practitioners in the state where the law will be in force, and proposing legislation that favors the members of the group sponsoring the legislation, as opposed to considering the interests of all practitioners in the state.

Many groups are interested in the outcome of legislative efforts. However, two national professional organizations have some of the strongest interests concerning these issues. These organizations, the AMTA and the ABMP, sometimes have different ideas about how the licensing process should proceed. From published articles and magazine editorials about licensing issues, the following seems true of the current situation regarding attempts to create governmental regulation for massage:

The AMTA (American Massage Therapy Association) initiates attempts to create new state licensing, but does not necessarily advocate licensure for every state.

The ABMP (Associated Bodywork and Massage Professionals) is not against licensing, nor is it against the AMTA, but it opposes unilateral attempts to impose massage licensing without input from the majority of practitioners who will be affected by the law.

Currently, the ABMP is maintaining a network to alert practitioners about attempts to enact laws regulating massage. The ABMP's goal is to be included in the process of formulating the law, so the law will be responsive to all groups within the profession. ABMP, as of this writing, was spearheading an effort to create statewide licensing in California, where massage is currently regulated under a patchwork of city and county governmental regulations (see pages 144–145).

AMTA has recently instituted an official policy urging chapters to build coalitions with bodyworkers and non-AMTA members. Before the national organization will provide funding to assist in legislative efforts, state chapters must show proof of coalition-building and must conduct a survey of both members and non-members to gauge support for the proposed legislation.

In the past, AMTA supporters have sometimes promoted laws that require practitioners to get their massage education at a school accredited by COMTA (Commission on Massage Therapy Accreditation), which is an arm of AMTA (see pages 126–128) West Virginia's licensing law originally required attendance at a COMTA school, but that provision was subsequently removed by the legislature.

Creation of laws requiring education at a COMTA-approved school has been one of the sources of discord between competing groups in the industry. In light of the current policy of AMTA to require coalition-building and non-member surveys, perhaps no future legislative proposals will include a COMTA-based educational requirement.

## Licensing, Certification and Registration

These terms can be confusing. Massage practitioners sometimes are certified, sometimes are licensed, and sometimes are registered. The three terms do not mean the same thing. In order to properly understand the political issues in the massage and bodywork field, you should understand the differences between these three terms. Once you read the following, their meanings will come clear to you.

First, ask yourself this question: When you speak about licensing, certification, or registration, are you talking about what a *government* is doing or what a *private group* is doing?

Governments can create *any* of the three kinds of regulations mentioned—licensing, certification or registration. Private groups or individuals can give only *certification*.

When a government requires a *license* to practice massage, then practicing without a license is a criminal act. The licensing law sets out the requirements for obtaining a license and establishes a procedure by which qualified individuals can apply for a license.

When a government *certifies* practitioners, that is usually a voluntary procedure that carries some benefit. For example, in Maine, certified practitioners may use the title "Massage Therapist" and non-certified practitioner may not. In Delaware, certified practitioners are exempt from the "Adult Entertainment Law" but non-certified practitioners fall under its authority.

When a government *registers* practitioners, they generally do not restrict the practice, but keep track of practitioners by requiring them to submit certain information to the government. (However, Texas requires registration as a mandatory condition to practice massage, so registration operates much the same as a license in that state.)

Private groups can give only *certification*. They cannot give a license or registration. Private groups that give certification are giving an individual their private approval. They are certifying that the person has completed a specific course of study or passed a specific test.

Certification is never a legal requirement to practice massage, but it can be a legal requirement to practice forms of bodywork that are protected by trade-name or service-mark protection, such as Rolfing, Trager, Feldenkrais, etc. As to those forms of bodywork, certification from the owner of the name is required to use that name in connection with your work.

Now that you understand the differences between registration, certification, and licensing, I have to add that the National Certification Exam complicates the picture by being part "certification" and part "license".

The National Certification Exam (NCE) is a standardized written test that is created by a private group (not by a government). However, it has been chosen as the written exam by governments in most of the states that regulate massage (see page 151). These states have other requirements, such as educational requirements, licensing fees, and sometimes character references, but they use the National Certification Exam as their written exam for massage.

The National Certification Exam (NCE) therefore operates both as a *private certification* and as a *governmentally-required exam*. A brief history of the creation of the NCE is the subject of the next section.

## A Brief History of the National Certification Exam

During the late 1980s, the AMTA announced its plan to create a voluntary, nationwide certification exam for massage. It was initially to be an AMTA project, and was to be a Swedish massage certification exam. Although the exam was to be voluntary, many therapists became concerned that it would nonetheless become a practical requirement, since the goal of the exam was to standardize the qualifications of professional massage therapists throughout the United States.

Some non-AMTA massage therapists became resentful that a standard was being created without their input, which could impair their ability to earn a living. Some were angered that this action was being taken without consultation with any industry leaders outside the AMTA.

In the wake of this initial controversy, some organized attempts at reconciliation took place, without much success. As time went on, AMTA decided to make the certification project separate from the AMTA. When it was launched as an independent organization, the certification project was funded by a loan from the AMTA, and seven of the nine members of the steering committee were AMTA members. These connections to the AMTA caused some non-AMTA members to believe that the project was still an arm of the AMTA.

After the exam had been created, the steering committee was dissolved and replaced by the National Certification Board, which now administers the test. The National Certification Board is incorporated in the state of Virginia, and Board members are elected by mail ballot from all nationally certified practitioners. The Board has a stated commitment to cooperate with the AMTA toward mutual goals, but it is administratively separate from AMTA.

The National Certification Exam certifies basic competence in massage, and does not test for competence in any specific area of practice, such as sports massage, medical massage, shiatsu or the like. There is no practical portion of the test, i.e., no test of manual skills is involved.

Until 2005, the only test offered by the Board was the "NCBTMB" or National Certification for Therapeutic Massage and Bodywork. Beginning in 2005, the board added a second exam, the National Certification in Therapeutic Massage exam, and entry-level, massage-only credential.

The exam is given on a continuous basis at locations with interactive computer terminals.

To be eligible for the exam, a practitioner must have completed 500 hours of education in massage or bodywork. Professional experience can substitute for a portion of the educational requirement. The exam covers anatomy and physiology, clinical pathology, massage assessment and technique, business practices and ethics. Continuing education is required to maintain certified status, but not to maintain state licensure in states that use the test as their written exam. For further information about the NCE, you can contact National Certification Board for Therapeutic Massage and Bodywork at (703) 610-9015 or Infoline (800) 296-0664 or on the Internet at **www.ncbtmb.com**.

## *Suggestions for the future*

In Chapter Two, I noted that the term "massage" is used to cover many different approaches to this kind of work. Boiled down to the most fundamental issue, the massage community is divided between viewing massage as a "personal service" and viewing massage as a "health care service". In other words, some identify with the idea that massage is mostly about wellness and relaxation, or "personal service". Others identify with the idea that massage is a medical or quasi-medical therapy, i.e., "a health care service".

A recent AMTA survey of public attitudes about massage found that roughly half of the general public thinks of massage as a health service and roughly half thinks of massage as a non-medical stress-reducing service. This same duality exists within the profession.

Therefore, I have for many years advocated for *specialized credentials* for massage therapists and bodyworkers, just like there are specialized doctors (surgeons, psychiatrists, dermatologists, etc.) and specialized dentists (orthodontists, periodontists, etc.). Specialists must achieve a separate certification to practice their specialty.

The licensing, regulation and certification of professional competence for "relaxation" massage should be viewed very differently from the licensing, regulation and certification of specialties, such as medical massage.

State licensing of massage aims at basic, or entry-level credentialing. Licensing is designed to assure basic professional competence so the public is protected from untrained practitioners. 500 hours of training (or the 300 hours required in Texas) is enough to provide this entry-level competency in massage, including basic anatomy, massage techniques, contraindications, proper hygiene, and basic business skill. However, 500 hours is not enough to provide training both as a massage practitioner and also as a specialist in a particular branch of massage or bodywork.

Forms of bodywork that are protected by trade-name or service-mark protection enforce advanced educational standards by limiting use of the trade name (such as "Rolfer" or "Trager Practitioner") to those who have met the governing organization's educational requirements. The possibility also exists for creating standard credentials for non-trade-marked modalities, such as medical massage, reflexology, sports massage, polarity, and others.

The American Manual Medicine Association, or AMMA (see page 130) has created a standardized credential for medical massage. If the AMMA medical massage credential becomes widely accepted, it will become easier to convince physicians, hospitals and insurance carriers to use credentialed therapists to offer this healing modality to medical patients.

If the massage profession evolves so that state governments license the practice of massage to assure basic professional competence, and the massage profession itself certifies specialists in the major modalities that are practiced, massage will have truly grown into its potential as a profession, and will have achieved a real maturity.

# II

# Career Options,
# Strategies
# and Tactics

# 4 Your Career in Massage or Bodywork
## Let's Get Organized

A surprising fact is that many, perhaps more than 50% of massage school graduates never create a massage practice that supports them financially. They either never make an organized effort to practice massage professionally, or they give it a try but abandon their efforts before they achieve a successful practice. The attrition (or drop-out) rate of massage practitioners is estimated to be 25% annually. In other words, large numbers of people are going to massage school and struggling with their careers and opting out of the practice of massage before they ever succeed in the profession.

The purposes of the four chapters in this section are:

1. To help you gain clarity about what it is you want from your professional life in massage or bodywork.

2. To help you make a sensible plan for achieving your goals.

3. To help you follow through on that plan with a minimum of wasted effort and a maximum of success.

## Common misconceptions

Many would-be massage therapists have certain wrong assumptions about the paths their careers will take. One very common expectation about a massage career goes like this:

> I will attend massage school, where I will learn everything I need to know to be a successful massage therapist. When I finish school, I will set up a practice. Clients will come to me and I will be busy and happy.

Several misconceptions are evident in this scenario. First, massage school will not teach you everything you need to know, either about giving a good massage or about operating in the business world. In fact, you should look at your first 1,000 professional massages as completion of your education as a massage therapist. Your skill level and confidence level will grow for years to come.

Second, you probably will not be in a position to set up a practice right out of school. Unless you have a very good reputation in the community, it will take time and effort to build your reputation sufficiently to establish a clientele.

Third, clients will not come to you just because you make yourself available. If you get yourself an office and say "Here I am, world!" the world will respond with a deafening silence. In order to be a busy massage therapist or bodyworker, you will need to take organized, affirmative steps to let people know you are there and make them want to take advantage of your services.

Finally, being busy and being happy are not necessarily the same thing. You want to attract those clients that most suit you. Even when you do not have enough work, there are still clients out there whom you do not want to have. Your clients will be a significant part of your life when your practice is going, so take the time to attract a clientele you will enjoy serving.

## Typical career paths

In imagining what your career will be like, and taking logical steps to reach your goals, it will help you to have the benefit of the experiences of those who have walked the path before you. Numerous interviews with successful massage therapists and bodyworkers have disclosed many common elements in their career paths.

Below are capsule versions of the careers of some actual massage therapists and bodyworkers. Some are more successful than others. All are earning their sole livelihood at massage or bodywork.

"A" started his career in massage when he had a wife and a baby and was very poor. His wife was very supportive. During the early years, he did very little else to earn money, except some painting work for Christmas money. He chose this approach so that he would be fully immersed in the profession and would be forced to overcome any obstacles. It took two years to achieve a steady client load. After four years, he was so busy he was turning away clients, and now travels with world-class athletes to international sporting events.

"B" went to massage school, then went traveling in Asia for 15 months. On his return to California, he found he was seriously depressed. After three months of depression, he pulled himself out of it and began working at a health spa and promoting himself locally, working out of his home and doing house calls. Newspaper coverage of him and his Asian trip helped his practice grow, and within eight months, he was doing upwards of 20 massages per week. His business is growing, yet he plans to spend only one or two more years in the area before moving on to some other location.

"C" had a marketing background, and when she graduated from massage school, used newspaper ads, coupons and flyers to gather a practice quickly. She worked out of her home in San Diego, and had 10 to 15 clients per week within a month of starting her marketing program. After two years, she got out of massage completely, finding she was "fed up" with dealing with men who were asking her for sexual favors. She currently works as a receptionist in a wholistic health center.

"D" opened a store-front massage office in Chicago right out of massage school. She did a great deal of personal promotion in the neighborhood. Almost all of her clients in the early days were men, many of whom presented her with requests for sex. Her husband supported her financially for the first few years, and despite aggressive promotion, it took about three years for her practice to reach a profitable level, especially in light of the very high rent she had to pay for a corner store-front business location. After four years in practice, she is seeing 20 to 30 clients per week.

"E" did massage for about five years as a hobby, accepting donations, before ever attending massage school. He has been out of massage school eight years, and does 6 to 15 massages per week. The slow growth of his practice and his current pace of activity are exactly to his liking.

"F" spent quite a few years not succeeding in the massage field. He worked as a physical therapy assistant for three years, and also tried to establish a massage practice in a hair salon. Then he "took some time off" from the profession. He returned to the profession and became involved in his state massage associations. He became active in the AMTA and went into practice with a prominent sports massage teacher and practitioner. His massage practice reached full capacity within three months of starting in this office, and he has since taken on a significant leadership role in the AMTA.

"G" had 10 years experience as a swimming trainer and worked as a case manager in a chiropractor's office while she attended massage school. She did some massage in the chiropractor's office for a few months after graduation. A cardiologist who had heard of her invited her to rent an office in his tasteful, downtown practice building at a very reasonable rent. She accepted, and once there, she was able to work on some very influential community members who spread the word about her skills. Within three months of moving to the cardiologist's office, she had a thriving practice.

"H" started out in the field as a new mother, and very poor. She was always moving from one home to another in search of cheaper rent. Her main priority was to be very good at her work, and it took her several years to begin to earn a living at massage. She has now been in practice 10 years, specializes in pregnancy massage, and works at a birthing center. She sees 15 to 20 clients per week, most of whom are regulars. She would welcome having more clients.

"I" made a point of having non-massage work that supported her when she began her massage career. She was concerned that if she were financially needy, clients would sense that neediness and be put off. Instead, having her financial needs met, she could approach her clients with warmth and openness. Within one and a half years, she was seeing 20 clients per week, and only then did she quit her other job. She has kept her practice at that level ever since.

"J" did house cleaning at the beginning of her massage career to meet expenses. The first year brought only enough massage income to pay expenses such as office rent and supplies. After fifteen months, she was earning enough from massage to stop doing cleaning work. After 18 months, her client load was 10 to 15 per week.

"K" was a public school teacher. She started gathering a practice during after-school hours, and as the practice grew, she switched to substitute teaching, and eventually was able to let go of substitute teaching, and be a full-time massage therapist. The entire process took four years, which was longer than she thought it would take. She currently sees 15 to 20 clients per week.

"L" has a practice as a polarity therapist, which she took six years to build. For the first year, she kept her job as a university teacher, and saw one to three clients per week to decide if she wanted to pursue polarity more seriously. For the next three years, she held a consulting job two days per week, and built her polarity practice up to about six clients per week. She currently sees 12 to 15 polarity clients per week, teaches four yoga classes per week, and markets her own yoga instructional tapes.

"M" opened a practice in the town she grew up in immediately after finishing massage school. During the next two and a half years, she worked in at least six different locations in and around the area, gaining experience and slowly gaining a client base. She then opened an office in a charming, wealthy seaside resort town a few miles away. She coordinated this new office with a direct mail promotion and a public speaking engagement. Within weeks of moving, her practice doubled, and within two months she was seeing 30 or more clients per week.

"N" worked for four years as a physical therapy assistant and sports therapist before going to massage school. She has been supporting herself with massage work during the first year after massage school, doing house calls and working in a chiropractor's office doing massage for $14 per hour. Her goal is to be a physical therapist.

"O" worked full-time for AT&T, and practiced massage in her off-hours, doing house calls in an affluent community. After about one and a half years, she left her job and went into massage full-time. She went to work in a hotel health spa to supplement her practice, and has a busy practice.

"P" went to massage school after several years in practice as a lawyer. After graduating from massage school, he took a job teaching law, and did one to three massages per week on the side. He did this for three years, and then set out to establish a massage practice in a new location where he knew very few people. It took two years for the practice to produce enough income to meet his living expenses. He used some of his spare time to work on a book about the massage profession. After three and a half years of practice, he is seeing between 12 and 20 clients per week.

## Elements these career paths have in common

The experiences summarized above display several elements that are repeated in more than one story. Consider the following:

- Those who had substantial experience in a hands-on field before going to massage school became established massage therapists much more quickly than those who had no such experience.

- For those without such prior experience, the average time needed to establish an income-producing practice varied quite a bit, but two years was about average. Some made it in a year, some took three or four years. Those taking longer than four years probably were not making an organized attempt to become established.

- Attempts at rapid growth through advertising tend to bring sexually-oriented male clients.

- It appears to take longer for most men to become established massage therapists than it does for women.

# Main causes of career failures

What factors explain the failure of most massage school graduates to create a successful professional practice? The two main ways in which would-be massage therapists sabotage their careers are moving too often, and being reluctant to promote themselves.

As you can understand from reading the career capsules above, success as a massage therapist comes only after a period of building a reputation in the community. The two essential elements in this process are 1) doing things to become known and 2) giving the process some time.

Recent massage school graduates are often very unsettled. Perhaps you are "in transition", having moved away from home to attend massage school, and not knowing where you want to settle to start a new life. Perhaps you are living in your home town, and you are apprehensive about becoming established, for fear that if you acquire a successful practice, you will never leave your home town and see the world. Perhaps you do not have confidence in your ability to give a professional massage.

If you are in such a situation, or in a similar situation that makes you unsure or reluctant about becoming established, you have at least three logical approaches you can take:

1. **The side-step.** Do some other kind of work to earn a living, and do massage on the side. This will give you the opportunity to see if you really enjoy massage work, and will give your skills a chance to slowly improve. It also will give you time to become better known in the community. If and when you decide to move to full-time massage work, you will have a stronger local reputation.

2. **The trial balloon.** Take any job you can get doing massage, such as working in a health club, resort, spa or chiropractor's office. These jobs will give you substantial experience doing massage, will give your skills a chance to grow, and may yield some contacts that can lead to a different job opportunity. While the pay usually will not be high, you retain the opportunity to leave town without sacrificing any time and energy spent in reputation-building.

3. **The leap of faith.** Act as if you have decided to stay in town for awhile. Commit yourself to staying for two or three years and take some steps to build a clientele.

If you don't know where you'd rather live, and you can't figure your life out, there is a good chance that three years from now you will either be right where you are now, or will move to a new place and still not be sure what you want to do. If you decide to take a stand wherever you are now, you may find that any major issues in your life are just as easy to wrangle with while you build a massage career as they would if you moved somewhere else or did something different.

## The golden keys to career success

Having discussed what holds some people back from succeeding in the field, what is it that generates success for those who succeed? There are four keys to success in this field, and all four are indispensable. Imagine them like the four legs of a table. If any of the legs is short or missing, the table is not of much use.

The four golden keys to success in this field are:

## Location   Personality   Skills   Desire

*Location.* You might be the greatest massage therapist on earth, but if you are in a town filled with people who cannot afford your services, or who have overwhelming resistance to trying massage, you will not do well.

Location refers also to the part of town your office is in. Neighborhoods have characters, as do streets, as do individual buildings. The character of the surroundings seeps into people's attitudes about you and your office.

*Personality.* Your clients are not simply coming to you for a physical treatment. They are coming to you for your presence as well as your skills. They may come in for work on the body, but it is the whole person who decides whether to come back for another massage.

Not only should your clients feel completely comfortable in your presence, they should look forward to coming to see you as a chance to be with you for an hour. Successful massage therapists develop personal, often warm relationships with their clients.

*Skills.* You need to have the ability to do a good treatment. The client must feel better leaving than coming in. The client must also feel there is some good reason for choosing your therapy over the competition.

In short, whatever type of massage or bodywork you practice, you need to know what you are doing and do it well. This can mean not just education, but experience. Your skills as a massage therapist will improve throughout the first few years of your massage career.

*Desire.* Consider whether you whole-heartedly want to succeed in your practice. If not, what is it that is holding you back? Your deepest and most honest desires deserve expression. If you honestly want to be a professional massage therapist, you will focus your efforts efficiently and effectively.

Do your best to look inside and discover what you really want from your massage career. If you have reluctance to really put yourself in the public eye and build a clientele, ask yourself why, or talk it over with a trusted friend. Understanding yourself is a valuable asset in making choices that will bring you a career you can really enjoy.

### *How do you rate yourself on the Four Golden Keys?*

Re-read the four golden keys to success. This is the most important information in this book. If you embark on a massage career with a significant weakness in any of these four areas, you should understand that you need to work on this area in order to become successful. Before you put yourself through any needless hardship, consider very carefully your assessment of yourself and your career.

## *Make a commitment to strengthen your weaknesses*

If any of these four keys is missing or deficient in your assessment of yourself, make a commitment to yourself that you will work on this area. Here are some suggestions for how to improve.

*Location.* Do some research about the town, neighborhood and building you are planning to be in. Find out about the residents' income and standard of living. Find out how well any massage therapists in that area are doing.

Generally speaking, it is more difficult to be the only massage therapist in town, because that indicates there is no established massage clientele in that area. On the other hand, if you are the first and only practitioner in an area, you will have a secure professional foundation once you do become established.

Imagine the best neighborhood, street and block for your massage office. What other businesses are on the street? What is the look of the neighborhood? Imagine yourself as a client coming to this office. Is it difficult to get to? Is it on the way to other places you may want to go? As you come onto the block and into the building, what thoughts do you have? How do you feel?

Coming to your office is what every client will do at the start of your sessions. Evaluate the experience of coming to your office, and make sure you choose a location that makes coming to see you a pleasant and comfortable experience.

*Personality.* If you have an abrasive personality, make a commitment to yourself to soften it. If you are shy, make a commitment to yourself to be a little more outgoing so you can put your clients at ease.

You yourself enjoy being around people who are caring, accepting, warm and easy-going. These traits are important for the massage therapist. If you are too talkative, judgmental, sarcastic, crude or angry, these traits will tend to discourage your clientele and make it difficult for you to become established.

Of course, you cannot become someone you are not. However, you can choose to suppress the aspects of your character that would interfere with your career. Remember that the tongue often acts as a sword, so when in doubt, say less rather than more.

*Skills.* Understand that your skills will continue to grow for years to come. Take continuing education workshops and professional trainings. Get massage often, not only to feel good but to learn from the skill of others. Continue to grow psychologically as well, as growth and maturity will lend their own added value to your manual skills.

Look for opportunities that match your skill level, and understand that your fees will rise with your skills and reputation.

*Desire.* Take steps that are consonant with your true desires for success—don't reach for the stars if you heart is not in it. You may not be ready for success today. If you are not ready, don't struggle—do something else for awhile and do massage on the side. When you have the desire that fosters organization and commitment, it will be much easier for you to get started in this profession. Be honest with yourself about what you want.

Weaknesses can be worked into strengths if you have the commitment to do so. These are the keys to success in your career. Use them well.

# 5 Career Options in Massage

This chapter's purpose is to expose you to the broad range of options for the kinds of massage work you can do, the types of clients you can work with, opportunities for self-employment, and what you can expect in various employment situations.

## Kinds of massage, types of clients

The six categories described below pretty much cover the field of massage at the present moment. Each of these types of massage attracts its own type of client, and requires its own set of skills on the part of the practitioner. You might practice several of these types of massage, but in most cases you will not practice more than one or two types in any one location.

1. Relaxation/stress reduction. The most common kind of massage, relaxation or stress reduction massage includes the types of treatments common in resorts, spas, private offices and clients' homes. This category would also include wellness massage, or preventative health massage.

2. Sports massage. This rapidly growing field encompasses athletic training massage and massage designed to help an athlete prepare for competition and recover from competing.

3. Medical massage. Working by prescription, or in a hospital, or in a physical therapist's office, the medical massage therapist works with pathologies, pain or recovery from injury. Medical massage can also be adapted to a non-medical clientele, and practiced in a home or office setting.

4. Chiropractic adjunct. Working in chiropractors' offices is becoming more and more common, especially on the West coast. Some practitioners operate relatively independently from the chiropractor, with a cross-referral agreement. Others work by prescription of the chiropractor, working on specific parts of the body that the chiropractor designates.

5. Psychotherapeutic massage. Some massage therapists focus on shifts in awareness and psychological insight that can be brought about with massage. These therapists often work by referral from

psychotherapists, and usually work out of a private massage office. They often combine another form of bodywork with massage.

6. Pampering. Probably a branch of relaxation massage, pampering refers to the type of treatment that might be found in some spas and hair salons. This treatment is usually thought of as more of a beautification treatment than a health treatment, and might include salt glows, loofa rubs, and light Swedish massage.

7. Chair massage. Massage or shiatsu done with clothing on, client seated, in any location. This can be done as an introduction to massage for clients who may not come in for an office massage, or can be a continuing form of stress-reduction therapy when done on a regular basis, as in the office setting.

## Settings for the practice of massage

The following are locations where massage is currently practiced. Some of these locations are traditional locations for massage, and the arrangements establishments make with massage therapists are fairly uniform. Others are not so well established, and the arrangements may vary from place to place.

In general, the more the owner of the location provides in terms of linens, booking service and client base, the less she or he will expect to pay the massage therapist. If the location has a built-in clientele, such as a resort, the owner will usually take at least half of the fee, and sometimes quite a bit more than half.

At the other end of the spectrum, if the massage therapist brings additional business to the location, or adds a sense of uniqueness to what the location has to offer, the owner may make a very favorable deal with the massage therapist, on occasion even allowing the therapist to retain 100% of the fee.

*Health clubs.* Home of the "rub down" in the old days, health clubs are increasingly being staffed by well-trained massage therapists, who may practice relaxation massage or sports massage.

Some clubs will hire a therapist for an hourly wage, usually between $8 and $15 per hour. Some give an hourly wage plus a small percentage of the price of the massage, and some pay the therapist anywhere from 45% to 100% of the price of the massage.

Generally, clubs where the massage therapist has to cultivate the clientele will offer the therapist a larger percentage of the proceeds. Clubs where massage is an established part of the routine, especially where there are two or more treatment rooms, will usually pay less to the therapist, since they are supplying the clients.

Common disadvantages of health clubs are relatively low pay, noisy environments, and clients who may not have a sophisticated understanding of the value of massage.

A major advantage of health clubs, especially for newly trained massage therapists, is the chance to get lots of experience in a short period of time. If your health club will allow you to bring outside clients in, it can also serve as an office location for you while you develop a private practice, and this can be a substantial advantage.

*Spas and resorts.* Many of the same comments that apply to health clubs apply to spas and resort facilities. When compensation is based solely on an hourly rate, spas may pay anywhere from $15.00 to $45.00 per client hour. When compensation is based solely on percentage, spas may pay anywhere from 15% to 50% of the client fee, although one therapist in Texas reports that resort hotels in his area pay between 50% and 70% of the fee charged to clients. Some spas may pay a combination of a small hourly wage plus a percentage.

The therapist in a spa or resort usually does not need to supply anything. The massage room will be equipped, and the spa or resort will do the bookings. The clients are supplied for you, but since they are vacationers, they seldom will become repeat clients for you in your local practice.

High-end resorts and day spas usually pay better and hire more experienced massage therapists. They may require uncomfortable uniforms, and sometimes therapists are booked with only ten minutes between clients, in which they must prepare the room for the next massage or spa service. If the company that owns the facility is a large one, an added benefit of employment may be discounted stays at the other locations owned by that company.

More modest resorts and day spas often hire recent graduates. Therapists may have unpaid idle time, and may be expected to be on call for appointments on short notice.

"Medi-spas" have become popular in some locations, offering cosmetic procedures such as laser hair removal, botox and permanent makeup, with massage also offered.

*Hair salons.* There are no reliable generalizations to make about the practice of massage in hair salons. Sometimes the service offered is a pampering-style light Swedish massage, and sometimes it is expert massage therapy.

Some salon owners expect a large percentage of the proceeds or a fixed monthly rental from the massage therapist, and some offer more reasonable arrangements to the therapist. It may depend in part on whether the salon owner sees the massage therapist as bringing new business or prestige to the salon, or as simply relying on the salon's established clientele.

The salon owner will often offer a "day of beauty" or "day spa" experience which includes a massage, usually a half-hour full-body massage. The price of the package will be discounted, and the salon owner will usually expect the massage therapist to offer her services at a discount for the day of beauty clients.

Common disadvantages of practicing in hair salons are noise, noxious odors, and an approach to massage as a "pampering" or beautification service. Advantages include a strong clientele for referrals (in an appropriate salon) and an atmosphere in which massage stands out as a unique service.

If you practice in a salon, some practical suggestions are: give demonstration massages to the stylists, who can be good sources of referral; give hand massage to salon clients during slow times; do chair massage in a location visible to salon clients; and confirm all appointments by phone, as no-shows and cancellations can be a particular problem at salons.

*Cruise ships.* The main advantages of working on a cruise ship are the excitement and exploration available to one traveling the seas of the world, and the opportunity to get a great deal of experience in the massage field in a short period of time.

Working conditions are usually cramped, a ten to twelve hour work-day is the norm, and pay is usually low. Many therapists on cruise ships concentrate on selling skin care products and their work may be classified as "beauty" treatments. Because of the long hours, low pay, and transient lifestyle, working on a cruise ship is usually considered a temporary job, although some individuals do choose this work as a long-term career option.

Hiring is usually done through a separate company. By far the largest of these is Steiner TransOcean (**www.steinerleisure.com**), which hires for the major cruise lines. Steiner owns and operates several massage schools: Florida College of Natural Health (four locations), Baltimore School of Massage, and Virginia School of Massage. Students who graduate from a Steiner school are eligible for employment on the cruise lines serviced by the company.

Steiner employees work 12 hour days with 1½ days off per week. Assignments last four to eight months. Weekly base pay is low and most of the therapist's compensation comes from tips and sales of a proprietary line of oils and beauty products.

It is also possible to apply on-line for cruise ship work. Visit **www.cruiseplacement.com** or do a search for "cruise line jobs". Beware of sites that have a fee to join or to provide their services. With the dominance of Steiner in the placement of entry-level massage therapists on cruise ships, the positions available through other sources are generally for experienced practitioners or on small cruise lines.

*Chair massage or on-site massage.* Chair massage, also called on-site massage, corporate massage, or seated massage, has grown rapidly into a substantial part of the massage industry. On October 17, 1989, the Wall Street Journal ran a front-page story about chair massage, which was the general public's first exposure to the concept. Ten months later, the Associated Press carried a photograph of an on-site massage session being given to a customer waiting in line at the new McDonald's in Moscow. Since then, the locations for practicing chair massage have become practically unlimited. During the first week of 2001, riders of the Paris subway received complementary 6-minute chair massages, along with green tea and crackers.

Large and small corporations recognize the value of on-site massage. It can improve employee satisfaction, reduce absenteeism, reduce repetitive stress injuries, and improve employee retention rates. These can all directly contribute to the profitability of the company. Major corporations such as Reebok, Rockwell International, and Boeing offer on-site massage to employees, and thousands of medium-sized and smaller companies are doing likewise.

A recent study found that about six percent of workplaces offer on-site massage, and that in those locations, 60 percent of employees take advantage of the service.

When practiced in the workplace, the practitioner usually offers a ten to fifteen minute session to employees. Sometimes the company hires the practitioner and provides the service as a fringe benefit, and sometimes the employees pay individually for their massages.

Other locations for chair massage that are gaining in popularity are shopping centers, airports, fitness fairs, music festivals, wine festivals, art fairs, craft shows, and store-fronts. A company called "Massage Bar" has locations at four airports: Sea-Tac, Nashville, Newark and Dulles (DC). The most recent entry in the field is the car wash – a tailor-made opportunity to provide a brief treatment to the driver who has nothing to do but wait for his or her car to be ready.

A chair massage treatment is usually a shiatsu-like treatment, using a specially designed chair that supports the client's chest and face, exposing the back and shoulders. Massage chairs were once a side-line for massage table companies, but have increased in popularity and sales of chairs now rival sales of massage tables.

There are two ways to approach on-site—as a practitioner or as an entrepreneur. As with other forms of massage practice, the hardest part of the job is acquiring a clientele. In this case, that means convincing a corporate executive that your services would be beneficial to his or her workers. The strongest incentive for a corporation is financial, so emphasize how on-site massage can reduce absenteeism, assist with repetitive stress injury, improve workplace satisfaction and increase productivity.

Once you have a contact to perform services in a workplace or other location, you can perform them yourself, or hire others to do so. If you establish a large number of clients, you can keep yourself and others busy, often making a percentage profit on the work done by those you hire.

There are opportunities for employment in chair massage as well. For example, Infinite Massage (**www.infinitemassage.com**) provides chair massage at companies and events in over 50 cities nationwide and advertises the ability to provide chair massage to any location in the United States.

Many massage schools include courses on practicing and marketing chair massage, and independent training in chair massage is also available (see page 226).

***Chiropractic offices.*** Especially in California, business relationships between chiropractors and massage therapists have become quite common. Chiropractors typically employ massage therapists to work in the chiropractor's office. The chiropractor most often prescribes massage for his or her patients, handles the insurance billing procedure, and pays the therapist either a commission or an hourly wage.

Some chiropractors pay the therapist 50% of the amount charged for massage. Some pay 50% but require the massage therapist to pay a monthly rental out of the therapist's 50%. Those who employ therapists at an hourly rate often pay in the neighborhood of $15 to $20 per hour.

Chiropractors have traditionally had great reluctance about prescribing massage for their patients. Some clients enjoy massage much more than chiropractic, or believe they benefit more from massage, and choose to stop going to the chiropractor and go to the massage therapist instead.

Chiropractors combat this by having the massage therapist in their office, and prescribing massage so that insurance reimbursement will cover the cost. The client receives massage as a no-cost added benefit of chiropractic care, and therefore has an added incentive to keep coming to the chiropractor.

The chiropractor not only gains a unique service to offer, but makes a large profit, since chiropractors can bill massage services to insurance companies at far more than they pay the massage therapist (often $80 per hour or more). The massage therapist, usually a recent massage school graduate, has a way to make a living wage and to gain a great deal of professional experience quickly.

The massage/chiropractic relationship varies greatly from state to state. In some states, like California, New York and Virginia, no restrictions exist on practice relationships massage therapists and chiropractors may enter into. In other states, some barriers do exist. Maryland and New Jersey chiropractors have all received a letter from their state boards advising them that only chiropractors can perform massage services in a chiropractic office, disrupting established relationships between chiropractors and massage therapists.

*Hospitals.* Hospital-based massage is experiencing a long-overdue phase of growth. Massage programs based in hospitals have existed for about twenty years, but until recently they were few in number. One writer estimated in 1993 that 50 U.S. hospitals had one or more massage therapists working in some capacity with patients. (*Massage* Magazine, March/April 1993) Three years later, in 1996, the newsletter of the Hospital-Based Massage Network estimated there were 100 to 150 hospitals using massage. That number has been swiftly rising since then.

Several different kinds of hospital-based massage programs exist. Some involve working only on staff members, giving chair massage for stress reduction. Some involve working on the general public, usually in a wellness center, in association with the hospital. Some involve working on hospital patients by physician referral as a part of the hospital's health care team. These are sometimes paid positions, sometimes volunteer. The paid positions may be employee positions or independent contractor positions. The departments most likely to employ massage therapists are pre-surgery and post-surgery, obstetrics & gynecology, ante-partum and post-partum, neonatal intensive care, oncology, physical therapy, occupational therapy, orthopedics, cardio-pulmonary, rehabilitation, out-patient pain management, speech therapy, HIV/AIDS, and fitness or wellness centers.

The acceptance of massage in hospitals is usually the result of a good working relationship between doctors or administrators at the hospital and educators or practitioners in the massage community. The exchange of information and ideas in personal and professional relationships brings about the possibility of establishing a hospital-based massage program.

Those who wish to work in hospital settings or who want additional information about this area of practice can contact:

Hospital-Based Massage Network
**www.hbmn.com or www.info4people.com**

*House Calls.* If you talk to massage therapists about house calls, you will find that most therapists either love them or hate them. The majority seem to hate them. I personally love them.

All of the massage therapists I have talked to who hate house calls charge only a few dollars more than they charge for studio massage. Those who love house calls generally charge 40% to 50% more for a house call than for a studio massage.

Clients expect house calls to cost more. If your price is $60.00 for a studio massage, consider charging $85.00 or $90.00 for a house call. Another method of pricing is to start with your basic fee for massage; add $5.00 for carrying and setting up your table, and add 50 cents per mile for your commuting fee.

House calls have several advantages. First, there is no office rental to pay. Second, the higher fee includes compensation for your time driving to and from the client's home. It's nice to be paid for driving time, especially if your body is feeling the effects of a busy massage schedule. Third, the client usually finds it easier to fit a house call into their schedule, and may have an easier time relaxing at home than she or he would in an office environment. Finally, you get to visit lots of people's homes, many of which are quite interesting.

Certain disadvantages exist as well. First, you have little control over the environment. The phone might ring, the kids might cry, the dog might bark, the room might be cramped and it might be too hot or too cold.

Second, people dawdle more at home than they would if they came to your office. They will take a phone call, or someone will come to the door, or they will be late getting home. It is not uncommon for a one-hour massage to extend to an hour and twenty minutes. Add commuting time, and you might spend well over two hours doing a one-hour massage.

Third, carrying the massage table in and out of the car, in and out of the house, and up and down stairs can be tiring. It helps tremendously to purchase a light table and a carrying case with side handle and shoulder strap.

The real beauty of house calls comes when you can establish yourself in a community, so that you have enough business to go from one house call to another, thereby reducing your commuting time. Another advantageous situation is the couple, each of whom wants a massage at home. Some therapists do house calls exclusively, and when they become established can make a very good living.

Suggestion: Keep your oil bottle in a zip-lock plastic bag when traveling to avoid messy leaks and spills.

***Office in your home.*** Home massage office practice has major advantages and major disadvantages. The advantages are fairly obvious—no commute and complete control over your massage environment. One disadvantage is the increased vulnerability of your home because of contact with the public. Another is that some zoning boards prohibit massage as a home occupation, fearing either that you will conduct a prostitution service in you home or that your business traffic will disturb the neighborhood.

A practitioner operating in a home office must have all the permits and licenses that would be necessary for any massage office. However, some communities will not issue a permit for a home massage practice, even though they would issue a permit to a dentist or psychotherapist in the same location.

In communities that refuse to permit massage practices in the home, some practitioners simply keep a low profile and hope they do not get caught violating the law. It is a shame that professionals are required to do this, but it results from local government officials who believe that massage equals prostitution. Consider organizing the home practitioner massage therapists in your town and trying to work through the governmental process to get the zoning restrictions changed. If you choose this option, consult your professional association for guidance and support.

Another potential obstacle to a home office is liability insurance, also called "slip and fall" insurance. Most homeowners' policies do not cover a home business. It may be possible to purchase a rider for your home business at a small additional cost, or you may have to purchase business liability insurance. See Chapter 17 for more information.

The challenge in a home office is to create a professional massage environment. This means no dogs barking, no music or television sounds wafting into the room. It also means keeping your massage environment separate from your living environment, and if possible, having a separate entrance so that clients do not have to walk through your living space to get to the massage room. If there is no separate entrance, the massage room should be the first or second room one comes to on entering the house.

If you are going to base your business in your home office, treat it as professionally as you would any other office space. Charge the going rate, have a separate phone line, and create the ideal massage room. Your efforts to create a professional atmosphere are just as important in a home office as in any other office you practice in.

***Group Practice.*** Joining in practice with other massage therapists or other health practitioners can be a great way to share expenses, generate cross-referrals, and create a sense of community in which each member draws support from belonging to the group.

One difficulty with a group practice is that everyone shares the responsibility for making decisions that affect the group, so there is a need for regularly scheduled meetings in which everyone must participate. This can be time-consuming, and can take lots of energy, especially when it comes in the middle of a busy week.

Some group practices hire a receptionist, and others use the group members to answer the phone on a rotating basis. A receptionist is a substantial expense that has to be split among the practice members, so sharing phone duties substantially lowers the overhead. However, for a well-established practice, having a receptionist can be a luxury for the practitioners who would rather not deal with telephones and scheduling. The presence of a receptionist also designates the office off as a successful and professional operation.

***Entrepreneur with associates.*** Similar to a group practice, several massage therapists or other kinds of therapists practice in a single location. Instead of being a group venture, however, it is the business venture of one or two who lease or own the establishment. The other practitioners either rent space or pay a percentage of the fees they charge. Payment of rent is much more common than fee-splitting.

The entrepreneur can often arrange things so that the rents paid by the other therapists cover the entire expense of the building, giving the entrepreneur a rent-free office. Generally, the entrepreneur is someone with a strong reputation in the community and good business skills.

*Individual massage office.* In an individual office, you have complete control over your environment and your schedule. You also have complete responsibility for getting done everything that needs to be done, including paying the rent and all other expenses. You have the most freedom and the most responsibility; the most potential for debt and the most potential for large income.

## Legal relationships

Any two people who have a business relationship also have a legal relationship. These relationships can apply to people in all of the categories discussed above.

*Sole proprietor.* When you are the only one in charge of your business, you are the sole proprietor. In the eyes of the law, you and the business are one. Business income and personal income are pooled together for income tax purposes, as are business deductions and personal deductions.

If you work in another person's office, you will need to understand whether you are working as an employee or as an independent contractor.

*Independent contractor/employee.* This refers to the two different legal relationships you can have when you make an agreement to work in another person or organization's location.

The main difference to you lies in how your income taxes are handled. If you are an *employee,* your employer is responsible for paying social security tax on your earnings, and must withhold money from your pay for this purpose.

However, if you are an *independent contractor,* you are responsible for paying your own contribution to the social security system, called a self-employment tax, and nothing is withheld from your pay. This can make a significant difference to you and to the person who may have to pay social security tax on your wages.

Another difference between employees and independent contractors relates to insurance. The person you are working for will normally have business insurance that covers employees but *not* independent contractors. For this reason, some massage employers will hire only employees, so that they will be covered under the business insurance policy.

The key fact that distinguishes between your status as an independent contractor or employee is who has *control* over the way in which you perform your services. If you are in charge of setting your hours and your fees, and choosing the specifics of the treatments you give, then you are an independent contractor. If the person or organization you work for controls your hours, your prices, and your therapeutic services, then you are an employee. You are more likely to be considered and *employee* if this is the only company you work for, or if you do not use your own equipment or supplies, or if massage is the main business of the person you work for.

If your situation has elements of both employment and independent contracting, then you have to examine it to see which definition it more closely fits. If you are truly an employee but your employer treats you as an independent contractor, the IRS can charge substantial penalties to your employer for failing to withhold the appropriate taxes.

# 6 Career Strategies

The purpose of this chapter is to help you acquire a "big picture" of your possibilities for a massage career. This chapter will examine the ways you can organize your career, from the investigation phase through the building of a practice.

The following four steps form a framework for your massage career:

1. Investigate the field—explore the field to see if you are interested in pursuing a career.

2. Go to massage school—make a choice based on geography, educational standards, or specialization.

3. Choose one of three approaches for professional growth: cautious exploration, planned transition or total immersion.

4. Create a business plan and follow it through.

## 1. Investigate the field

This book contains some of the flavor of a career in massage, but your own experience is the most reliable guide you can consult. Supplement the resources and ideas in this book by finding people who can complete your picture of the field. Get a professional massage. Talk to professionals about their careers. Listen to what people say about massage.

Imagine yourself in the profession. Can you? Is it easy, enjoyable and exciting, or awkward and unnatural? Ask yourself why you want to go into the field. Are your motives based in service and a desire to connect with other people, or are you thinking more about what you can get from the profession?

This is the time to be as honest with yourself as you can. Choosing massage as a career can be very rewarding for the person who wants to grow and serve. It can be frustrating for the person who does not have the determination to make a commitment and follow it through.

## 2. Going to massage school

Some massage schools offer evening programs so that you can go to school without changing your life. Others require full-time attendance.

If you are unsure about pursuing massage as a career, you might consider taking some adult education massage classes, or classes for the general public offered by the massage school in your area. This can be an excellent way to "get your feet wet" without risking your whole lifestyle. It may also have the advantage of making the rest of your professional education tax-deductible (See Chapter 19).

Your choice of a massage school will set the tone for your career. Use the resources provided in Section VII (page 243) to locate, evaluate and choose the best massage school for you.

# 3. Choose your approach:

## *permanent part-time, cautious exploration,*
## *planned transition or total immersion*

Your massage career will take some time to grow. Your skills as a therapist will mature for years after you finish massage school. Your reputation in the community will likewise take time to build. It is best to have a plan that will allow you to integrate that period of career growth into the context of your life.

### *Plan A: Permanent Part-Time*

Massage is a career that lends itself well to part-time practice, and a great many massage therapists—possibly more than half—choose to keep their career permanently part-time.

In 1999, ABMP conducted a survey of its members and found that about half of those surveyed had a second, non-massage job. In 2000, AMTA did a survey of its members and found that more than half of the respondents practiced massage part-time. A 1999 job analysis conducted by the National Certification Board found that 65% of massage practitioners earned $20,000.00 per year or less.

Full-time massage work can be physically demanding. Repetitive strain injuries can be a problem, and giving out your energy all day can be depleting. While some practitioners can give six or seven massages per day with no ill effects, others know that they must stop after three or four massages per day in order to stay healthy.

If you can acquire either a house-call practice or an office practice with low overhead costs, a part-time massage practice can support you, and can give you the freedom to pursue your other interests as well. For parents of small children, those with other part-time jobs, aspiring writers, dancers, actors, and people in a variety of other work situations, a part-time massage career can make a lot of sense.

### *Plan B: Cautious Exploration*

This is a low-risk alternative. The idea is to make no significant changes in your current lifestyle, but integrate massage education and exploration of massage practice into your life.

You can do this by going to a massage school that has evening or weekend classes, and using your after-hours time to experiment with doing massage professionally. You can charge for your services or not, as you see fit. (In states that require a license, you can charge only after licensure) The idea is to gain experience, and to learn whether massage is a field you want to put some real energy into.

After exploring the field in this way, you will be in a position to know whether it is something you enjoy and can commit to pursuing for a living. At this point, you can move to Plan C or Plan D, or make an informed choice to remain a part-time massage practitioner.

### Plan C: Planned Transition

This is for those who are committed to pursuing a career in massage, yet want to do it in a way that creates a minimum of disruption in their lives. It is a plan that is particularly well suited to teachers, part-time and flex-time workers, and others with substantial free time to pursue a massage career.

A teacher might build her massage practice after working hours. When it reaches a good level, she can switch to substitute teaching. When the practice will support her fully, she can quit teaching and rely fully on massage. Similarly, a waiter or waitress can cut back on hours as the massage practice grows, eventually giving up waiting tables completely.

In order to make this option work, you will need to be committed. Making a living at your "day job" can take a lot out of you, yet you need to have the energy and drive to become established in your new field during your after-hours time. In the next chapter, you will read about the many marketing techniques available to you. Make sure you will have the energy to keep your current job and also apply yourself to building a massage practice. The transition may take several years, so be sure you are prepared.

### Plan D: Total Immersion

This is a sink-or-swim approach in which you quit your job, rely on whatever financial support you have, and focus 100 percent on establishing yourself as a professional massage therapist. This option requires some means of financial independence—either a bankroll, a generous spouse or benefactor, or a talent at living without much money.

Most marketing techniques require you to have an office setting for the practice of massage. To pursue Total Immersion, you should have an office. This will of course add a significant expense for which you must be prepared. Give some thought to the economics of the situation, and decide whether you could essentially go without any income for a year. There is a good chance that your first year will be a very lean one, and that your second may not be a great deal better.

Some prefer this approach because it forces the person to do everything possible to make a success of their massage career. To pursue this option requires a clear sense of commitment, and also an understanding of the balance between self-promotion and patience. You should also be prepared for some long, lonely days.

This option will be easier for the individual who has lots of contacts and a strong local reputation. Such a person will have the best chance of establishing a practice relatively quickly. It is not advisable for someone who is new in the community.

## 4. Create a Business Plan and Follow it Through

A business plan is like a blueprint. You can build without one, but having one is likely to make your task easier and your result better.

The specifics for creating a business plan, and a form you can use to create your own, are provided in the next chapter.

# 7 Marketing Yourself as a Massage Therapist

This topic mystifies more massage therapists and bodyworkers than any other. Books, marketing kits, seminars, instructional videos, and other items are on the market to teach you how to acquire a following in your chosen profession.

This guide will give you the benefit of my experiences, as well as those of many other therapists I have interviewed, as to principles and techniques you can use to market your professional services. Before examining the specific techniques you can use, however, there are a few questions you should ask yourself.

## 1. Preliminary questions

### *Are You Ready?*

Do you feel your massage is worth $60.00 per hour (or whatever is the going rate in your area)?

How would you feel about having a strong clientele in the town you are now living in? Are you prepared to call this place home?

Imagine introducing yourself to a variety of people in your town. You tell them you are a massage therapist. How does that feel to you?

The above questions touch on the chief reasons that massage practitioners, even after they have gone to massage school, are reluctant to make a commitment to building a massage practice. If you are not ready to present yourself to the public as a professional deserving their time and money, take the time to grow before making a sincere effort at professional marketing.

That growth may mean gaining new professional skills. It may mean confronting issues of self-image or self-esteem. It may mean learning to be comfortable relating to a broad variety of people. Your growth on all these levels will continue for a long time, well into your professional career. You do not need to be perfect to succeed as a massage therapist—just ready.

### *How Long Do You Expect This To Take?*

How much of a hurry are you in? Are you expecting to throw yourself into a marketing campaign for six months and then have a thriving practice? Are you willing to spend two years or longer creating a practice for yourself? If you are looking for the six-month version, you will probably be disappointed in the results. These things take time.

Consider advertising, for example. One study has shown that the average consumer will notice your ad only one out of three times you run it, and that the same consumer has to *see* your ad nine times before she is ready to purchase the advertised goods or services. Therefore, you may need to run an ad 27 times to have your client actually come in for a massage.

Word of mouth can be similarly time-consuming. A client coming to me for the first time told me that a friend had been urging him to try my massage for *two years*. Two years is an exceptionally long delay in accepting a referral, but I include this example to give you the idea that some aspects of marketing simply cannot be rushed. Successful marketing involves a blend of *commitment* and *patience*.

## *What's your plan?*

Make a plan for your career—what your practice will be like in six months, one year, two years, three years, five years. Use the form below or create your own planning form.

All sources of professional business guidance will tell you, as a business person, that a business plan is an essential part of your growth process. Advantages of a business plan are:

- It helps you know where you want your career to go;

- It helps you keep track of your progress toward your goals;

- It helps you organize your efforts toward meeting your goals;

- It gives you the clarity to express your goals to others so that they will help you find opportunities.

At the same time, it is important to stay flexible and be quite willing to depart from the plan. In fact, every few months or so, you may want to completely rewrite your plan to reflect what you have learned or how your goals have changed.

For example, let's say you make a business plan that emphasizes house calls in an affluent suburb. It includes working at a health spa in that area part-time and using advertising in a community newspaper to try to break into the house call market. Midway through this project, you meet a cardiologist who offers you an office in his group practice. This is a terrific opportunity that you had not even realized was possible.

Do you pass up the cardiologist because you are in the middle of a different plan? Of course not. You change your business plan. At the same time, it was important to have the business plan even though you changed it; you might never have met the cardiologist.

When you make your plans for six months, one year, two years, three years and five years from now, be as detailed and specific as you can. Include your best predictions about all of the following:

- Location for doing massage

- Target clients

- Type of work you want to be doing

- How clients will learn about you

- Number of clients you want or expect to have

- Workshops, professional trainings and meetings to attend

- Advertising and other promotional plans

- Expenses you are likely to incur

Mark on the top of each plan the date you write it, and the target date for the goals you create. Take your group of plans out every few months and see how things are going. Revise your business plan at least once a year.

### Sample Business Plan

On page 42 is a sample business plan for Mary Jones. Mary has been out of massage school one year, and is seeing 8 to 12 clients per week. Some of these are house calls, and some are in a resort 15 miles from her home. She has a part-time job doing cleaning work to supplement her income.

## Create Your Business Plan

Use the form on page 43 as a sample to create your business plan. If you feel the form does not suit your particular needs, by all means modify it to take into account the planning you need to do.

You will be creating more business plans as time goes by, so you may want to create a form that suits you and make a few copies of it. Keep your business plans in a folder and keep the folder with your other business materials, such as business receipts, client records, and professional books.

## 2. Nuts and Bolts of Marketing for Massage and Bodywork

You have examined your readiness for success, your expectations about your career path, and your plans for making your goals take shape. You now have an understanding of the larger picture that your marketing efforts will fit into.

Before discussing the specific marketing techniques you might use, there is one broad principle to consider:

### Person-to-person contact is the most effective.

Because massage is a personal service, and because it is relatively expensive, people want to have a good idea that they are going to like both the person and the person's treatment before they come in for a massage. It is much harder to convey this level of confidence with impersonal contact, such as advertising, than it is with person-to-person contact.

To overcome people's natural shyness and resistance to the idea of nudity and being touched, you need to let people know enough about you to trust you, and enough about your work to have confidence in it.

Keep this in mind as you consider the following techniques you can use to promote your professional services.

**MARY JONES' BUSINESS PLAN**                              May 7, 2006

**Goals:**

　　To increase clientele to 25 per week
　　To keep commuting distances to a minimum
　　To emphasize sports massage in my practice

**Target clientele:**

　　Amateur and professional athletes
　　Local residents
　　Professionals and their spouses

**Possible new locations to work in:**

　　Hospital wellness center
　　Sports injury clinic
　　Country club

**Means of reaching new clients:**

　　Ads or feature story in country club newsletter
　　Person-to-person contact with physicians and attorneys in the area
　　Contacts with personal fitness trainers and athletic trainers in the area
　　Ads or feature story in local circulation newspaper

*Six month goals:*

Acquire a local office at a low cost where I can see clients; meet at least four personal fitness trainers or athletic trainers and give them complimentary demonstration massages; meet at least four doctors or lawyers in the area and introduce them to myself and my work.

*One year goals:*

Take advanced trainings in neuromuscular therapy and sports massage techniques; expand contacts with personal fitness trainers and athletic trainers; expand athletic clientele to at least 12 per week; obtain a quality office environment where I can create the ideal setting for sports and rehabilitative massage as well as doing relaxation massage.

*Two year goals:*

Have firmly established sports/rehabilitative massage office, seeing 20 clients per week. Supplement practice with occasional house calls for professional clientele. Work with world-class athletes in preparation for competitive events.

*Three year goals:*

Travel with athletes to sporting events, hire other sports massage therapists to work in my clinic when I am away.

*Five year goals:*

Offer sports massage trainings; employ at least one full-time massage therapist in my clinic; work exclusively with competitive athletes.

SAMPLE BUSINESS PLAN _____ date: _____

Items to consider:
>       Location for doing massage
>       Target clients
>       Type of work I want to be doing
>       How clients will learn about me
>       Number of clients I will have
>       Current fee structure
>       Workshops, professional trainings and meetings
>       Advertising and other promotional plans
>       Expenses I am likely to incur

**Goals:**


**Target clientele:**


**Possible locations to work in:**


**Means of reaching target clientele:**


**Six month goals:**


**One year goals:**


**Two year goals:**


**Three year goals:**


**Five year goals:**

# *A. Person-to-person Marketing Techniques*

All professions depend chiefly on referrals, or word-of-mouth, and massage is no exception. A certain amount of word-of-mouth marketing happens naturally. If you give one client a great massage, she naturally wants to tell her friends, and some of them may be curious enough to try you out sooner or later.

The art of marketing yourself, however, lies in accelerating this process as much as possible. The main task to accomplish in that regard is to become widely known and accepted within as many groups as possible in your community.

The following are some proven methods for making people familiar with you and comfortable with you, and interested in trying your therapy:

## *1. Demonstration/lecture at health clubs, professional groups and social groups*

These can be a very effective way to become known and accepted, and to increase your clientele. The idea is to present a short speech on the nature of massage, the benefits it can have, and what is to be expected during a session. This is followed up by a brief demonstration on a volunteer.

If you are doing it in a place where a massage room is available, such as a health club, you might consider following it up with an offer to do a ten-minute foot massage on anyone who is curious.

A presentation of this sort accomplishes many marketing goals all at once. As you establish rapport with the group, you become known, familiar and accepted. They learn the theory of massage and how it can help them, and they gain an understanding of the process and what to expect. Then, after your demonstration, they see and hear from your client how wonderful a person feels after one of your treatments.

For someone who is curious about massage but fearful about nudity or about being touched by a stranger, the lecture/demonstration is perhaps the only marketing tool that will give that person the confidence to try a massage. By creating confidence in yourself, taking the mystery out of the massage process, and giving the person a clear idea of what she has to gain by having a massage, you can effectively break down some strong barriers to using your services.

One therapist gave several lecture/demonstrations at her health club, a women-only club. She made such an impression that practically each time she went into the club for a workout after that, one or more members came up to her asking to schedule a massage appointment.

Other locations for this type of presentation are civic, professional and social groups. Ask your friends and clients about any groups they are members of, such as the Rotary, local women's club, yoga group, exercise class, or toastmasters. These groups are often glad to have outside speakers, and the fact that one of their members recommends you will be an advantage.

Many people have a great fear of public speaking, and will feel it is impossible to do a lecture/demonstration in front of a group. If you can't, you can't. However, if you can't you are missing out on one of the most effective and successful marketing opportunities you can use. Remember that the group you speak to will be there because they are interested in you and in massage. They are on your side and they want to like you. Prepare in advance what you are going to say and do, and just be yourself.

A group that can help you overcome your fear of public speaking is Toastmasters International. They have regional meetings everywhere, usually early in the morning, and each participant gives short talks and receives constructive criticism. You can find your local groups at **www.toastmasters.org**.

## 2. Free introductory massages for selected individuals

Anyone who is likely to be the source of repeated referrals should be cultivated as a contact. Such people are psychotherapists, medical doctors, chiropractors, acupuncturists, wholistic practitioners of all sorts, team coaches and sports trainers, dancing teachers, real estate agents, other massage therapists and bodyworkers, and people who are well-known and well-respected members of the community.

Any of these people, who are in a position of trust with their friends, neighbors, clients, and patients, will generally be listened to by those they know. Therefore, once they believe in you and your work, they can be a good source of referrals.

You may wish to seek out these people and try to introduce yourself, or you may wait until you meet someone in the natural course of events. Either way, offering a complimentary massage can be an excellent way of introducing that person to you and your work. Once they know you and your work from their own experience, they will be more willing to refer clients to you.

## 3. Gift Certificates as a mass marketing tool

Consider using gift certificates creatively as a promotional tool. Some ways to do so are:

- give out gift certificates with your business card

- give gift certificates to charities and fund raisers to use as prizes

- give gift certificates to a local radio station to be given away to callers

Even though you may give out a large number of gift certificates, most will probably not be redeemed. You may find that only about one in five certificates is actually used. The recipients who do use the certificates are interested in becoming massage clients, and a significant percentage of these are likely to become repeat customers.

Hopefully, at least ten percent of the people who redeem your gift certificates will become repeat clients. If so, you will have acquired a very valuable practice boost for no cost to yourself, and the publicity generated by your promotion will have boosted your reputation and good will in the community. Consider the following true story about using gift certificates as a marketing tool:

> I did a small mailing to CPAs at tax time, empathizing with their stress and enclosing a gift certificate for massage. Of the ten CPAs I mailed to, only two responded. Only one actually made an appoint-

ment, and, after several cancellations and reschedulings in a row, I was about ready to give up on her. However, after her massage, she made regular appointments for herself and her husband through the end of that year, then referred her neighbors, both of whom come every week for massage ... and then *they* referred some folks ... short version of the story is that one give away ended up providing about two-thirds of my income that year! Since that time I have formed a relationship with a local high end real estate agent. I have given her probably a hundred or more certificates to give to her clients as closing (or other) gifts, and she continues to send me a small but steady flow of folks who like and can afford massage.

### 4. Discounts to clients for referrals

One therapist gives a ten-dollar discount on the next massage to any client who refers another client. She believes this fosters referrals, as it gives clients a motivation to spread the word about massage.

In a similar vein, one therapist offers a "buy two gift certificates, get your massage free" promotion. I have not tried either approach. My hunch is that clients have a natural desire to tell their friends and neighbors when they like you and your service. However, it is possible that a financial incentive would give them more of a reason to do so. Those of you who do try it, let me know your experiences.

### 5. Join the local Chamber of Commerce

Consider joining the Chamber of Commerce in your community. These are local business people who are getting together to share matters of common concern. You are such a person, and there is no reason you should not be involved in such a group.

The contacts you make in a group like this will be valuable for your career, since these people know many members of the community. The more you become known and accepted as a "normal" business person, the less resistance people will have to the idea of coming to you for a massage.

### 6. Do on-site promotional massages

This means going where the people are and working either for free or for a small amount, doing brief treatments.

You can rent a booth at a health fair, craft fair, workshop center or convention and offer five or ten minute massages. You can arrange in advance to set up at the end of a sporting event, or at a shopping center during busy times. If your office is on a busy street, consider doing chair massage on a volunteer in front of your building to draw attention to you and your practice.

The exposure you get from such activities may bring you clients immediately, and also may have a long-term benefit in getting you known in the local community.

### 7. Join as many organizations as you comfortably can

The goal is to meet large numbers of people and to become known. Don't join organizations just to accomplish a marketing goal. You won't have fun, and you may seem pushy. Join organizations you are interested in, but don't be shy about telling people what you do, and never get caught without your business card handy to give out to an interested person.

## B. Person-To-Paper Contact

There are some people who are your potential clients, whom you cannot reach in person or through a personal recommendation. Reaching them through the printed word may be your only means of making contact.

Advertising is a quick way to reach large numbers of people. The difficult aspects of using advertising effectively are *avoiding* the people you do *not* want to find you, and making a persuasive impression on the people you do want to find you.

Advertising has the disadvantage of being impersonal contact. It will let people know who you are and where you are and perhaps what you offer. However, it will not tell them that they will like you, that they can trust you, that you have a great touch and tremendous skills, or that they will feel much better after one of your treatments.

Therefore, advertising will most effectively reach those clients who are already familiar with massage but do not currently have a massage therapist whom they go to. This is a relatively small percentage of the general population. However, it takes only one new regular client to make any advertisement worth its cost.

The biggest disadvantage of advertising is that it opens you to sexually--oriented massage clients. A great many men have had sexual experiences that were billed as "massage." In many areas of the United States today, it is easier to find sexual massage than it is to find legitimate massage. Though great progress has been made in legitimizing the profession in recent years, confusion persists.

Doing any general advertising virtually guarantees that you will be confronted by at least some men calling to find out if they can get sexual services from you. Every massage therapist I know finds this to be draining, degrading and infuriating. However, at this point in the history of massage, it is an unavoidable side-effect of using advertising as a tool to build your practice.

**Suggestion:** In any person-to-paper advertising you do, consider including a photo of yourself. This will do several things. First, it will help dispel any idea that you are offering sexual massage. Second, it will convey some information about you—it is the best substitute available for personal contact. Finally, it is an eye-catcher. In a print medium, a photo tends to draw attention, and it can help clients see an ad they might otherwise miss.

### 1. Flyers and Business cards

Flyers and business cards are best used after you have made person-to-person contact, to further explain your work or to serve as a reminder about you and your services.

Most therapists who have tried leaving flyers for the general public and posting business cards in places like health food stores and supermarkets find that the results are poor. You may find that your business cards mainly reach the other therapists who see your card when they post theirs.

One flyer that worked was the one used by Wes Boyce in southern California. That is reproduced on the following page. Wes used this flyer as part of his plan to become established quickly from the ground up. This flyer brought him 100 clients within seven months, and at that point he canceled the promotion. His promotion had raised $1,000 for Meals On Wheels.

He did not make much money directly from these massages, although some clients tipped him, and a few became paying customers. However, he was able to get a lot of practical experience in a short time, and also generated a great deal of public awareness about himself and his work.

### 2. Direct mail

This refers to those packets of ads and coupons we all get in the mail from time to time. Some massage therapists have used these very effectively to build their practices.

These direct mailings generally go to 10,000 homes at a time. The cost to have your ad or coupon included will usually be a few hundred dollars. This may sound like a lot of money, but consider that one weekly client will repay the entire cost of the promotion in two to three months.

Two useful approaches to direct mail are to use it when you open a new office, and to use it at holiday times to advertise gift certificates. It can also be used as a major promotion to boost an existing practice.

To get in touch with direct mail companies, look in the mailers for their phone number and address, or get the Business-to-Business Yellow Pages if there is one for your area. (available free from your local phone company's business office) Look in the listing for "Marketing Programs and Services."

The direct mail sales person will help you design your promotion. Most such promotions include a special offer or coupon, such as an introductory massage for new clients at a reduced price.

### 3. Yellow Pages

All of the massage therapists I interviewed who have yellow pages listings agreed that the listing more than paid for itself with the business it generated. However, they also agreed that the quality of calls that came from the listing was poor. A large percentage of these calls are from men seeking sex, and a significant amount of time and energy is taken in screening these calls.

Some localities have two listings in the yellow pages—one for massage, and one for massage therapists. The idea behind the distinction is to tip off the sex-seekers that those listed as massage therapists are legitimate. Unfortunately, the sex clients either don't see the distinction, or figure that you're really offering sex and you put the listing under "massage therapist" to fool the police. If your listing has the word "massage" in it, you can count on sex calls.

# *Treat Yourself!...*

## *Treat the Senior Adults of North County*

Receive a **FREE One-Hour MASSAGE** if you donate a minimum of $10.00 to the Senior Adult Services - North Coast - Meals On Wheels program.

 WES BOYCE, M.S., Ms.T., is an experienced, state certified Massage Technician licensed in the City of Encinitas. He is offering a **FREE**, one-time, **Full-Body Massage**, normally valued at $40.00, when you support Meals On Wheels. Your $10.00 donation will feed one senior for two days — meals delivered by M-O-W volunteers.

If you are in need of ENHANCED ENERGY, BODY RELAXATION, STRESS REDUCTION or SPORTS MASSAGE, contact Wes. He'll help to relieve your stiffness, aches and pains, in the neck, back and shoulders. Treat yourself and/or a friend to this unique opportunity and experience the wonders of massage.

You'll feel better — for supporting a worthwhile cause and for giving your body the freedom from tension that it deserves.

## *Call today for an appointment*

# **(619) 436-1569**

You can help create the image you want by carefully selecting the name and information you present in the yellow pages. One practical option is to choose a business name at the beginning of the alphabet, since you will get more calls if you are listed first.

Another practical option is to choose a name like "wholistic health center" to attract only legitimate callers. The business name you choose for your yellow pages listing need not be the same as the one on your business cards or bank account. The people who publish the yellow pages will accept most any business name you supply.

Yellow pages ads are expensive. A basic listing with no more than name and phone number will cost around $20 per month. A small block ad with some basic information can cost around $60 per month. Larger ads can cost a great deal more. This will be more economical for a group practice than for an individual.

Getting into the yellow pages requires some advance planning. In my area, the deadline for new orders is in March, and new books are distributed in July. If you are opening a new office, or changing locations, you may want to coordinate your move with the schedule of the yellow pages publisher to minimize the disruption in your practice.

### 4. Newspaper coverage of you and your practice

One way to become better known is to have a local newspaper reporter write an article about you, about massage, and about any particular aspect of you or your work that is unique or interesting.

Make contact with a reporter for your local newspaper, and give her or him a massage. Discuss anything about yourself or your work or training that may be of interest, and let the reporter decide what angle might serve as the basis for a story. You may also want to discuss the role of massage in society; its popularity, its many uses, the confusion between legitimate massage and illicit massage, etc. As an "expert" you have greater credibility and interest with the general public.

After the story appears in the paper, frame it and put it on your office wall. Your clients will be gently reminded that you are a special person worthy of respect.

### 5. Placing ads in newspapers

Many successful massage therapists never advertised in newspapers and never will. Others have found newspaper advertising to be a way to shorten the time needed to build a practice to a self-supporting level. Others have advertised and been so frustrated by the clients who responded that they have burned out on massage as a profession. The following information about newspaper advertising should help you make the most of newspaper advertising.

#### Two types of newspaper ads—classifieds, display ads

Two types of massage ads are available in newspapers—display ads and business classified ads. Display ads (also called block ads) appear in the body of the paper, with the news and features articles, and therefore are seen by more readers than business classifieds. Display ads are larger and substantially more expensive than business classifieds. Display ads make sense in small-circulation newspapers, when you are trying to break into a new market. In larger newspapers, massage ads almost always run in the business classifieds.

### Business classifieds

Business classifieds is a separate section of the classifieds, devoted to business services such as painting, carpentry, cleaning and hauling. While these ads are much cheaper than display ads, they cost a great deal more than a normal classified ad.

The response to advertising in the business classifieds tends to be immediate. If the response to your classified ad is going to be good, you will know within the first few days. Start with a short run for your ad, so that if the response is not good, you have the opportunity to try a different newspaper.

Generally speaking, business classified advertising is cost-effective for massage therapists. In other words, you will generally make more money as a result of placing the ad than you spend on the ad. The other question, however, is how much grief you will have to put up with in the process.

### Display advertising

Display advertising is quite different from business classified advertising. Someone looking up massage in a business classified is ready for a massage—today, if possible. Someone just reading the news or features, who sees your display ad in the newspaper, was not thinking about massage until she saw your ad. She may not be ready for massage for quite a while.

In fact, it may take many exposures to your ad before this person feels you are sufficiently "familiar" to give you a try. After seeing your ad a few times, she will begin to get the idea that you are not just a passing fad, but a true fixture in the community.

The more times a person sees your ad, the more familiar and accepted your name will be to that person. After five to ten exposures to your ad, the person may be sufficiently comfortable with your print image that she would consider trying a massage. The more nervous the person is about massage, the longer it may take for her to begin to feel comfortable about you by repeatedly seeing you ad.

Therefore, display advertising is generally best used in small circulation newspapers, where you have a particular desire to break into a new market that you feel has a good potential for your practice. Choose your newspaper and plan to place your ad many times. Keep your ad the same each time you run it, so that the "familiarity" factor works best. Use a picture of yourself in the ad—this will be an eye-catcher, will help the person feel she knows you and will give more of a sense that you can be trusted.

## Types of Newspapers

Many types of newspapers exist, and you can use each differently in aid of your marketing goals. The different types of newspapers are general circulation dailies, special interest newspapers (usually weekly or monthly), and local or regional papers (usually weekly).

### General circulation newspapers

These are the daily newspapers read by the general population. The general circulation newspaper I advertised in is the Asbury Park Press, which serves a region within about a 25-mile radius of Asbury Park, New Jersey. Their business classified directory includes a listing for massage, and at the top of the massage listing each day is the following notice:

---

ATTENTION ADVERTISERS: The only copy permitted in a massage ad is: name, address, phone number, rates & hours. The only exception is a licensed spa listing their facilities (sauna, steam room, etc.)

The terminology 'Professional or Licensed' can be used if customer sends copy of certificate from a school of massage prior to ad running.

Ads must be paid in advance.

---

This notice appeared for the first time shortly after the same newspaper ran a story about a prostitution ring that had operated through the massage classifieds. The management placed the notice at the top of the massage listing in an attempt to prevent the use of its massage ads for prostitution.

I advertised in this listing immediately before and immediately after the story about the prostitution ring operating through the massage classifieds. Despite the notice at the top of the listing, and despite the story in the same newspaper about prostitution arrests, roughly ninety percent of the calls I received from this ad were men looking for sexual massage. This percentage did not seem to change as a result of the prostitution story or as a result of putting the notice at the top of the massage listing.

Phone calls at 7:00 A.M. and 11:45 P.M. in response to my ad were not uncommon. I chose to answer my own phone, although some therapists who advertise leave the answering machine on and selectively return calls. I found that, in general, people calling at unusual times were looking for unusual massage services. My first name (Martin) indicated I was a man, and my ad apparently attracted a great many gay or bisexual callers. Calls for sexual massage dropped off dramatically after the first week.

Most of the clients looking for sex had the sense to stop trying when I explained in no uncertain terms that my massage was completely legitimate and did not include any sexual contact. A few, however, apparently regarded that as a challenge and made appointments anyway.

These men would wait until the end of their massage, or in some cases until their second or third massage, to verbally or non-verbally make their wishes known. This was quite a growth experience for me, as I had to learn how to deal with my own feelings of anger and resentment in such a situation.

My growth brought me to a point where I could comfortably take charge of the situation. I learned to discuss any suspect signs of arousal immediately, carefully watch the client's attitude about the subject, and terminate the massage immediately if the client was being inappropriate. Once I realized that I had control of the situation, my emotional response lessened dramatically.

The several regular clients I acquired through this advertising exposure are lovely people whom I appreciate very much as clients, and who never would have found me without the ad. The total expense for the ads I ran was about $250 over a period of several weeks. Despite the irritation factor, on the whole it was well worth doing.

### Special interest newspapers

There may be newspapers for special interest groups in your area that can be good sources of massage clients. Such papers include:

- New age or holistically oriented newspapers

- Religious or community oriented newspapers

- Homeowners' association newsletters

- In-house newspapers for corporations

- In-house newspapers for institutions such as retirement communities and hospitals

- Magazines or newsletters targeted to women, mothers, families, athletes, or other groups

- Real estate mailings sent out by local agents

The cost involved is usually low, and the response level probably will also be low. However, such exposure can be useful in gaining entry into a new market. I placed small ads in two local newspapers targeted to the Jewish community in my area. These generated enough new business to at least pay for the ads, and also served to gain some name recognition.

If there is a corporate headquarters or large corporate office near your practice consider advertising in their in-house corporate newspaper. This can be a good source of clients who can afford your services and are near your office on a daily basis.

### Local and regional newspapers

Many communities have small local papers, which are published once or twice a week. These are sometimes mailed to all households in the community at no charge. These papers often have a "business classified" section similar to the one in general circulation newspapers.

Before advertising in one of these, get the flavor of the other ads in the paper. If a massage ad would seem distinctly out of place in comparison to the other types of ads that are currently running, it may not be a good idea to place your ad in that paper.

As with special interest newspapers, the circulation of local papers will be small, as will be the cost to advertise. One advantage is that you can be sure that any potential clients who see this ad will be close to you and able to conveniently reach your office.

## C. Broadcast Media

Radio, broadcast television, and direct access cable television are also possibilities for massage marketing. Generally speaking, the cost of commercial advertisements on radio and television is too great for an individual massage practice.

Direct access cable, however, can provide opportunities for exposure. A pair of chiropractors in my area produced a multi-part feature on wholistic health modalities that was broadcast on direct access cable. One segment was on massage, and the therapist they chose for that segment received significant exposure at no expense to her.

## D. Internet Marketing Opportunities

The Internet will not provide a majority of your massage referrals, but it can provide your practice a boost if done properly.

How successful is Internet marketing? There's an old saying "The more things change, the more they remain the same." With the Internet, as with pre-Internet massage marketing, there are some success stories and some flops, and many in-betweens.

One massage therapist in Southern California has a successful website at **www.MassageDirect.com**. She has actively promoted the website and has also listed her practice with several referral websites (referral websites are discussed below). She reports receiving several clients per month from the Internet. A practitioner in Denver has a website which is listed with many search engines, yet he has received only one Internet client in six months. Another practitioner has entirely given up on Internet referrals because most of the clients who found her from the Internet were seeking sexual massage, and most of the appointments made were not kept.

A husband and wife who are both bodyworkers in Rutland, Vermont have a website, and although they are listed on many search engines, their community is so sparsely populated that the Internet does not provide them with client referrals. However, their website has proven to be a good marketing tool in other ways; when a new client calls, after giving some preliminary information, they can refer the person to the website for further information and details. They believe this gives them an edge over other local practitioners who do not have a website. In addition, they have sold gift certificates to out-of-town people who want to give gift certificates to their central Vermont friends and relatives.

As far as I know, no one supports a massage practice exclusively with Internet referrals. How successful your site becomes will depend partly on where you live, partly on how well you produce your site, and partly on the skills and services you have to offer to the public.

There are two basic strategies for using the Internet to market your practice. One is self-promotion and the other is getting listed on sites that promote your practice for you. Following are some of the basics for each approach.

*Strategy #1—Make a website and promote it.* If you have ever created a website, you know it is not as intimidating as a novice might think. Free software is available on the Internet that you can use to create websites. Even Microsoft Word can be used to create a basic web page.

If you don't have good computer skills, find someone who is computer-savvy to make a website for you. It's not that big a job for someone who knows how to do it—you can hire someone to make your website, or you may even find someone willing to trade massage for website creation services.

### Designing your website

Your website should reflect who you are and what services you offer. Design it the way you would design your massage room—think about how the visitor will feel at your site and choose words and images that reflect the best about you and your work. Your website should also "sell" you to potential clients; it should convince them that you have something valuable or unique to offer them, and it should give them a sense of personal connection with you and a basis for trusting you.

One crucial element of a successful website is a good quality photograph of yourself. The old saying "a picture is worth a thousand words" has some truth in it. Don't you get a "feeling" about a person when you see their photograph? With a service as personal as massage, it is crucial that a potential client has a reason to trust you and feel comfortable with you, and putting your photograph on the site goes a long way to starting that personal relationship.

Your site should also act like a good résumé does; it should get across your strengths and talents so the potential customer feels interested about trying your work. Put your best foot forward when you describe yourself. Be positive and self-confident without misrepresenting yourself or your work.

Finally, make sure your site is attractive and easy to use. If you are not talented in this way, invest a little money in a graphics person who can give your site an appealing overall look and a functional design. A site that is beautiful and well-organized will make the visitor feel comfortable and attracted to you and your work.

For a good sample practitioner website, visit **www.MassageVermont.com**. When I visited this site, it opened with a professional-quality photograph of the two practitioners that own the site, and their names, phone number, address, and certifications. Following that were their fee schedule displayed in a very easy-to-follow format, and a brief bio of each of them. Next came a brief description of the types of work they do and the benefits of the work, accompanied by the logos of all the professional organizations they belong to. Finally, there was a brief "Q & A" section.

### Your website's "address"

If you are creating an Internet presence, your domain name is an important part of that presence. Choose a domain name that you can keep as your permanent Internet identity. You may think the good ones are all gone, but think again—if you invent an unusual name, it may still be available. For example, in June, 2005, the domain name "mygreathands.com" was still available. You can also choose your own name or a variation of your name as your domain name.

The owner of a domain name must pay an annual fee to register the name. Shop on the Internet for the best price—you can find domain name registration services for as little as $15.00 per year. Likewise, shop around for a company that will "host" your site on their server. Hosting plans continue to come down in price, some just a few dollars per month.

*Promoting your website*

Now that you have put the time and energy (or money) into creating your website, you want people to come and visit. There are two ways of promoting your website on the Internet—through search engines, and through links. The links that will most directly help you promote your professional website are "referral" sites discussed below.

Google and Yahoo routinely search the Internet and save (or "cache") all the sites on the Internet, and then search their compilation upon request by visitors.

Once you create your website, you can manually submit it to search engines, or use services (some are free, some charge a fee) that submit your site to multiple search engines. Alternatively, you can just wait for the search engines to find you, since all of them routinely "sweep" the Internet to update their compilations.

One key to being ranked higher in search results on Google is to be linked to many other web pages. You might want to keep this in mind when creating your site, since a site composed of many inter-linked pages will score higher on search results than a single page that has all the same information.

When you design your website, also investigate how to choose the "meta-tags" that describe your website. These are words that are invisible to the users of your site, but are read by the computers accessing your site. Some search engines use these words to rank your site's usefulness to the users doing a search. Choose key words for your meta-tags that people would use in searching for you, such as the type of work you do or your location. If your meta-tags match the terms used in a search request, the search engine will place your site at the top of the list of results for that particular search.

You can also seek out local websites, such as city websites and local directory websites. These sites focus strictly on what is available in your local or regional area, so any visitors to these sites are there because they are interested in your location. These sites have less traffic than sites of national interest, but may provide you with better results, since all the visitors to a local area website are potential clients for your practice.

***Strategy #2—Join referral websites.*** A number of websites provide searchable "directories" of massage practitioners. The owners of these websites may do publicity or advertising to attract potential clients to their websites. Alternatively, they may have a domain name that a potential client might "guess" at and visit on a hunch, such as "iwantamassage.com"

Someone seeking a massage practitioner visits the website and searches the site's database for a massage practitioner in a particular location. They are then provided with a list of all the practitioners in that location who have signed up with the website. It is then up to the person seeking massage to reach out and contact the practitioner.

Most of these referral websites are fairly new, so they don't have well-established track records. Some of the sites provide basic listing (name, address, phone) at no charge, but then offer to sell you a "featured" listing consisting of your practice details and fees. Some of the sites will include a link to your personal website and others will not.

The Internet, like the Yellow Pages, is used by both legitimate clients and clients seeking sexual massage. As with any massage advertising, you must be prepared for the occasional errant caller who must be re-directed.

### Will Internet marketing pay for itself?

As you can see, Internet marketing is not expensive. You can create your website for no cost if you know your way around computers and software, or you can have someone create a site at a modest cost. The only out-of-pocket expense I had when I created **www.CareerAtYourFingertips.com** was $40.00 for the software (called "WS-ftp") needed to communicate between my computer and the computer hosting my website.

At $15.00 per year for domain name registration and $8.00 per month for hosting services, you can have a basic web presence for $111.00 per year. You could subscribe to several paid Internet referral services and still have a total Internet budget of about $250.00 per year. Keep in mind that since this is a business expense, it is tax-deductible, so you will receive a tax credit worth about 30% of this amount when you do your income taxes the following April 15th (see pages 154–155).

The Internet is still growing, and will continue to grow in importance for a number of years. The time has come for any "serious" massage professional to create an Internet presence for their massage or bodywork practice. Just being able to refer potential clients to your website for "further information" is a big plus in credibility and prestige. Massage practitioners without websites—even in this "high-touch" profession—risk being looked on as not being serious about their careers.

Even if you are already an established practitioner, creating a website for your practice will help you continue to thrive by attracting new clients to your practice. As a relatively inexpensive way to lend prestige and credibility to your practice, I recommend establishing an Internet identity to anyone seeking to earn a living practicing massage or bodywork.

## E. Ethereal Marketing Techniques

"There is more to the world" says Shakespeare, "than is dreamt of in your philosophy." Many successful practitioners believe there is more to making contact with another person than operating in the world of the physical senses.

These are some of the unorthodox marketing tips used by some successful massage practitioners:

- Visualize an open field, and see clients coming across that field to you.

- Meditate, tell the universe you are ready for people to come into your life.

- Imagine that you have a dial you can turn to control the flow of your practice. Turn it up to become busier, turn it down when you need freedom from your practice.

If this sounds like so much hocus-pocus to you, don't bother with it. You may find, at some point, that it has meaning for you. For example, several therapists have said that when they find themselves feeling frantic and wishing they had spare time instead of appointments, their clients often call in and cancel.

A skeptical person can always see something like this as coincidence. It is not scientific and cannot be proven. If it intrigues you, simply suspend disbelief. Allow the possibility that it is hogwash and allow the opposite possibility that it is a real phenomenon. Then stay with your experience, see how things go and form opinions later.

## F. Joining Managed Care Networks

Reimbursement for massage by insurance companies is covered in Chapter 21. This section deals with becoming a provider in a managed care network.

### Massage and Managed Care

In recent years, the medical insurance industry has developed a means of offering massage to its customers without actually reimbursing for massage. The "managed care" movement in the insurance industry has come to regard massage therapy as an added service it can offer to attract customers to its medical insurance plan. Massage, acupuncture, chiropractic, and some other "alternative" or "complementary" therapies are being added by HMOs and PPOs to make their plans more attractive to consumers.

A few of these companies cover massage as a reimbursed service, usually by offering a "rider" to their customers at an additional cost to cover alternative therapies. However, most HMOs and PPOs do not actually pay for massage services. Instead, they offer massage to their customers by creating a discounted referral network.

Massage offered by HMOs and PPOs usually works as follows: First, a network of "providers" is assembled by the insurance company. These networks usually include chiropractors, acupuncturists, massage therapists, and other kinds of practitioners. Either the insurance company assembles the network or they make a contract with an independent company to assemble a network for them.

The members of the network must agree to offer professional services to clients of the insurance company at a discounted rate. Sometimes the fees are set by the insurance company; more commonly, the provider agrees to work on the company's clients at a discount, usually approximately 20% less than the provider's regular fees.

The insurance company offers this discount network at no cost to its members, and supplies all its members with a directory of network providers whom they can contact directly to make appointments for services at discounted prices.

Clients use the directory to locate a practitioner in their area. They call the therapist directly for an appointment, and all future arrangements are between the therapist and the client. Usually no paperwork is required by the insurance company.

The insurance company does not pay the therapist; its only role is to assemble the network of providers and give the directory of providers to its customers.

### Advantages and disadvantages

The major advantage to the massage therapist in participating in this type of network is having a source of client referrals without any marketing effort on the therapist's part. This can be an advantage for a new massage therapist or someone who has not built their practice to the level they would like it to reach.

Some therapists receive a substantial number of referrals from these programs, while others receive only a few calls as a result of being listed. I have been listed with Oxford Health Plans, Inc. as a participating provider for several years. During the first year I received very few calls. More recently, I have been receiving about one call per month. Participating in this network has not been a major source of clients. However, I live in a non-metropolitan area, and I suspect that therapists in a more urban setting may do better with these referrals.

Another benefit to being on a referral list of this type is that you can use the listing in your marketing materials. For example, if you have a brochure that describes you and your work, you can state that you are an official provider for the "such-and-such" insurance company. Additionally, if you are on one or two insurance company lists, this may lend additional credibility when you contact physicians to seek referrals for insurance reimbursement work.

There is no limit on how many companies' lists you can be on; you could theoretically be on all the referral lists in your area, and get clients from all the companies that offer referral services in your region.

The main disadvantage is that you must give a substantial discount from your regular fee. The discount is fixed by the referring insurance company. Busy therapists may regard working at a discount as an imposition, since they have to take time away from other clients who would pay full price for their services.

Some therapists also find that the clients referred by these networks are "bargain hunters" who may be looking more for a price break than for a professional relationship with a qualified therapist. For this reason, you may find a difference in the quality of client you receive from these networks compared to other sources.

### The Credentialing Process

All of these programs use some type of credentialing process to assemble the network of massage therapists providing services for their clients, to assure they are referring their clients to trustworthy professionals.

The pioneer of this trend on the East Coast was Oxford Health Plans, Inc., a large HMO/PPO that was the first to offer discounted alternative therapies to its members. Oxford has the most rigorous credentialing process I know of. They require proof of national certification, massage school diploma, malpractice insurance, liability insurance, résumé, photographs of the inside and outside of your office, examples of your record-keeping system and progress notes, and a personal visit by an Oxford representative.

Many insurance companies hire outside companies to create their network. These companies take on the job of finding massage therapists and making sure they are qualified providers. Two of the largest credentialing companies is Complementary Care Company, 111 Yorkleigh Rd., Towson, MD 21204, 888-862-3223, 410-825-6665 (**www.c3online.com**).

### The Trend Is Toward More Massage

A recent study indicated that about 11% of HMOs offer massage services, usually in the form of a discount plan. Most HMO directors surveyed said that "consumer demand" was the main reason they offer these services to their members. This same survey also showed that the trend is toward greater and greater inclusion of "alternative" or "complementary" therapies in the managed care industry.

### Is Managed Care For You?

If you are in need of increasing your clientele, and willing to offer a discount on your services in return for referrals, this may be something for you to pursue.

To become listed in a referral network, contact either a credentialing company or one of the health insurance companies in your area that maintains a massage referral network. The company will guide you in the process of becoming credentialed and being added to their network. This process can take several months, so start early if this may be something you want to do.

## G. Fostering Repeat Business

The first goal of your marketing efforts is to get potential clients to try you out. The next goal is to have them realize they should come back and make massage a regular part of their lives.

Client retention, or fostering repeat business, is an extremely important part of success in your career as a massage practitioner. You will spend a great deal of energy getting your clients to know you, trust you, and try your services. The extra energy you devote to client retention will produce major rewards by giving you a full schedule of regular clients.

The main ways you can foster repeat business are to create an understanding of the benefits of massage, encourage re-booking, and stay in touch with your clients.

### Create an understanding of the benefits of massage

After receiving a massage, the client's body will understand how healthful it is, but the person's mind may not. Many people guide themselves primarily by their mental processes, and unless these people have an understanding of the value of massage, they may not become repeat clients.

You can help them understand the process by honestly explaining how massage benefits people in general, and how they specifically could benefit from a regular program of treatment. There is no need to be a salesman, or to be pushy. If you are honest and forthright, people will respect your professionalism and appreciate the information—they want to take care of themselves once they understand how.

Your massage school education will teach you the benefits of massage (see Chapter 20 for further information), and your work in particular will take on certain unique characteristics that promote health and well-being. Part of your job as a massage practitioner is to educate your clients about the benefits your work offers them. Teach them enough to understand the value of your work, and why they should come to you on a regular basis.

### Encourage re-booking

Keep client retention in the back of your mind from the moment of your first contact with a client and at all times thereafter.

Make sure you find out what each client needs each time a client comes to you and do your best to provide it. Make sure the client understands the value of your massage for her specific issues or conditions. Create a treatment plan tailored to this client. Emphasize the importance of consistency and follow-through.

Finally, ask the client to make her next appointment before leaving your office. After receiving your work, the client is in a receptive frame of mind and is relaxed. Rather than relying on phone messages in the future to communicate, this is the best time to make the client's next appointment.

Many massage practitioners are uncomfortable doing these things, feeling they require too much "salesmanship." But the fact is, you have something of value for this client, and you should do all you can to create the opportunity to provide your unique services to this person. If that includes mastering communication techniques to educate your client and encourage her to return regularly, you should embrace those techniques as part of your therapy practice.

### Stay in touch with your clients

Some therapists call their clients a day or two after their first massage to ask how they are feeling. This is especially appropriate with clients who have come in for relief from a specific condition.

Other ways to stay in touch with clients are:

- Send birthday cards

- Photocopy an article of interest about massage and send it to all your clients with a short note

- Send holiday greeting cards at Christmas or Rosh Hashanah

- Send a flyer or post card reminding clients that you offer gift certificates at holiday time

- Send flyers or post cards advertising any special offers you are making on your services

- Send announcements to your clients when you begin working in a new location or take on an associate in your office

- If you have a seasonal clientele, send thank-you letters to your clients at the end of the season for their patronage.

### Other ideas on client retention

- Send a "Welcome" card after a client's first session offering $5.00 off on the next session; this lets the client know you value them and encourages them to re-book.

- Give out promotional items with your name on them. One such item is a bottle of spring water with your label on it; clients can re-use it, and will have a constant reminder of your name and phone number on hand.

- Send clients a gift certificate on the yearly anniversary of their first visit.

Make sure your sincere desire to help shines through in all your promotion. People will see through a tactic that is insincere, but will respond to your communications if they sense that you are motivated by a real desire to help and to be of service.

### For further information about marketing

Magazine articles and books about marketing massage appear on a regular basis. For the most part, they all have basically the same advice presented in this book, although each author filters and expresses the information through their unique perspective. An excellent new book called *Marketing Massage* by Monica Roseberry (Delmar Publishing, $39.95) provides a book-length discussion of the subject matter covered in this chapter, and it presents its own version of the "golden keys to success" (see page 24) with a different slant.

You will also see marketing kits and seminars on marketing advertised in trade journals. These tend to be expensive, and you should be cautious about them. The best marketing devices you can obtain are education and motivation—these turn *you* into your own best resource.

It is more worthwhile to invest in training yourself about marketing than it is to buy the expensive videos and packets you may see advertised. Even the best materials, ideas and suggestions will not create your career success—it is your own energy, effort, enthusiasm and talents that will ultimately bring you a full practice.

# 8 Opening a Massage Office

Opening an office is a big step. It is the mark of maturity of a massage career. It requires confidence in your professional skills, your business ability, and your commitment to your practice.

When the time comes in your career to open your own office, it should be a joyous venture. It will bring you the chance to make a better living and have a clear professional identity. This chapter will help you be fully prepared and ready to take this step, and will give you the basic information you will need to make the best choices in bringing your office to life.

The topics covered in this chapter are governmental requirements, practical requirements, and business decisions. Business decisions include measuring your readiness to open an office, choosing a location, and negotiating a lease. In addition, you will find a checklist for office opening, and discussions of opening a group practice and buying an existing practice.

## Governmental Requirements

You are becoming a local business owner, and as such you are taking on a new identity in the eyes of your local government. One of the main functions of local government is to regulate the operations of businesses. By the same token, a substantial source of revenue for local government is license fees and taxes paid by local business owners.

So you are in a two-way relationship with your local government. On one hand, the government wants to exert its authority over you to make sure you do things to their liking. On the other hand, the government wants to see you succeed, so that you will make money and share it with the government.

Your first step is to visit your local government, whether it is a town hall, city hall, municipal complex, or village governmental center. Bring a note pad and pen. Ask for assistance about the following items:

### 1. Massage licensing law

Most towns and cities do not have laws regulating the practice of massage, but many do. These laws often were written more to guard against prostitution than to realistically regulate massage practice. You may find that the local law regulates massage quite heavily. Some local laws prohibit massaging members of the opposite sex. A few towns prohibit the practice of massage completely.

If your town has a restrictive law, you will have to choose 1. meeting all of the restrictions, 2. giving up the idea of practicing there, 3. fighting to have the law changed, or 4. practicing there and risking being penalized for violating the law. If you think you may choose number 4, it is probably not a good idea to march into city hall and identify yourself as a way of getting information.

## 2. Practitioner license, establishment license

If the town has a licensing law, it will probably have two parts to it. One will give the requirements for a massage practitioner license, and the other will give the requirements for a massage establishment license.

The practitioner license applies to your right to practice massage within the town, and the establishment license applies to the office in which you will practice massage. Each will have a separate procedure and a separate fee.

## 3. Zoning requirements

Almost all towns have zoning laws, which regulate the types of "uses" that may take place in different "zones." In other words, zoning laws restrict the kinds of businesses you can operate in different neighborhoods. Certain neighborhoods are set aside for residences only. Others may be zoned for industrial uses, such as factories and warehouses. Others will be for stores or professional practices. A sample zoning map is on page 65.

Before committing to a particular location for a massage office, you should be sure that the location has the proper zoning for use as a massage business.

Different communities will use different zoning classifications for massage. Some will call it a personal service. Others will call it a profession. Others will call it a health service. Still others refer to it as "adult entertainment." What they call it will have an effect on which zones you will be allowed to locate in.

The town clerk can direct you to the zoning map for the city. If the zoning board can tell you exactly which category massage is considered to be for zoning purposes, you can check the map to see which neighborhoods are open to you for an office location. If there is doubt about which category they consider massage, you may need to go before the zoning board to get a definitive ruling before choosing your office location.

If you are opening a home office, the zoning board may require a hearing before deciding whether to allow you to operate a massage practice in your home. They may consider factors such as the burden placed on neighborhood parking, the percentage of space in the home devoted to your business, and whether you will be the only one who performs massage services in your home. If you need to appear before the zoning board, consider consulting an attorney beforehand to advise you about how to proceed or to represent you before the zoning board.

## 4. Health, police and fire department inspections

Inquire of the health department, police department and fire department what their policies are about inspecting a massage office before it opens. Ask about any requirements you will need to meet. Write down the answers you receive, the name of the person who gives you the information, and the date.

BOROUGH OF
# BRADLEY BEACH
MONMOUTH COUNTY                    NEW JERSEY

THE ZONING MAP

R-A    RESIDENTIAL ZONE – A
R-B    RESIDENTIAL ZONE – B
RCT    RESIDENTIAL COMMERCIAL TRANSITION ZONE
GB     GENERAL BUSINESS ZONE
B-R    BEACH FRONT – RESORT ZONE
O-P    OFFICE – PROFESSIONAL ZONE
BOR    OFFICE AND RESEARCH ZONE

## 5. Local business taxes

Ask the clerk about any local taxes, such as sewer tax, business property tax, or other local business taxes. Make a note of this information, as you will want to know what your expenses will be in operating your business.

# Practical Requirements

## 1. Fictitious name statement (also called "assumed name" or "doing business as")

If you will give your business a name other than your own name (such as "Wholistic Massage Center" or "Beams of Light Massage") you will need to register your fictitious name with the county government. This allows the public to know who owns a business when the owner's name is not included in the business name. This certificate does not give you exclusive rights to the name. For that you must seek trade-name or service-mark protection.

To register your fictitious name, you must go to the county seat, the town in your county that houses the county government offices. If you do not know where that is, someone in your bank or city government office can tell you. Contact the county clerk, and find out the cost for registering a fictitious or assumed name, the hours you can go and do so, and the procedure for doing so. In some places, the procedure includes advertising your fictitious name in local newspapers.

In most cases, you will be required to do your own checking through the county's records of business names to make sure that no one has already chosen that business name. This can take awhile, so give yourself enough time to take care of this. After you have checked the records, you pay your fee (bring cash and keep your receipt) and you will receive a "fictitious name certificate" (or "assumed name certificate").

## 2. Business bank account

Your bank will require a fictitious name certificate in order to open an account in the name of your business. It is a good idea to have a business checking account, and to pay for all business expenses with your business checks (or business credit card). Your business will appear more credible and established than it would if you pay for business purchases with your personal checks or credit cards. Having a separate account will also make your task easier when it is time to prepare your year-end income taxes.

## 3. Business stationery, cards, gift certificates, flyers

Choose a print shop that you can be comfortable with. You will probably be a repeat customer for your printer. You should have a printer that you have confidence in, as to quality, prompt completion of orders, and competitive price. Consider recommendations of others and your own observations when in the shop.

The bare minimum you will need to open your office is business cards. Consider whether to also invest in customized gift certificates and business stationary.

Also consider: A rubber stamp with your business name and address, a rubber stamp with your bank account number to endorse the back of checks, flyers that describe you and your business, a printed coupon for purchasers of pre-paid series of massage, and promotional items to publicize your office.

# Business Decisions

## 1. Financial and Professional Readiness

### Start-up costs

First consider that you will need some money up front in order to open an office. You will need money for office furnishings, first month's rent, security deposit, telephone and utility deposit, printing needs and advertising or other promotional costs. If you have established credit, you may be able to get a loan. Otherwise you will need to use your savings to meet these start-up costs.

As a guideline for planning purposes, the following figures are estimates of the amounts you will need to spend on start-up costs:

| | | | |
|---|---|---|---|
| Massage table | $500 | Desk | $175 |
| Table or shelf | 80 | Hamper | 35 |
| Phone/ans. mach. | 75 | Music system | 250 |
| Sheets/towels | 200 | First month rent | 400 |
| Security deposit | 400 | Phone deposit | 150 |
| Utility deposit | 75 | Printing | 100 |
| Ads/promotion | 300 | Miscellaneous | 100 |

Any of these items can be more or less than the amounts shown, depending on your particular circumstances. The start-up costs in the sample above total $2,840.

### Monthly expenses vs. income

Next examine your ability to meet the continuing financial obligations of operating a professional office.

Perhaps you work in a health club, hair salon, or doctor's office. Would most of your clients stay with the new massage therapist who replaces you or would they follow you to your office?

### Estimated Monthly Business Income

Take an honest look at your client list, and imagine the first month in your new office. Examine your records to see what your business income has been for the last few months, and any upward or downward trends you notice.

Consider, also, that once you have an office of your own, it may be easier for you to create new growth. First, you will have strong motivation to do so. Second, you will have a location that is conducive to the kind of work you want to do. Third, you will have an established office that will serve as the focus of your marketing efforts—promotional ideas such as direct mail, lecture/demonstration and advertising will be more open to you than they would be if your were working in an employer's space.

Make an estimate of your first month's income. If in doubt, choose a lower figure for planning purposes. For purposes of making a sample financial projection, we will assume you can start in your new office with an income of $1,200 per month. This is your "estimated monthly business income."

## Other Monthly Income

Calculate your other sources of income, apart from your business. Include any sources of income you know you can count on, such as interest, alimony, pension, or the like. Total all this income, and figure how much you receive in an average month. For purposes of this example, we will use the figure $150 per month for your "Other Monthly Income."

## Total Estimated Income

Add your "estimated monthly business income" to your "other monthly income." In this example, the total is $1,350.

## Estimated Monthly Business Expenses

Calculate the amount you must spend each month for your office rent, telephone, and yellow pages. Also include a twelfth of your annual business expenses, such as advertising, oils and linens, business taxes, professional association dues, accountant fees, insurance costs, and the like.

The total of your monthly business expenses is likely to be between $300 and $1,200. This is the amount you need each month to support your business. We will use the figure of $600 per month as an example of "estimated monthly business expenses."

## Estimated Monthly Personal Expenses

This is the amount you need to live on each month, for such essentials as home rental, food, automobile, health insurance and taxes. One way to calculate this is to look through your checkbook for last year. Add up all the money you spent on personal expenses, plus your best guess for how much cash you spent, and divide by 12. Another way is to add up your fixed expenses and then add an estimate for your spending money.

Let's say you come up with a total of $1,000 per month for your "estimated monthly personal expenses."

## Estimated Total Monthly Expenses

Add the "estimated monthly business expenses" of $600 per month to "estimated monthly personal expenses" of $1,000 per month to find your "estimated total monthly expenses." This is the amount you will need to earn each month in order to support your new office and your current lifestyle. In our example, this is $1,600.

These estimated figures are summarized in the chart on the next page.

*New Office Financial Projections*

**INCOME**
|  |  |  |
|---|---|---|
| Estimated monthly business income | $1,200 | |
| Other monthly income | 150 | |
| Total estimated income | 1,350 | |

**EXPENSES**
|  |  |  |
|---|---|---|
| Estimated monthly business expenses in new office location | 600 | |
| Estimated monthly personal expenses | 1,000 | |
| Estimated total monthly expenses | 1,600 | |
| **NET DEFICIT** | $250 | per month |

This projection shows expenses will be higher than income. Subtracting income ($1,350) from expenses ($1,600) shows an estimated deficit of $250 per month for this person's overall lifestyle after opening the new massage office.

If your financial planning estimate shows a net deficit per month, you should plan to have a reserve of at least one year's worth of deficits before you decide to open your office. It may take a year for you to see any significant increase in your business, so plan to start with the ability to sustain your practice at its current level for at least a year.

In this example, that would mean you should have a capital reserve of $3,000 to supplement your income for the first year.

Consider choosing a larger figure for your capital reserve, since it is possible your second year may also produce a net deficit.

## Additional Reserves For Business and Personal Expenses

In addition to the predictable expenses, you should ideally be prepared for the unforeseen ones as well. For example, your car's transmission falls out. You need $600 to fix it. You decide it would help business to do a direct mail promotion. You need $400 for the cost of the mailing.

This kind of expense can come up without warning, so you should plan on at least another $1,000 to draw on for such emergencies.

## Total Needs for Financial Readiness

Add your Start-up Costs, your first year's Net Deficit, and Additional Reserves. This is the amount you can expect to need in the first year to start your business and supplement your income. In the example above, this total would be $6,840.

If your skills, personality and location are good, and you approach your marketing with commitment and organization, you should find that after the first year you begin to see some increase in your practice. You may still have a net deficit each month in the second year. If you proceed with organization and commitment, you should have a net profit after the second year, and have a net operating profit for the rest of your massage career.

## *2. Location*

There is an old joke in the real estate business:

> *Question:*  What are the three most important factors in the value of real
>                   estate?
> *Answer:*     Location, location and location

This expresses a basic truth about the business world. Location counts for a great deal in business. Choose a location that is central, easy to get to, enjoyable to go to, and that conveys a positive image for your practice.

**WIZARD OF ID**

Take your time finding a location. Consider a broad range of questions.

### Consider the town:

- Is the town one that can support a massage therapist?

- Are any massage therapists currently earning a living in this town?

- Will I be in direct competition with them or will we draw on different client bases?

- Is there another town in the area that would afford a better image or a more receptive client population?

### Consider the neighborhood and building:

- What is the ideal location within my town for my particular practice?

- Will this location be one my clients are comfortable coming to? One they will look forward to coming to?

- Is the building attractive and well-maintained?

- Is the building visible to large numbers of people on a daily basis?

- Are the other offices in the building ones whose images fit comfortably with the image I want for my practice?

- Is the neighborhood safe and pleasant?

- Is parking convenient?

- What other businesses are nearby?

- Will this location support my plans for future growth?
- Do I feel comfortable thinking of this as "my" office?

Your choice of an office location can make your whole professional life easier or more difficult. Do yourself a favor, and make the selection of an office your highest priority. Investigate, think, feel and take some time with this decision. Your efforts will pay great dividends for years to come.

## 3. Negotiating a Lease

Look for items in a lease which give you flexibility and control and avoid items which give power to the landlord and obligate you excessively.

For example, your lease should include a statement that the office provided will be suitable for use as a professional massage office—as to noise level, temperature control and good repair of all fixtures. This gives you a legal right to complain if the landlord fails to provide you with a quiet and warm massage environment.

If you have any doubts about the zoning for the location, put in the lease that it becomes void if the city refuses to approve zoning for a massage business at that location. Otherwise, you could be stuck with a lease on an office in which you cannot open your business. Also consider making the lease conditional upon being granted a local massage practitioner license and a massage establishment license.

You also may want to negotiate for a lease that is renewable at your option. After all, you do not know for sure that you will succeed in your business, or that you will like the location. Give yourself the option to leave after a year. At the same time, give yourself the option to renew for a second and third year at the same rental (or a small increase) so that you know you will be able to enjoy the reward for your efforts if your practice is very successful.

Spell out in the lease any other items that you consider of special importance to you, and make sure you understand all of the provisions of the lease you sign. As a precaution, it is good practice to show the lease to a lawyer or experienced business person to get an informed opinion before signing.

One further thing to keep in mind is that, while your lease gives you legal rights, these may not amount to anything in practical terms if you wind up having a conflict with your landlord. If you need to hire a lawyer and file a lawsuit, your expenses in suing will almost certainly be more than you would recover even if you win. You can sue in small claims court if you meet the local requirements. However, even that takes preparation, time, energy and expense. While your lease should afford you legal protection, steering free of conflict is worth much more than having right on your side.

The lease on page 72 is the one I signed when I moved into a massage office in a beauty salon. It's not perfect, and the rent was too high, but it is as an example of the kinds of items you may want to include in a business lease.

## 4. Taking Credit Cards

Consider taking Visa and MasterCard in payment for your services. The disadvantage is the cost—there are setup costs, either purchase or rental, and transaction costs for each charge. If you process a small amount of business on credit cards,

## LEASE CONTRACT

This contract is entered into this 15th day of January, 1988, between Martin Ashley (Martin) and Anthony Marzarella, doing business as Anthony Louis (Anthony). The parties agree as follows:

1. Anthony will furnish a massage room in Le Club salon on Route 88, Brick, New Jersey. He will also furnish a receptionist to take appointments for massage and to collect clients' payments for massage. The receptionist selected shall be a courteous individual who presents a positive image of massage and of the massage therapists employed to work at Le Club.

2. Martin will pay a monthly rental to Anthony of $400.00 per month, payable on the 1st day of each month. Martin will also pay Anthony 17% of the cost of advertising which advertises massage at Le Club.

3. This contract shall be for a period of three months, and shall be renewable at Martin's option for additional periods of three months, up to a total of one year. In addition, after the first year, the contract shall be renewable for an additional year at a monthly rent not to exceed $500 per month.

4. Anthony shall obtain a Brick massage establishment license, and Martin shall obtain a Brick massage practitioner license. All massage therapists employed by Martin at Le Club shall have Brick massage practitioner licenses. Martin shall have the right to transfer or sell his rights under this contract to any other individual who has a Brick massage practitioner license.

5. Permanent improvements to the premises made by Anthony shall be the property of Anthony, and furnishings placed in the massage room by Martin shall remain the property of Martin.

6. Collection of the amount due to be paid for massage shall be the responsibility of Anthony. The receptionist shall collect payment from massage clients.

7. Liability to clients and customers for any accidents or injuries shall be Martin's if the accident or injury occurs within the massage room, and Anthony's if the accident or injury occurs elsewhere on Le Club premises.

_____
date            Anthony Marzarella

_____
date            Martin Ashley

the setup fees may make it too costly for you. But if you process a large amount of charges on credit cards, these costs are spread out over many transactions and will not be much of a burden.

In order to take credit cards, you first need to establish a "merchant account", and you next need either software or hardware that will allow you to process credit transactions. Hardware (the "swiper" and printer) can be purchased for several hundred dollars or leased for $15.00 to $50.00 per month. There may also be a monthly minimum processing fee, a per-transaction fee, and a percentage of each sale taken as a processing fee. Shop around, as prices vary considerably from company to company. As a target price, try to find a merchant account that charges 2 percent of credit charges with the least additional per-transaction and monthly fees.

Clients usually find it convenient to write a check or pay cash, but you may find there is some business you will do only if you take credit cards. Credit cards make it very easy for clients to buy gift certificates—they can order them much as they do flowers from a florist. It also facilitates sales of series coupons, and can make it easier for a client who finds herself without checks or sufficient cash. An office that takes credit cards also presents a very established and professional image.

To investigate taking credit cards in your business, go to the bank where you have your business checking account, and ask for assistance. Check with other banks, and check the Business-to-Business Yellow Pages under "Credit Card Equipment and Supplies." Costco offers low-cost merchant accounts to executive members (1-888-474-0500). I joined Costco just to obtain a merchant account and have been satisfied with their services and their cost.

You can also search the Internet if you are seeking a merchant account. There are literally hundreds of websites offering merchant accounts, with terms that vary greatly. Some providers, like PayPal, offer accounts that operate only on the internet, and others offer accounts you can use in your office.

One final option to consider is to "piggy-back" on someone else's merchant account; make a deal to use someone else's merchant account for a fixed per-use fee. The fees charged by your clients will be credited to that person's bank account, and you will need to settle up periodically to transfer the fees earned to your account. If you are a low-volume credit merchant, this arrangement may be the cheapest alternative you can find, assuming you have a good relationship with the owner of the merchant account.

## 5. Furnishing Your Office

The furnishings you choose for your office will reflect your personality and your preferences for a setting in which to practice your particular type of work. You might choose pastels and crystals if you lean toward the ethereal, and whites and stainless steel if you lean toward the clinical. Only you know the atmosphere you want for yourself and your clients. Certain basics, however, apply to most or all massage rooms:

- In general, you should keep your office spacious and uncluttered, as this generally promotes a more comfortable and relaxed feeling.

- Arrange for lighting that is not harsh. Avoid ceiling lights, as these will be too bright for clients when face up. Dimming switches are inexpensive and easily available. One type installs in the wall switch and another screws directly into the bulb socket. Also consider stained glass lamps designed to hold low-watt bulbs and night lights that plug into wall sockets.

- Your diplomas will add an air of professionalism to the walls. Consider also some artwork to create an appropriate atmosphere.

- Keep a desk in your office. The desk is the place for your telephone and answering machine, phone books, schedule book and client files.

- Linens can be kept on a shelf, in a cabinet, or under the massage table. Choose your linens after you decide on a color scheme for the office, or use white linens, which can go with any office colors.

- Have a mirror available to your clients.

- Give your clients ample hooks for their clothing. Have a table or counter where clients can put their jewelry and personal belongings.

- Have a computer, word processor or typewriter in the office so you can do paperwork between appointments if necessary.

- Have your business cards out in a spot where clients will see them and can take one.

- Consider having bottled water available for you and your clients in your office.

### Checklist for office furnishings

| | |
|---|---|
| massage table | mirror |
| linens | desk |
| hamper | table or counter space for |
| oil | client's use |
| chair | music system |
| clothing hooks for clients | |
| business card holder | telephone and answering machine |
| bottled water cooler or other dispenser | computer |
| lighting system | artwork, diplomas or other decorations for walls |

## 6. Telephone Reception

One advantage of a group practice is that the group can pool resources to either hire a receptionist or rotate duties on phone reception. This assures that callers will reach a person who can answer their questions about massage and schedule an appointment.

If you are practicing alone, it is much more difficult to answer your own phone. Hopefully, you will be too busy doing massage to be serving as your own receptionist. The choices available to you are hiring an answering service or using voicemail or an answering machine.

Practically all therapists, faced with this choice, choose voicemail or an answering machine over an answering service. The service may seem to have the advantage of presenting the caller with a live human to talk to, but the person who works for the answering service is not likely to be familiar with massage. Therefore, she or he cannot answer the potential client's questions about your services. The answering service can take messages for you, but that is about all.

A new service has recently come on the market, "My Receptionist." This is a company in Eau Claire, Wisconsin that provides your personal phone line, so that their employees can answer your line with your business name, answer questions about you and your services, and schedule your appointments. Cost for the service starts at $39.95 per month, with additional charges for individual calls and for credit card transactions. Contact information is in the reference section on page 213.

### Caller I.D.

Caller I.D. is an especially useful feature in a massage practice. It allows you to say, when making an appointment with a new client for the first time, "Can I call you at 555-3456 to confirm?" The fact that you know their phone number will be a strong deterrent for any sex clients who may be calling you. If the caller has chosen to block his identity from caller I.D., this may be someone you want to be especially careful with.

## Checklist for office opening

The items in this checklist are arranged in chronological order—in other words, do number one first, number two second, etc. Begin this process three to six months before your target date for opening your new office.

*Three to six months before opening:*

1. Contact local government for information about zoning, and any regulations of health, fire and police departments

2. Contact direct mail company to learn the date of their next mailing; contact phone company to learn deadline for next yellow pages listing

3. Consider possible locations and look at offices for rent

4. Negotiate a lease for your office location, select starting date with enough lead time to make all preparations

5. Obtain all necessary governmental approvals, licenses and permits

*Two to four weeks before opening:*

6. Register fictitious name with county

7. Establish business checking account

8. Contact telephone company to connect new service

9. Order stationery, business cards and any promotional items you plan to use to publicize your office's opening

10. If appropriate, plan an advertising push when you open to create an increased clientele for your new venture

11. Shop for office furnishings

12. Notify all your clients of your new office opening and any introductory promotions you may be having

13. Get to know the neighbors in your new location and use any opportunities to gain clientele through your neighbors

## Opening a group practice

Group practice refers to several massage therapists or related professionals sharing a suite of offices. Group practices have some significant advantages over individual practices, as well as some disadvantages.

The two main advantages of group practices are shared expenses and cross-referrals. The main disadvantage is the group decision process.

Renting an office suite and sharing the cost usually results in a lower price to each member than she would have to pay for a similar office space rented individually.

A group practice has the potential to become well-known as a center, thereby attracting a larger clientele through the reputation of the group. Once such a reputation is established for a group practice, it will generate a significant walk-in trade, and all the group members will benefit.

The disadvantage of a group practice is that decisions must be made by the group as a whole. This usually means devoting one evening per week to the process of group decision-making. After a busy week of massage, an evening of group process can seem like a burden. However, if you choose carefully which other practitioners you associate with, these group meetings can be an enjoyable opportunity for learning and socializing.

## Buying an Existing Massage Practice

Occasionally, practitioners sell their practice. You may have an opportunity to purchase an existing practice. This may seem like an appealing way to have a ready-made practice. However, buying an existing practice is risky, and you should be extremely careful if you choose to do so.

Ask yourself several questions:

1. Why is this person selling her practice? She may not be giving you the real reason. Ask to see her appointment book, and take a minute to look at it. See how busy the office really is.

2. Will she take any of her clients with her? This can be a problem if the selling therapist plans to stay in massage and to stay in the area. You could find you have paid for a practice that evaporates as soon as you arrive.

3. Will her clients like you? It was the selling therapist's style of massage and personality that attracted her current clientele. If your massage and your personality are different from hers, her clients may be dissatisfied with you and may leave to try other therapists.

If I were buying an existing practice, I would want to first become an associate, and work in the office on a part-time basis. By so doing, I would get the feel of the clientele, and know whether they would accept me, and whether I would feel comfortable working with them. I would also have the opportunity to see first-hand how busy the practice is.

Ask the seller if such an arrangement is possible. You could try it for a couple of months, at which time you would decide whether to buy the practice for a pre-set amount of money.

The real value of an established practice is the client base, the group of people who are in the habit of coming to this practice for massage on a regular basis. The client base can be a valuable asset if you are new to a community and want to become established quickly. I suggest you base a purchase price on the number of clients you believe will stay with you after you take the practice over. You will need to make your best estimate of this.

If the client base will give you only enough income to meet the office rent, it is not worth much to you. On the other hand, if you will be able to step in and immediately earn enough to meet expenses and take home an income of $500 per week, that has a substantial value.

Figuring the value of an existing practice is tricky, but consider this formula. Project the income you expect to earn immediately after taking over the office. To do this, you must have some basis for knowing how many clients will stay with you after the selling therapist leaves.

Assume your projected income for the first month is $1300. Next, total the expenses you will have for rent, phone, yellow pages, insurance, taxes and supplies. Assume this is $750 per month. Subtract the expenses from your expected income. You can project your estimated profit to be $550 for the first month.

Offer the seller three to five times the amount you expect to take home as profit for the first month. If your assessment is correct, you will be able to recover your investment within a year or so, and you will then have a successful practice with a minimum of marketing effort on your part.

The figure you offer will probably be less than the seller was hoping for. The seller may hope for a figure that represents a year's profit, or even more. In the "business world", a going business is commonly sold for three or four times the net annual income. However, it is hard to imagine a situation where that would be an appropriate formula for the value of a massage practice.

If the business is very attractive and you can afford it, you may want to agree to more than a few months' net income. However, you should only offer what the business will be worth *to you*. If you were buying a store that sold brand-name goods, the established trade would be reliable. In your case, the value of this business depends very much on how much it will change after you take it over.

# III

# Sex, Gender
# and Touch

# 9 Sex and Massage

About half-way through my massage school course, I began to wonder when we would have the class about sexuality and massage, to help us understand and deal with sexual feelings that may arise for the client or the therapist during a session. I kept waiting for such a class, but it never arrived.

When I set up a practice in the "real world," I encountered sexual issues that deserved to be discussed in schools. While some schools now include a discussion of sexuality and massage in their programs, many programs still do not give students meaningful preparation for what they can expect in the "real world."

## *Differences in approach*

The approach I suggest for a professional massage therapist or bodyworker is to set up clear boundaries for the therapeutic session. Any sexual intention by the client or the therapist is outside those boundaries. A client who presents sexual intentions should be confronted, and if the client acknowledges sexual intentions, the treatment should be ended.

Some authors and some educators differ with that approach, and regard a client's sexual desires not so much as a problem, but as an opportunity to foster the client's growth by exploring the psychological issues he has concerning sexuality. Be aware that if you choose such an approach, you are crossing the line between massage and counseling, and you should do so only if you are professionally qualified to work in that way. I don't have psychological training, and most massage therapists don't. Therefore, my advice is to simply terminate a massage when a client presents the wish for sexual gratification.

## Clients who want sexual massage

Occasionally, a woman massage client attempts to initiate sexual contact, either with a male or female massage therapist during a massage session. Instances in which men attempt to initiate sexual contact, either with a male or female massage therapist are, unfortunately, much more common.

It is likely that at some point in your career, you will have a client attempt to initiate sexual contact. The following suggestions and observations are offered as guidelines for what to expect and how to deal with what takes place. Since the great majority of sexually oriented clients are men, the male pronoun is used throughout this chapter.

## *Arousal need not be considered a problem*

A few men experience a partial erection at some point during a massage. These men are not necessarily after sex, and may actually be somewhat embarrassed by their arousal. The simple fact of a male client having an erection should not be seen as a problem, as long as the man's attitude is appropriate and he presents no verbal or non-verbal sexual expressions.

## *Arousal plus inappropriate action is a problem*

Signs to watch for if a male client has an erection are: touching the genitals; grinding the hips into the massage table; moving the hips in any way; using muscular contraction to flex the penis.

These activities should alert you that this client will probably present a request for sex. You should confront him immediately about his arousal. Unless he can explain his actions to your satisfaction, terminate the massage immediately.

A subtler signs of sexual intention is very shallow breathing. If you have some experience with clients who want sex, you will learn to "feel" that desire coming from them. It may be a subtle change in the mood in the room, or a change in *your* breathing or thinking, or a sense of anxiety that you cannot explain.

## *If in doubt, confront*

If a client has an erection and you perceive signs that lead you to believe this client wants sex, ask your client questions to find out if you are right. Mention that he seems to be aroused and ask his feeling about that.

If the client's response tells you his attitude about the arousal is one of enjoyment, terminate the massage immediately. If the client continues to make any voluntary movements of a sexual nature, such as grinding the hips or touching the genitals, terminate the massage.

Your massage room is your environment, and you are in control of what does and does not happen there. Do not allow a client to threaten that control. Do not be afraid of losing business—any client who is sexually oriented is a client you want very much to lose anyway.

If you are alone in your office, you may want to have a phone number handy for someone you know you can reach in an emergency. It may help you to feel more at ease to know someone is available to help you if necessary.

## *Understanding the big picture*

Sex and massage have undoubtedly been linked for thousands of years. One explanation for the persistent connection between the two has been offered by David Lauterstein, co-director of the Lauterstein-Conway School of Massage in Austin, Texas:

> … we rather awkwardly encounter the one good reason massage
> and prostitution were ever associated. Both address people's need for
> love. However, prostitutes simply don't deliver—selling sex as love
> is robbery. That's a good reason why it's illegal. Massage therapy

recognizes that underneath each person's tension, stress, even illness
and injury, is an unmet need for energetic nourishment, i.e., love.

Unfortunately, many men are not aware of the distinction Mr. Lauterstein refers
to. They *think* that what they need to be happy is sex, and there are plenty of
"practitioners" who are willing to indulge them in their illusion.

In some parts of the world, a manually-stimulated orgasm is the normal and
accepted conclusion of a professional massage. In many parts of the United States,
a sexual massage is more common and easier to find than a legitimate massage. In
some areas (San Diego, for example) the sexual massage ads in the yellow pages
completely overwhelm the few listings for massage therapists.

In recent years, newspapers have carried stories of "acupressure" parlors fronting
for prostitution in Los Angeles County, California, and massage parlors fronting for prostitution in the Oyster Bay area of Long Island, New York. The New
York parlors were closed only after a march by licensed massage therapists, who
announced plans to hold a press conference in front of their local senator's office
unless action was taken.

Millions of men have had sexual massage experiences, and continue to have them
today. As such, it is understandable that they would have some confusion about
what it is you do. That is why you should be 1) non-judgmental and 2) completely
clear in your communications before beginning a massage.

## *Screening new clients*

It is a good practice to ask anyone who calls you how they heard about you. First,
you want to be able to thank clients for referrals, and keep track of how successful
your various promotional activities have been. Second, if the person does not come
as a referral from a trusted client, you want to be able to make sure the person does
not have the wrong idea.

Most sex clients will find you either through the yellow pages or through a
newspaper ad. With male callers who have located me through advertising, I make
a point of stating at the beginning that my massage is strictly non-sexual. I may
use terms like "legitimate" or "therapeutic" to reinforce the message. I then ask
them if this is the type of massage they are looking for, and pause to give them an
opportunity to answer.

Massage clients understand the need for such an explanation, and are not put
off. Most of the sex callers will hang up at that point, but some persist. During
the conversation that follows, I have learned to watch my breathing. If my own
breathing becomes shallow, and my heart starts beating fast, I have learned that
this means my unconscious is getting the message that there is something dishon-
est about the caller.

Clients looking for sexual massage will try to find out what they can get without
saying anything incriminating. Typical questions the sex caller may ask, in an
attempt to find out if he can get a sexual massage, are these:

Is this a nude massage?

Is this a "complete"?

Is this a sensual massage?

What will you be wearing during the massage?

How much do you weigh?

Is tipping allowed?

Are there extras?

Can I get a release?

What else is included?

Does a girl give the massage?

Can I shower after the massage?

If you hear any of these questions, politely tell him he has the wrong office, and hang up.

To minimize sex clients, get a first *and last* name for any first-time clients, and a phone number you can call to confirm the appointment.

Try to avoid same-day appointments with first-time male clients. Clients who want same-day service are less likely to become regular clients and more likely to demand same-day booking again. In addition, a significant number of same-day appointments turn out to be no-shows.

Be cautious with male internet referrals. If the client will not give his name and phone number, be suspicious. These calls may have a high no-show rate as well.

Phone to confirm the appointment the day it is to take place. If any difficulty or confusion results from your attempt to confirm the appointment, be prepared for a no-show or a client who may be using a fictitious name.

### *One Massage Therapist's Story*

The following essay is one of four essays in a work called Massage Portraits, originally published in 1984 in CoEvolution Quarterly/Whole Earth Review, issue No. 43. It is written by Anneke Campbell and is reprinted with her permission. I include it here because it captures well many of the aspects of dealing with a client seeking sex.

### *CHIP*

It was nine in the evening when the phone rang, and a male voice asked if he could come for a massage. "How did you find out about me?" I asked, always cautious. "Connie usually works on me when I'm in town, but she's out for the evening."

I knew Connie did good work, so I relaxed. "My old football injury is acting up," the man continued, "Could you see me tonight?" "Well …" I didn't much feel like it, but my rent was due at the end of the week. "Alright then." "I sure do appreciate it."

The fellow who walked in my door was a massive six-foot-four, dark-haired, jowly. I was going to have to work for my money. Chip had played football at college in the sixties, and nearly gone pro. Partly due to his back problem, he had opted for business, and was doing quite well, if he did say so himself. He also told me he was divorced. He took off all his clothes with bravura, as if to let me know he had no hang-ups about his body, not him.

His back was a sheet of lumpy, tight muscle. I stood close to the massage table and leaned all my weight into my hands. I began by pushing on the bunched-up erector spinae, and to my surprise, they softened up right away. Chip was responsive. I concentrated with my fingers on the vertebrae, which were buried in fibroid connective tissue. While I worked, Chip told me about the injury which had left him with some weakness in the sacral area. He had experienced both numbness and aching in his legs for years.

"There's nothing I can do about nerve impairment, if that's what the problem is," I explained, "but your entire back is a mess, probably due to compensating for the injury. And I can do something about all these tense, bunched-up muscles." I used long, firm strokes down the erector spinae and up the latissimus dorsi. I kneaded the well-padded abdominal obliques and trapezius. I worked so hard that the muscles in my own arms started aching, and drops of sweat ticked at the small of my back.

After about forty minutes, he began to moan. I was feeling pleased with the results of my work; his back was definitely less rigid than when I started. "Doesn't it feel better?" I asked. "It does, oh yes, but you're not getting to where most of the pain is." "Which is?" "Lower down."

I chased an uncomfortable thought from my mind, and moved my hands down to his sacrum and pelvic brim. I focused on the tiny muscles that lie over the sacrum; they were mushy in texture, a mushiness I associate with damage, and I could see that these could well be the source of his "weakness." Underneath, my fingers discovered some cyst-like formations. Here I worked carefully, but thoroughly. "Lower," he said.

I ignored the request. Chip's heavy body seemed suddenly disgusting to me. "Massage my thighs, that's where the problem is, on the inside of my thighs." "I've only a few minutes left." "How about another hour?" "I don't work two hours in a row," I lied.

I did some long, firm strokes down the length of his legs, trying to ignore the slight grinding of his pelvis into the massage table. I moved up, and took his bullish neck into my hands. Muscle like rock. He needed another hour, that was clear, but he wasn't going to get it from me.

"My masseuse in Florida, she does a full-body massage." I felt a sudden stab of hatred for the masseuse in Florida. "Yep, but she's a strong lady," Chip continued, "bigger than you are. You're just a little thing, aren't you. Well, what this lady does, it doesn't take much strength really."

I remained silent, kneading away at his sterno-cleido-mastoids. "She massages me down there, you know …" "I don't do that kind of massage." "I'll give you fifty dollars." "Thank you, but no," I say, clear I would never do such a thing. "One hundred dollars then." "I don't do that kind of massage," I repeated, thinking, good Lord, one hundred dollars for a hand-job, he must be filthy rich.

"Please," he said, "One hundred and twenty?" Half a month's rent, I thought. Is it really that different, rubbing his penis or rubbing his trapezius? What's a little come on my hands? And what difference would it make to anyone but me?

"No," I said, and left the room. As I washed my hands, I noticed they were shaking. I felt a little sick to my stomach, and worried about being alone in the house with this huge man. I sat down in an easy chair in the living room. After a while, Chip appeared, fully dressed. He handed me a twenty-dollar bill. "Thanks," he said, "my back feels a hell of a lot better."

For the first time in that hour, I looked him fully in the eye. The cringing I saw there took away my fear. He was obviously embarrassed, but more to the point, terribly lonely. I knew what he needed was not sex, but warmth, contact, friendship. I nearly wished I could help him, but I had no desire to be his friend. "I'm glad your back feels better." I said, getting up. I opened the door, and extended my hand. Chip held it between his for a moment. "Good hands," he said.

## Therapists who have sexual feelings toward clients

Very likely, at some point in your career, you will feel sexually attracted to a client on your table. It is your responsibility to your client and to your practice to work with your own feelings and control your thoughts and actions.

### *Your touch transmits your thoughts*

Your touch communicates an unbelievable amount of information to the person you are touching. If you are viewing them with sexual intention, they will feel that in your touch. They may not be consciously aware of what they are feeling, but the communication will take place nonetheless.

If you have ever had the experience of receiving a massage from someone who had sex on their mind, you know what I mean. You can feel it in their touch. It is a totally different experience than being treated by a therapist.

Transmitting sexual feelings in your massage can sabotage your practice. The client whom you approach sexually will feel uncomfortable, and is not likely to become a repeat client. He or she is also likely to communicate to others a feeling of discomfort, uneasiness, or general dissatisfaction with your massage.

As you practice massage with clients where there is the potential of a sexual attraction, either by you or by the client, monitor your own thoughts and feelings. If you start to slip into sexual thoughts about a client, simply choose to stop. Remind yourself of your therapeutic intention, and focus your thoughts on your techniques and therapeutic goals for this client.

The fact is that all massage practitioners and all clients are human beings, and human beings are sexual beings. Neither the client nor the massage therapist leaves their essential nature outside the massage room. The challenge for both people in a massage is to be who you really are, which has many facets—including a sexual nature—but to understand that a professional massage is a context in which any expression of your sexual nature or your client's sexual nature is inappropriate.

## *Create a safe and non-sexual environment in your practice*

Be alert to your own feelings of sexual attraction and to signs that a sexual attraction may be taking place for clients. Subtle signals and comments that pass unnoticed can create an ambiguity which invites confusion about these issues.

Make sure your dress and general appearance convey a professional, not a sexual intention. Do not allow your desire to be comfortable or casual to create the wrong impression; avoid low-cut blouses and exposed waists, excessive jewelry or make-up. Make sure there are no items in your massage room that could invite sexual confusion, such as suggestive artwork.

It is advisable to outline in advance what the client can expect during the massage session, including draping. Communicate in advance about whether to massage the abdomen and other potentially provocative parts of the body.

Choose language that does not invite confusion. Use scientific names for body parts, and avoid personal or evaluative comments about the client's body, such as making statements about how they look.

Avoid careless contact with the client's body. Do not contact the client's body with your trunk or legs.

If you feel sexual attraction while giving a massage, do not deny to yourself that you have these feelings; do not act on the feelings; acknowledge the feelings and make a conscious choice to sacrifice this sexual attraction for the sake of your career and the client's therapeutic experience.

## *Never initiate sexual contact with a client*

Occasionally, stories are reported about professionals, including massage therapists, who sexually accost their clients. This is damaging to the profession as a whole, and disastrous to the lives of the therapists involved.

It is one thing to date a former client, and to create whatever personal relationship you both decide to have after you're therapist/client relationship has ended. That presents no particular moral or ethical problem. However, dating a current client which presents ethical conflicts and dangers.

Much worse than socializing with a client is to attempt to initiate romantic or sexual activity with a client *during* a professional massage. This is immoral, unethical, and illegal. The massage relationship involves trust on the part of the client, who becomes vulnerable to the therapist. In this sense, the relationship resembles that of a doctor and patient, or priest and penitent. The trust placed in you by your client gives you a greater responsibility to be honest and above board in your dealings.

If you feel a desire to initiate sexual activity with your clients, seek professional help. You may be able to learn something about yourself in the course of working with this desire. If you are unable to control this desire, your best course of action may be to stop practicing massage, or to limit your practice to men only or women only.

# 10 For Men Only

## The challenge for a male massage therapist

In the massage field in general, attracting clients and becoming established is more difficult for a man than for a woman. This is not true in certain specialties, like sports massage, on-site massage, Rolfing, Trager, polarity, and other forms of bodywork that do not involve nudity and stroking. It is also not true in some other countries, such as Germany, where men tend to be accepted as massage therapists more easily than women.

However, in the field of Swedish massage in the United States, experience shows that most clients prefer having a woman give them a massage. Most women are shy about becoming undressed and being touched by a man they are not intimate with. Many also have self-image issues and are embarrassed to have a man see their bodies. Many men feel uncomfortable being touched by another man, and prefer the nurturance they receive from a woman's touch.

## Some groups of clients that prefer male therapists

Some men prefer a male therapist because they want to avoid any possibility of arousal. Such groups include Catholic priests, orthodox Jewish men, and men with strong conservative moral principles.

Many gay men prefer a male therapist, apparently because they are more comfortable in the company of men.

Many athletes and very muscular men prefer a male therapist, having the belief that most women lack the strength to give them a satisfyingly deep massage.

## Some clients are gender-neutral

A certain number of clients do not care whether their massage therapist is male or female, but choose a therapist on personality and skill level. Such clients are a minority. Generally speaking, such clients are probably more common in cosmopolitan areas and on the west coast.

## The task for a male massage therapist

Because the available client pool for men is smaller, men have to try harder, be better, and have more patience than women when establishing a massage practice.

Men can and do succeed in the field, and some men become tremendously successful. Do not allow the challenge to discourage you. Knowing the situation in advance will allow you to better plan your career and focus on target groups which are likely to produce clients for you.

## The male as pursuer

Societal conditioning, and perhaps instinctual patterns, result in men generally pursuing women sexually and initiating sexual contact in relationships. As a result, men tend to be in the habit of seeking sexual encounters.

One very successful male therapist told me that he considers it a great advantage to him that he is married. His desire to couple is focused on his wife, and he feels much more relaxed than he otherwise would about working with his women clients.

If this issue is a problem for you, there is no magic solution. Simply be honest with yourself, and exercise your will and creativity to avoid confronting your clients with sexual energy that will create problems in your professional life.

## Avoiding allegations of impropriety

Although only about one in five U.S. massage practitioners is a man, male massage practitioners are the subject of more than half of the allegations of improper conduct. An allegation of this type, even if eventually proven to be untrue, can nonetheless be terribly traumatizing, embarrassing, and costly.

A male massage therapist must be very clear and very careful to ensure that he will not be the subject of an allegation of improper conduct. Clear communication with clients will help. Having clear intention to work solely in a therapeutic way will help. Having strong and well-defined boundaries will help.

Male therapists should pay close attention to the advice in Chapter 9 (Sex and Massage), Chapter 11 (Working with Survivors of Childhood Sexual or Physical Abuse), and Chapter 13 (Ethics and Boundaries). Together, the awarenesses and recommendations in these chapters will give you a framework for practicing in a scrupulously ethical way that will greatly reduce any possible confusion on the part of you or your clients, and will be your best "insurance" against allegations of impropriety.

# 11 Working with Survivors of Childhood Sexual or Physical Abuse

Recent years have seen a dramatic increase in society's awareness of childhood abuse as a prevalent social problem. Those who have been abused as children may or may not remember being abused. They may have been abused sexually or non-sexually, and may or may not have begun the journey of healing the effects of that abuse.

As a massage practitioner, chances are you will come in contact with a number of clients who experienced childhood abuse. There are no definite figures about the extent of the problem, but some studies have estimated that 20 to 30 percent of females and 10 to 15 percent of males in the U.S. and Canada are sexually abused before reaching age 18.

Some of these individuals become massage clients, and they may or may not have a conscious awareness of the abuse they endured. If they come to a massage practitioner without any awareness of their childhood trauma, treatment by an unprepared massage therapist can result in the client having extreme reactions that include terror, convulsions and withdrawal. The purpose of this chapter is to learn about these potential clients, their sensitivities and vulnerabilities, and the precautions and procedures that will assist you in avoiding re-injuring such clients.

Most massage clients are women, so the female pronoun is used throughout this chapter. Also, most childhood abuse is sexual in nature, but many clients have also experienced non-sexual abuse as children.

I wish to thank Mary Ann DiRoberts, who provided substantial assistance in the preparation of this chapter, and also Diana Lonsdale and Anya Seerveld, both of whom provided useful information.

## Childhood abuse and the damage that results

Children have natural mechanisms to deal with stress, but extremely strong experiences can overwhelm these mechanisms. Sexual or physical abuse is too much for the child to deal with, and it can prevent the normal integration of the psyche as the child matures.

One aspect of this process is numbness, or dissociation. Minor dissociation is a natural part of life for most people, taking the form of spacing out, daydreaming, or similar behaviors. However, more significant dissociation can result in a state in which the person is not aware of the physical sensations of the body, or is not consciously present in the experience of the body. In extreme cases, multiple personalities are created and the person lives a life as different personalities who may not even know each other.

Psychologically, childhood abuse destroys the child's sense of safety and trust, and drastically violates the child's boundaries. The child may grow into an adult who has difficulty trusting and is confused about boundaries. One who experienced childhood sexual abuse may have guilt about the sensations she had during the abuse, feel shame or responsibility for the abuse, and have terror buried in her body from these childhood experiences. As an adult, she may feel like "damaged goods" and may believe that sex is all she is good for, or that she is not even good for that.

While you should not attempt to diagnose someone psychologically, certain traits can provide clues that childhood abuse *may* be an issue in someone's life. Signs to look for include depression, lack of emotion, extreme changes in emotion, feelings of being different or defective, dysfunctional relationships, irresponsible sexuality, anorexia, bulimia, obesity, childishness or excessive vulnerability, inability to take care of oneself, workaholism, compulsive rituals or other compulsive behaviors, and anxiety attacks.

It is important to remember that unless you are trained as a mental health professional, you should not attempt to be a psychotherapist for a person who experienced childhood abuse. In fact, unless you have specialized training in practicing massage with abuse survivors, you should consider declining to practice massage with such a client. Without the understanding and skills necessary to work with such clients, you may do more harm than good by giving a massage.

## The intake interview

When initially interviewing a client, do *not* directly ask if she experienced childhood abuse. Asking this question violates the client's boundary; it requires her to either lie or disclose something she may not wish to share with a person she does not yet trust.

It is better to ask generally whether bodywork brings up feelings for her. You may tell her orally or in your printed information that you invite her to let you know if she is in psychotherapy. Rather than probing too deeply, carefully listen and watch for signs that may alert you to a history of abuse.

## During the massage

The abused child has been dis-empowered, has had trust violated, and has not had boundaries honored. When massaging this adult client, be careful to empower her and to operate with clear boundaries. Be scrupulous about giving control of the session to the client. Be clear about your permission to touch in specific places or in specific ways. Check in often with your client to be sure she is comfortable with the session and is present in her body. To feel safe is the primary need for a client who has been abused, and a lack of safety can cause such a client to dissociate even before being touched.

Even a client who is not an abuse survivor will appreciate being empowered, respected, and given control. Since you likely will not know that a particular client is a survivor, consider these guidelines with all clients.

It is especially important to check in often during the massage with a client who has a history of abuse or who shows any indications of such a history. When your touch triggers an emotional response or a memory of abuse, this client may be unable to tell you what is happening. The abusive experience often includes training in "not telling," and when a memory of that experience is triggered, the training to be silent may prevent the client from letting you know what is happening.

If a client recalls a portion of the abusive treatment during a massage session, it can be extremely upsetting for the client and a difficult situation for the massage therapist. A "flashback" can feel to the client like a flood of terrifying feelings. She may dissociate from current time and reality and be completely immersed in an experience of the childhood events. She may shake with terror, convulse, go into tetany, curl up in a ball, or shout at the perpetrator.

If you as a therapist find yourself with a client having such an experience, remember that this person is re-experiencing a terrible event from her past. If you can, talk to her in simple language, telling her where she is and what is happening in the present moment. Suggest that she open her eyes and describe the room you are in, or make eye contact with you, or change her position to sitting or lying on her side.

If she tells you about her experience, let her know you understand what she tells you by rephrasing it in your own words. Maintain boundaries and give her control over what happens, and assure her that you will stay with her and keep her safe as long as she needs you. After the experience has passed, she may still need your support and attention. Help her make specific plans for the rest of the day, and encourage her to use whatever support is available in her life. If the client is not in psychotherapy, this would be a good time to make a referral to a qualified practitioner.

Because flashback experiences can be so very unsettling, it is advisable to assure that a client with a history of childhood abuse has a psychotherapist if she is going to work with you doing massage. Because of the likelihood that your work will bring up such an intense experience, the client should have the services of a professional who can help process such an event if it occurs. If you intend to specialize in working with clients with histories of childhood abuse, you should have additional training in this area, be in supervision, and have done your own psychotherapy.

## *One survivor's experiences with massage*

The following is excerpted from an article that appeared in The Journal of Soft Tissue Manipulation. Written by Tess Edwards, it describes the experiences of a woman who experienced ritual satanic abuse as a child, and became a massage therapy client as an adult.

Her descriptions of various massage experiences and suggestions for therapists have great value. As you will see from reading the following, Tess is a client who dissociates during massage. Her massage therapist practices safe touch work, which requires specific training to do.

I wish to express my gratitude to the Journal of Soft Tissue Manipulation for permission to reproduce this essay.

### One trauma survivor's experience of massage
### by Tess Edwards

I believe strongly in the importance of massage for survivors of child abuse. I feel very lucky that I am one of the few survivors I know who can both afford and tolerate a weekly massage.

In my search for healing, I saw an applied kinesiologist who told me that my trauma has settled mostly in the muscle and skeletal systems instead of the organs, as is more common. So for me, I believe that massage is crucial to the healing process because the toxic effect of the trauma is lodged in my muscles. Even when the toxic effect of abuse is primarily in the organs, I believe that massage is essential to the healing process—not only because safe touch is an important and unusual experience for most survivors, but also because trauma is held in the body.

Dancers talk about muscle memory—that is how they learn the intricate moves they must make on stage. We all have muscle memory. I have never been comfortable placing my arms above my head—I have never been able to paint a ceiling or hang curtains without going into a state of panic. Similarly, I usually postpone washing my hair for as long as possible. I always called myself lazy, stupid or other nasty names because I could not do these tasks. And I never understood that this had any meaning.

I now understand that many of my worst life experiences took place while my hands were tied above my head for long periods of time. I still have trouble with this. In fact, as the memories surface, difficulty with these tasks has increased. Now even in aquabics class I have tears rolling down my face when I try to do the above-the-head arm exercises. This is typical. As the memory surfaces, the symptoms intensify.

I've always thought that massage would help me, but it has been a long battle to allow myself to afford it and to learn how to tolerate it. For three or four years, I got massage treatments about three times a year. For the most part, I don't think they helped me at all because I simply left my body during them. Touch of this type is really a re-enactment of the original abuse and in fact gives me even further to go in my healing journey. In one case, the massage I received was truly a re-enactment of the abuse and for months undermined the healing work I was doing.

One massage therapist really upset me when she was giving me her new-age philosophy about how we all choose our lives—have choice even about abuse in childhood. One of the hardest things to recover from is the guilt and shame that every survivor I've met feels about the abuse. Hearing their stories, I have noted that in most cases, the abuser blames the victim: "You're too sexy." "You make me do it." "You love it." "You know you want it."

"You're making me evil" was what my father used to say to me and he even taught one of my personalities to beg him for intercourse at an early age. So for my massage therapist to tell me that I chose either to come back in this life as a victim of child abuse, or that I as a child had some choice in the matter, pushes all my shame and guilt buttons. If I'm lucky, this makes me very angry. If I'm not, I feel despair.

My biggest difficulty with massage, although it took me a long time to realize it, was that any touch was triggering. Two years ago, a group of four survivors of sexual abuse started a self-facilitated group based on giving and receiving safe touch. In our weekly five-hour sessions, we would ask for what we wanted that night—anything from getting a back rub, to being rocked while we sang lullabies, to massaging just a hand, to building a protective igloo with pillows, to brushing hair. Any activity involving touch that the survivor could accept that evening.

During these sessions two of us began retrieving new memories of abuse while in the group. Instead of being a group for safe touch, the group became, temporarily, a group for memory retrieval. The memory work triggered by the touch was so intense for the other two members of the group that they asked us to stop. We then formed a group specifically for memory retrieval, which has been going on for over a year now and from which I have benefited enormously. Another survivor I know began the process of retrieving memory when she began to receive massage. This is why I feel that massage is so very important and so very tricky for survivors.

Currently, I see a massage therapist once a week, and it is helping enormously. Three nights ago, I had a dream that my body turned from metal into flesh. Last Sunday in my memory retrieval group, I was able to feel and express many more of the feelings that I felt as a child than I have before.

The massage is still hard sometimes. We're still trying to develop a system so that I can ask her to stop. We haven't found a good way yet because when I need her to stop, I'm in a child part who was trained not to speak; stopping wasn't an option, no matter how desperately she wanted to. It's hard for my massage therapist to help when I go there because the signs are subtle to non-existent. This is partly because I received tons of training on how to pretend everything was alright.

I think my massage therapist is learning my body enough to notice when I hold my breath or, more often, when my flesh just feels dead or uninhabited. I don't know how she does it. She checks with me a lot, which for me is great because it can sometimes give me permission to say that I am in trouble.

I have learned to set some boundaries. We do not work on my bum. I allowed her to work on my upper legs once and got so badly triggered that I was unable to say so until a week later. During that week, I wandered around in flashbacks. My inner thighs are now off limits.

My massage therapist tells me a lot of things about my body which are very useful to me because I've spent most of my life outside of it. She is helping me to learn about my body, making it easier to reside there.

There are a number of things I feel that a massage therapist should do when working with me. I am sharing these ideas so that other massage therapists might learn about how to help someone who has been abused.

- First and foremost, I am more important than your technique. If I can't lie face down, I need you to accommodate me. Maybe massage me while I'm on my side, even if it means you can't give me what you feel is your best work. Give me what is best for me, not your best work.

If I leave my body, you can make my circulation shoot around better, but that's it. For me, the purpose of massage is to get more into my body, not leave it more. If I'm not present, I'm not getting what I need. I need to learn to feel pleasure in my body. Pleasure is something that has never been safe for me.

- Be creative. If I can't tolerate lying down, you could have me sit on a chair with my arms on the table and do just my head and neck. If I need to keep my clothes on, figure out how you can help me with my clothes on. Encourage me to bring my teddy bear if I am terrified.

- Help me to feel safe and comfortable. I love to be rocked and so do my inner kids. I love to be warm and adore my massage therapist's heating pad and the warm blankets she covers me with.

- Find out what you need from me in order to help me. Find out my other support systems. You can't be all things for me. You're not my therapist and you're not responsible for my healing or the bad things that happened to me. If you sense that my support structure is weak, be careful if you trigger memories that you can't take me through.

- Respect me and my process. I know best about me, just as you know best about you.

- One of the skills I value the most in my massage therapist is her understanding of emotional release. It is wonderful to know that she can handle anger, grief or terror as they come up and work with them, instead of being terrified by them. She has a big bucket with a pillow on it for resting my hands on when I am on my front or hitting if I need to release some anger.

- Learn to detect the difference between re-enactment and release. Re-enactment and release can look the same but have an opposite impact on the survivor. Both re-enactment and release can cause the survivor to show physical symptoms of grief, fear or anger. However, in re-enactment, the survivor is lengthening the work she has to do. She has yet one more incident of feeling powerless and victimized to recover from. In release, she is letting go of some of the abuse and actively reclaiming her life.

Being placed in a re-enactment can help enormously if I am ready for it and I choose it. I went to my massage therapist once after a particularly nasty memory where my hands were tied. I specifically asked her if she could work on my wrists and as she did, it felt as though hundreds of wrist restraints fell off as I cried. The relief was wonderful.

- Learn about triggers: what they are, how they work and how to cope with them.

- Please refer me if you are uncomfortable working with me. Don't sabotage my courageous act of attempting to find safe touch and learning to re-inhabit my body.

To me, my healing process involves recalling my life and integrating the sensory information that I blocked or dissociated from my awareness. This includes my emotions, my spirituality and the events, sights, sounds, smells, tastes, textures that I have been unable to allow into conscious awareness. I want to experience my life as a whole.

One of the most useful parts of healing is massage. To be touched without sex, without violence, is a first for me and a great gift. To learn that it is safe to allow someone into my space is incredible. To begin to release the trauma is a relief.

# IV

# Business, Practical and Legal Information for the Practitioner

# 12 Business Basics and Practice Pointers

Practicing massage means operating in the business world. If you have no significant experience doing business, certain expectations of the business world may not be familiar to you. The purpose of this chapter is to give you enough information to avoid pitfalls and facilitate your success.

The subjects covered in this chapter are *Steps You Can Take Toward Professionalism, What to Expect From Clients,* and *Pricing Your Services.*

## A. Steps You Can Take Toward Professionalism

### 1. Communicate Clearly and Keep Agreements

The business world operates by mutual agreement. In order to run smoothly, agreements must be unambiguous, and both parties must be able to rely on the other to keep the agreement.

In practice, this means you and your client should have no confusion about where or when appointments are to take place, how long they are for, how much they cost, and what sort of therapy the client is expecting you to provide. Keeping your agreement means arriving on time to all appointments with all the equipment you will need.

If an appointment is tentative, make sure both of you know when you will speak again to make it definite. If there are any questions in your mind about an agreement, speak to the client about them. The chances are that your client also has questions.

### 2. Present a Well-Groomed Image at Work and After Work

Most massage therapists understand the need to present a professional image at work. Your physical appearance announces who you are, and if you are proud of your work the image you present should convey that pride.

As a community member, you will see and be seen by your clients after working hours at unexpected times. Your appearance and your actions at these times will also have an effect on your clients' perceptions of you. While you need not constantly look over your shoulder, keep in mind that anything you do in public reflects on your professional character. If you have a wild side, you might want to keep it indoors.

### 3. Answer Your Phone in a Businesslike Manner

Even if you have separate office and home phone numbers, you should answer both your home and office phones in a polite way. You never know who is calling with what opportunity, and it is a shame to spoil an opportunity by creating a poor first impression. Never let young children answer a line on which you take business calls, and make sure that your outgoing message is a professional-sounding one recorded in your own voice.

### 4. Return Phone Calls Promptly

Make a point of returning your phone calls as soon as you can. Keeping people waiting for a return call will train them to expect you to be hard to reach; they may think twice about calling you next time. You also run the risk that the person who is trying to reach you will find someone else to meet her needs, and you will have missed an opportunity.

### 5. Make Cleanliness a Priority

Massage clients are very sensitive to the issue of cleanliness. If they find you or your office unclean, they will not tell *you*, but they will tell others.

Since massage is such a personal service, clients will want to be sure the linens are fresh, the carpet is clean, and your clothing and body are clean. If in doubt, go overboard, as some clients have a very critical eye when it comes to hygiene.

### 6. Avoid Talking Too Much During a Massage

If your client wants to talk, let her talk. It's her massage and her hour. However, do not use the massage as a time to talk about yourself, your problems and your opinions. If your client is being quiet, then you should be quiet as well, unless your conversation concerns an issue related to the massage session.

Several of my clients have told me they left their previous massage therapist because he or she would not keep quiet during a massage. Notice that they did not tell the talkative therapist—they told their new therapist.

### 7. Watch the Details of Client Comfort

Show concern for your clients' experience. Their perception of their entire experience with you is important, not just the result of your hands working their muscles.

On a physical level, make sure your clients are warm enough. Be aware of any modesty issues. Avoid getting oil in their hair, and offer to towel off excess oil. Avoid causing any pain during the massage, unless you and your client both agree that aggressively working a body part is the best thing to do.

On the level of emotions and boundary issues, make sure you honor the right of your clients to reveal or not reveal facts about themselves, to have portions of their body worked or not worked, and in general to be in charge of their session. Don't let your desire to give override the client's wishes about what to receive.

### 8. Finish on Time

Clients are often on a busy schedule. You may want to do that extra five or ten minutes, but your client may feel it's more important to be on time for her next meeting. If you want to go past the agreed ending time, get the client's permission beforehand.

### 9. Get to Know the Other Therapists in Your Area

Become acquainted with as many massage therapists, fitness trainers, physical therapists, bodyworkers, chiropractors, acupuncturists, psychotherapists and medical doctors as you can. The more people who know you, the more opportunity there is for them to assist you in your professional growth.

Remember that you are becoming a service professional. Allow yourself to assume membership in the community of those who are serving others' health needs. Knowing a large number of health professionals gives you a broad perspective on the field, and on the level of activity in your community. Be as involved in the total picture as you can.

### 10. Foster Your Own Personal and Professional Growth

As one therapist told me "There are massage therapists, and there are massage therapists, but the ones who make it are the ones who are working on themselves."

Examine what it is you offer your clients—what benefits your work gives them, and what kinds of difficulties your work helps them get through. Chances are, you are offering your clients help with the kinds of issues you also face in your life.

Acknowledge that you are also a client. Practice what you preach. Nurture your own growth through finding therapists and healers and teachers who help you grow. In the process, you will also learn new techniques that you can incorporate in your bodywork. The process of growth has no end.

## B. What to Expect from Clients

### 1. Cancellations

Clients will cancel; plans change. It is an unavoidable fact of life. You can minimize cancellations by calling to confirm each appointment the day before. Even so, you will sometimes encounter last-minute cancellations.

You can create a cancellation policy to protect yourself, so long as you communicate it to your clients. One fair cancellation policy is to require 24 hours advance notice, and to charge a penalty (such as $25) for canceling on shorter notice. A sign on your desk or office wall, where it can be seen by your clients, is adequate to communicate your policy.

Consider a "one-miss" policy—each client gets to cancel or miss one appointment without penalty, and is then told that your standard procedure will be enforced for all subsequent times. Another option is to encourage clients to give their appointment to a friend if they cannot use it to avoid any cancellation issues.

Whatever policy you choose should be fair to you and fair to your clients. You must be able to manage your time so that your practice supports your life. At the same time, your clients' lives may be complicated and they may have to deal with emergencies and unexpected events. Try to create a policy that balances your need for a predictable schedule with clients' needs for flexibility in extraordinary situations.

## 2. Great Expectations

One lesson I have learned over and over is not to place any importance on statements by clients like "I'm going to get a massage every week" or "I've got half a dozen friends who have been looking for someone like you." If I had the fee I would have charged all the people who told me they were coming in for a massage, I'd be considering retirement by now...

I'm sure they mean it when they say it, but the fact is people talk about getting massage much more than they actually follow through. Once you are an established therapist, these "great expectations" are not of great importance. However, if you are seeing four clients a week and needing the rent money, it can be harder to keep this sort of thing in perspective.

## 3. No-shows

Some clients make an appointment, do not cancel, and do not show up. This is about as frustrating a situation as you can get practicing massage, and there is very little you can do about it.

The great majority of no-shows are clients who have never been to see you before, and who learned about you either through the yellow pages or a newspaper ad. One way to control the problem is to require that all people making appointments give you first and last name and a phone number where they can be reached to confirm the appointment.

If you call the number and they never heard of the person, don't be surprised if he does not show up. If you call the number, and they sound shocked that the person is getting a massage, don't be surprised if he never arrives. With experience, you will learn to evaluate the likelihood of the person showing up for the appointment based on your experience in calling to confirm.

When a first-time client fails to cancel or to show up, let that person go. This is a person you will not hear from again, and it will not do you any good to try to track him down. Put your energy into those who want and need your services.

The decision what to do when a regular client fails to cancel or to show up for an appointment is more difficult. If you have discussed your cancellation policy with your clients, it is a simple matter to remind them of your agreement and to proceed according to it. If you have not established a cancellation policy, you do not have a strong ethical position for holding the client financially responsible for the missed appointment.

## 4. Angels

Once in a blue moon, you will get a client who takes it upon herself to be your fan club, publicity agent, networker and marketing strategist. Say a prayer of thanks.

An angel is someone who thinks so much of you and your work that she is inspired to do anything she can to help you succeed. This person will be thinking about you and talking about your work many times a day. Some are able to do more than others, but all act out of a feeling of love and caring.

My angel is one of my less affluent clients, and as a gesture of my appreciation, I have never raised his rate from the low introductory rate I was offering when he first became my client several years ago.

## 5. Constructive Critics

Most clients will not let you know that you caused them pain, or that they were too cold or too hot, or annoyed about something in your massage room. Although they will not tell you, such unspoken dissatisfactions cause many clients not to return for another massage.

That is why you should be grateful for the very few clients who ask you not to do a certain stroke, or complain about the temperature, or ask you to change this or that about your massage or the surroundings. In all likelihood, these clients speak for many others as well.

One such client of mine is a chef with a very acute sense of smell. One day while I was seated and working on his face and head, he asked me to please breathe to the side. Apparently, he was able to identify just what I had eaten several hours ago.

Until this time, I had not realized that I have a tendency to breathe through my mouth, and to exhale onto my clients' faces. Most clients probably did not notice any breath odor, but they probably did feel my breath on their faces. Either way, I no longer breathe on people's faces. Unless my constructive critic had spoken up, I would never have realized what I was doing.

# C. Pricing Your Services

Pricing your services can be a difficult issue. This discussion is meant to give you guidance in what to consider in order to find the most appropriate price for your services.

Several factors enter into a decision about pricing. The factors to consider are the "going rate" in your community, your expenses involved in providing the treatment, the price you feel comfortable charging, and the effect your price will have on your clients' ability to come to you.

## 1. The "Going Rate"

This refers to the customary charge for your kind of services in your area. The "going rate" for a one hour massage may be as low as $30 in some areas, and as high as $90 in other areas. Usually, there is a variation of $5 or $10 between the low and high ends of the "going rate." In my area, for example, the price for a one-hour massage ranges from $55 to $65.

Consider that the "going rate" is the rate charged by established professionals who have a clientele. A time-honored custom among newly-trained professionals is to slightly undercut the going rate when they are first attracting a clientele. To the cost-conscious consumer, the lower fee is an incentive to try this therapist. In addition, the lower fee is an acknowledgement that a newly-trained professional is still learning, and has not yet acquired fully mature skills.

If you choose a rate *far* below the going rate, for example $15 per hour, people will become suspicious that you are not really a trained therapist, and it may actually be harder for you to attract clients than if you charged a fee nearer the going rate.

As your skills and reputation grow, you will naturally raise your rates to a level that reflects your growth. Your clients will adjust to your new rates without much difficulty, especially since your new rates will be in line with the rates established therapists are charging. While some clients may find it hard to accept a rate increase after becoming accustomed to a lower price, most clients who know and like you will not leave you when your rates rise to the "going rate."

## 2. A Price You Are Comfortable With

For you to be comfortable with the fee you charge for your services means at least two different things. It means, first, that you are comfortable asking your client to pay your fee—you believe your service is as valuable as the money you receive for it. This touches on issues of self-worth. Your fee should be one that you can ask for and receive without mixed feelings.

Second, being comfortable with your fee means that it creates an income for you that meets your needs. You should feel that it compensates you for what you have given in your therapy session, and that it provides you with the means to have the material things you need to keep your life and practice going. If you feel you are not being nourished in your professional life, you may find yourself resentful and unenthusiastic about your work.

## 3. Effect of Pricing Decisions on Clients

Many years ago, a client told me "If massage costs $40, I'll come in twice a month. If it costs $60, I'll come in once in six months." I suspect this client speaks for many others.

Massage clients are generally quite cost-conscious. Many people would like to have massage on a regular basis, but feel they cannot afford it. Compared to items like a bag of groceries, a movie ticket or a tank of gasoline, massage is an expensive item to fit into a budget.

Even the wealthy are often quite cost-conscious. Many wealthy individuals either do not believe they have enough money, or resent people trying to charge them a premium because they are wealthy. They will shop for the best price, and reject a therapist who charges what they consider too high a price. This may not apply to a celebrity clientele, or the enormously wealthy, but the run-of-the-mill millionaire often watches prices very closely.

Therefore, your pricing decision may well affect the amount of business you get, the ease with which you generate new business, and the frequency of your repeat business.

## 4. Working on a "Sliding Scale"

Sometimes it is not possible to meet all the goals mentioned above with one set fee. In some cases, you may need to make exceptions to your price or work on a "sliding scale." This means that you charge some clients a lower fee because that is all they can afford.

Some clients refuse to pay a reduced fee as a matter of pride. Others may ask you directly for a reduced fee. If you are comfortable working at a reduced fee for those with a financial need, there is nothing wrong with doing so. Charge a fee they can afford and you can comfortably accept. Do not price your work so low that the client no longer places a value on it, or that you become resentful of the imbalance in the relationship.

My normal fee is $65. For clients with financial hardship, I will reduce my fee as low as $40. If I worked for less than $40 I would feel taken advantage of. However, for someone who cannot afford $40, whom I feel really needs my services, I will work without charge.

## 5. Discounts for Series Purchase

A common device therapists use is to offer a discount to clients who purchase several massages in advance. For example, if the cost of one massage is $60, a therapist may sell a series of five massages for $250 ($50 per massage).

This benefits both parties. The client saves $50, and the therapist has the use of the money in advance for any necessary expenditures. The client has the option of giving one or more of the series massages to a friend, which brings potential new clients to the office.

To offer a series, you can have a coupon printed up and sell the coupon. It may have five places to punch holes, or five numbers to cross off, or any system you prefer for keeping track of when the massages are used up. You can also create a system without coupons, by keeping track in a record book.

## 6. Other Discount Arrangements

Create any discount arrangement that serves a business purpose. This can include discounts for those who refer new clients, or promotions in which you give a free massage to someone who buys two gift certificates, or any other such idea that makes sense to you. One discount I offer is $15 off the second massage in one week for any client.

Sometimes it is appropriate to offer a discount to a client for becoming a "regular." Take the example of Ray, one of my early clients. Ray came for massage an average of once a month. Sometimes he would come more often, sometimes less often.

At the end of a massage, I asked Ray if he would come in regularly if the price were lower. He said he would, and we discussed possible agreements.

We decided that he would like to come twice a month, and could afford to do so if he paid $30 per visit instead of the $40 I was then charging. This seemed advantageous to both of us, and we agreed to adopt this plan. Ray began coming in twice a month. He enjoyed receiving more massages and I appreciated the added business and income.

I would not make this offer to most of my clients. It felt right to do so with Ray, in part because Ray did not know any of my other clients, so I knew I would not be presented with multiple requests for the same arrangement. I offer this as an example of the creative marketing you can come up with to fit a particular situation.

## 7. Barter for Goods or Services

Bartering—exchanging your service for the product or services of another—can be a means of gaining clients who would not otherwise receive massage. It can also be a good way for you to receive valuable goods or services without a cash outlay. In addition, clients with whom you barter may refer cash clients to you.

Barter can be done on an equal basis—one hour for one hour. It can also be done on an unequal basis. For example, if you barter with your physician, you may have to give more massage time than you receive from your doctor. On the other hand, if you barter for house-cleaning, you may receive more house-cleaning time than you give in massage service. One starting-point for negotiations is to compare the hourly rate for your services and the services you are bartering for, and adjust your barter arrangement accordingly.

Massage therapists who use barter find they can receive some great products and services through barter. Following is a list of services and items therapists have reported bartering for:

> Accounting services, advertising banner, airline tickets, auto repair, Barbie clothes, bodywork & massage, candles, chiropractic, computer equipment, contact lenses & eye exams, decorated cake, dentistry, dinners, electrical work, facials, gluten-free bread, graphic design, hair styling/haircuts, house cleaning, landscaping, legal services, linens for the office, manicures, medical services, office shelves, office sign, opera tickets, pedicures, prayers, printing services, psychic readings, sewing, stained glass, sweet corn, swing, teddy bears, trip to Cancun, voice coaching, waxing, wedding flowers & wedding cake, wristwatch.

You should be aware that the IRS treats barter as a taxable transaction. You are required to include the fair market value of the goods or services you receive as "income" when you file your year-end tax return, and pay taxes on it. It is true that the lack of a paper record of the transaction makes it difficult for the IRS to prove, but their policy is to prosecute those who do not report barter transactions when they can. Several years ago, pop artist Peter Max pled guilty to tax fraud, partly as a result of having bartered his artwork in partial payment for several homes without paying the proper taxes.

Another concern about barter is the issue of dual relationships. If you do emotional-based work, structural work, or work that involves any aspect of psychotherapy, barter may be an inappropriate way to interact with your clients because of boundary issues in the therapeutic relationship. Most psychologists will not barter for massage for this reason. Ethical issues about bartering for massage services are explored more fully in the next chapter.

# 13 Ethics and Boundaries

In simplest terms, having ethics means doing the right thing, or acting morally. In ordinary relationships, this means such things as telling the truth, being honest in business and keeping your promises.

In a professional relationship with patients or clients, you have a stricter standard of ethical conduct as a result of your professional relationship with your clients. For example, psychiatrists and psychologists encourage patients to share their secrets; therefore they have a special duty to protect their client's secrets. Lawyers encourage clients to entrust financial affairs to them; therefore they have a special obligation to be careful with clients' funds. All professions have special ethical rules and obligations based on the nature of their relationship with clients or patients, and the special kind of trust the professional requires to do their work.

As a massage therapist, the extent of your ethical obligations depends on the type of work you do. The more vulnerable your clients become, the higher your ethical obligations. The more your work requires clients to trust you in order for the work to succeed, the higher your ethical obligations.

If your work involves encouraging clients to access emotions, or if you work at a deep level with clients' bodies or psyches, your ethical obligations are stricter than someone who does only chair massage or relaxation massage.

## The Fundamentals of Ethics for Bodyworkers

What are the basic ethical requirements for a massage practitioner? The most essential ethical obligations can be summarized in the following three categories: (1) confidentiality, (2) integrity in your business practices, and (3) respect for boundaries. Let's look at each of these items individually.

### Confidentiality

In some professions, the law creates a formal guarantee of confidentiality—lawyers, doctors, priests, and psychiatrists have a *legal* obligation, not just an ethical obligation, to protect any communications between themselves and their clients, patients, or parishioners.

As a massage therapist or bodyworker, you do not have the same legal obligation of confidentiality, but you do have an ethical one. Your clients should never have to worry that anything about their relationship with you will ever embarrass or injure them.

That means that all discussions with your clients should be considered confidential and should not be repeated. The details of a client's personal life should never be repeated outside the office. Even repeating the facts in a story without naming the person can be risky, as the person you tell the story to may have enough information to "put two and two together" and figure out the identity of the person in your story.

Consider the idea that confidentiality might even extend to the question of whether a certain person is a client or not. Is it possible that any of your clients would not want a certain person to know they are a massage client? Perhaps you have a high-profile client whose privacy is extremely important to him or her? Perhaps you have a client who comes from a social group in which massage is not accepted and has chosen not to let her friends or associates know she receives massage. This is a "gray area" in a practitioner's ethics, but give some thought to this question, and you will see how important it is to safeguard your clients' confidences in general.

### *Integrity in Your Business Practices*

In Chapter 12, we discussed the basics of business for a massage practitioner, including such topics as being on time and keeping agreements. Some of these topics overlap with ethics.

One important part of integrity for a massage practitioner is making sure that your clients understand in advance what service you are providing and what compensation you expect. If you give a "one-hour" session, does that mean you schedule appointments on the hour—including time for intake, undressing, and dressing—or does it mean you have a session lasting one hour on the table? This should be discussed in advance so there is no chance for confusion to arise.

If your gift certificates have an expiration date, explain that when you sell them and let the purchaser know the reason [but note that some states have laws against expiration dates on prepaid gift certificates]. If you have a cancellation policy that requires full or partial payment for a missed appointment, make sure your clients understand the policy clearly before you enforce it.

The key elements of business integrity are standing by your word and clarifying the terms of your agreements. Practice these two traits and clients will be better able to relax about the business aspects of your relationship and focus on receiving the healing and nurturance you are there to provide them with.

## Boundaries

Sometimes part of a massage education is learning to become intuitive and "merge" with your clients at some level.

Another aspect of your work as a massage therapist is to recognize and enforce the separation between yourself and your clients. Protecting the "sovereignty" of your clients will help them feel safe in their relationship with you. Protecting your own "sovereignty" will help you to focus your full healing abilities on your clients without distraction or confusion over personal issues.

In short, boundaries ensure that, as a massage practitioner:

- your clients are safe

- you are comfortable

- you are not distracted in your role as therapist

The term "boundaries" may not be familiar to you. The word boundary usually means the border, or edge, or limit of something. In the context of a massage practice, "boundary" refers to the separation between you and your client; respect for the separateness of the two of you and for the areas within each of you that should remain off limits to the other. In this chapter we are discussing boundaries both for you and your clients; each of you needs to be able to set limits.

## The Primary Boundary Is the Client's Right to Set Limits on Touch

The first and foremost "boundary" in a massage relationship is that the client is in control of where and how to be touched.

In other words, whatever the client asks you not to do must be scrupulously honored. This may be something as simple as not getting oil on her hair, or not touching her feet, not doing deep work without permission, or any other request the client may make. In addition, touching any body areas that could be considered sensitive—such as abdomen or inner thigh—should not be done without first specifically asking the client.

You create safety for the client by establishing that boundary between the client and yourself, so that the client knows her privacy and safety will be respected.

The primary boundary of inappropriate touch means of course that any sexual contact during a massage is unethical. However, it means much more than that. It means that any unwelcome contact during a massage is unethical. Some clients may be uncomfortable with massage on their chest, abdomen, buttocks, inner thigh or upper leg. Some clients may feel uncomfortable with the degree of pressure you are using, but may be reluctant to ask you to lighten up until the pain is intense. Some clients may have modesty issues about draping and remaining partially clothed.

As the therapist, it is your ethical obligation to make sure that you understand the client's wishes about being touched. You should ask about any possibly sensitive or questionable areas before massaging them.

## Beyond the Primary Boundary

Touch is not the only subject that raises boundary issues for a massage therapist. Let's look at some examples of day-to-day activities in the life of a massage practitioner that can also raise the issues of boundaries:

- Do you allow clients to phone you at home? If so, what times of day are OK and what times of day are not?

- Do you work in a home office? If so, does it have a separate entrance or do clients walk through your home to get to the office? Do you allow pets into your office? Are the sounds of your home audible during sessions? Do clients encounter pets or other family members as they enter or leave?

- How much do you tell your clients about your personal life? Do you volunteer information about yourself or only answer their questions, or not answer any personal questions at all?

- Do you socialize with your clients?

- Do you barter with your clients?

## Dual Relationship

Socializing or bartering with your clients creates a "dual relationship". The term "dual relationship" refers to the situation where you have a therapist/client relationship, and you enter into another, different relationship with the same client. The second relationship may be a social or romantic relationship, or it may be an employer/employee relationship, where the client works for you in a barter arrangement.

A number of ethical concerns need to be addressed regarding dual relationships to assure you do not endanger your basic therapist/client relationship when you also engage in another kind of relationship with a client.

The major risk in dual relationships is that your therapist/client relationship will be compromised by some aspect of the new relationship. For example, assume you trade massage services for lawn mowing services. You agree that each hour of your services will be compensated by two hours of lawn mowing.

What if you feel your grass needs to be cut on Thursday, but your client is not available to do it until Sunday? What if the client does not mow to your satisfaction, missing an edge now and then, or leaving too many clippings on the lawn? What if you sense the client is working slowly and you feel you are not receiving full value in return for your services?

Any of these could cause you to feel resentful, or to feel like you should hold back and not give your finest work to the client because you are not being properly compensated in the barter relationship. Anything that causes you to hesitate in giving your best work creates a problem in your therapeutic relationship with your client.

On the other hand, what if your client feels taken advantage of because she is spending more time mowing than you are massaging? What if the client feels your standards about how she performs her lawn cutting are too high and she resents you telling her how to perform the work? These feelings can easily carry over to the massage relationship and make the client uneasy about continuing as your client.

I used the example of lawn mowing, but similar problems could creep in for any kind of barter relationship—if you trade for hair cutting, accounting services, house cleaning, or any other kind of service, there is always the possibility that the way the service is performed will create an issue for you or for your client, which will affect your therapist/client relationship. It helps to be as detailed and specific as possible in creating your barter contract, and I suggest a written agreement so both of you will be very clear about the agreement and what each of you expects.

Barter for goods is less of an ethical problem, because goods can be objectively valued, but even so you still need to be careful of ethical issues. If you and your client decide in advance on the value of your service and the value of the item you are bartering for, you might avoid conflicts.

But what if you "really" feel you should give only three massages for an item, whereas the client wants four? If you agree to four massages instead of three, will you skimp on the time or hold back to make the deal seem fair to you? If not, will you feel resentful about the arrangement? Such a feeling could hinder your work and unconsciously create a situation where your therapist/client relationship is compromised.

Your client also may have difficulties with the barter relationship—she could feel that she is not receiving your "best" professional services, or that the terms of the exchange are not fair to her.

## Power Imbalance in the Therapeutic Relationship

To complicate matters further, there is a natural tendency in a therapist/client relationships for the therapist to be "in charge". After all, you set the fee, you direct the activities during the session, you are the "performer" and the client receives your work. Because the relationship has you as the "expert", there is a tendency for the client not to speak up when troublesome feelings creep in, or to defer to your judgment or authority within the context of the massage relationship.

Therefore, if a client with whom you are bartering has some discomfort about the way the barter transaction is going, she may not feel free to express these feelings, and these unresolved feelings can become an irritation to the client and damage the working relationship you both have with each other.

## Romance and Dating

Another kind of dual relationship is the social or romantic relationship with a massage client. We all know that social and romantic relationships can have their ups and downs, and can get complicated. Combining social or romantic relationships with a therapeutic relationship can create confusion and even turmoil in the therapeutic relationship.

To avoid difficulties, I recommend that if you are interested in dating a client or seeing a client socially, you first refer that person to another therapist and stop your therapist/client relationship. There is no ethical barrier about dating an ex-client. This does not involve a dual relationship and it does not raise any ethical questions (unless your work is psychotherapeutic in nature).

## Find Your Individual Answers to Ethical Questions

Not all massage practitioners need to set up exactly the same boundaries. The need for boundaries depends in part on the kind of massage work you do, and in part on your personality and the way you relate to your clients.

For example, are you naturally a very open person, sharing your life with friends and acquaintances alike, comfortable opening up without first forming a close personal bond? Or are you more reserved, needing to feel comfort and trust before revealing the feelings and ideas that are important to you, reserving such communications for close and trusted friends? Your personal style may dictate how open you are with your clients and how much of your life you will allow them to share without risking your comfort zone.

With these considerations in mind, make policies that are appropriate for you as to:

- The times at which you will take calls at home

- The extent to which you socialize with clients, either individually or in group situations

- Whether to barter your sessions for goods or services

- What kind and how much personal information you tell your clients

Do you work with vacationers, or on-site clients, or other people whom you probably will not see on a regular basis? Or do you work with people in distress, those experiencing emotional problems, survivors of touch trauma, or those who are seeking more than just massage, but some form of healing?

The kind of work you do dictates the level of trust your clients need and deserve, and should guide you in establishing boundaries that make your therapy room a safe place for your clients to become vulnerable and receive your deepest work without risk.

Consider whether it is appropriate for you to:

- restrict or eliminate dual relationships with clients

- research or study the issues of transference and counter-transference

- engage a supervisor who can oversee and guide your professional conduct

It may seem contradictory, but many therapists have found that limiting their relationships with clients improves their work. By having clear boundaries, both parties are able to keep their focus on the therapy and not be distracted. Clients can remain clients longer and can receive your best work.

## Supervision

A common practice among psychotherapists is to hire an experienced colleague to provide supervision. Supervision involves meeting on a regular basis to discuss with your supervisor the work you are doing with your clients. It is a time to bring up any difficult, confusing, or unclear elements of the relationships with your clients, and receive objective evaluation and guidance.

If you are doing relaxation massage, you probably do not need supervision. If you are doing medical massage, you likewise probably do not need supervision. However, if you are regularly working with survivors of abuse, or touch trauma, supervision may be an important part of your professional life. Work such as this, which can evoke strong and unpredictable feelings in the client, requires a degree of attention and skill that may not be natural to you unless you have had specific training in working with clients such as these.

Even with less sensitive clients, supervision may be helpful to a practitioner in developing communication skills that allow clients to be heard more fully about how they need the therapeutic relationship to change. This type of supervision is akin to coaching, in which a more experienced practitioner can show you opportunities you may be missing to listen more carefully to your clients' needs and provide your clients with a more comfortable and effective relationship. This can have a very positive effect on your practice, improving the effectiveness of your work and helping with client retention.

## *Transference and Counter-transference*

These are terms psychologists use to discuss aspects of the therapist/patient relationship. Transference refers to the client bringing feelings into the relationship from experiences earlier in life, and experiencing those feelings about the therapist. For example, a client's feelings about a father or mother may unconsciously be "transferred" to the therapist, and the client's relationship with the therapist can be colored by these feelings.

Counter-transference is when the therapist brings feelings to the relationship which become "transferred" to the client, such as identifying with the client, or trying to "fix" the client instead of providing the client with the tools to solve her own problems.

Dr. Ben Benjamin, head of Muscular Therapy Institute in Cambridge, Massachusetts, has written:

> Normal personal boundaries and cultural taboos of touch are automatically transgressed in massage. For this reason, massage is a relationship in which therapists need to be cognizant of transference and counter transference, boundaries, abuse, and therapeutic dynamics.

To a certain extent, the simple act of touch, especially coupled with disrobing, creates the possibility for feelings to arise and cloud the relationship between the client and the therapist. Because massage inherently transgresses boundaries, perhaps all massage practitioners should undertake supervision to improve their professional relationships and provide the best possible care to their clients. However, supervision would probably be regarded as an unnecessary refinement by most practitioners of pure relaxation massage.

However, anyone who works more deeply than the basic levels of muscle, fascia and physiology should seriously consider supervision, or at least a study of transference, counter transference, abuse and therapeutic dynamics. Once you enter the realm of emotions and the psyche, you can find yourself swimming in deep waters before you know your way around.

If your work is intended to provide healing, or emotional or psychological growth, you should invest in some study of the therapeutic relationship so you have a better understanding of the predictable issues that will arise both for you and for your clients as you do this work.

If you wish to further explore the issues discussed in this chapter, you may want to read *The Educated Heart*, by Nina McIntosh, published by Lippincott, Williams and Wilkins ($29.95). This book is a detailed instructional guide about ethics for bodyworkers by a certified Rolfer. It is written from the perspective of one whose work is intended to be deeper than relaxation massage, and if your work is of that type, it contains many insights and awarenesses that may be useful to you in your practice.

Another useful ethics text is *Ethics of Touch*, by Ben E. Benjamin, Ph.D. and Cherie Sohnen-Moe, $28.00 at **www.sohnen-moe.com**.

# **14** Staying Healthy in a Demanding Field

Every successful massage therapist I have spoken to has had to deal with some kind of physical or psychological problem that resulted from doing the work.

The most common physical problems are wrist injuries, back strain, neck and shoulder pain, and nodules (ganglia) in the fingers. In addition, some therapists suffer depression, some take on pain in places where their clients have it, and some "burn out" from the stresses involved in a massage practice.

There are practical ways you can avoid these problems. Successful therapists offered these tips from their experience:

## Exercise

Do yoga, tai chi, aikido, stretching, jogging, swimming, aerobics or some other exercise to improve your own bodily well-being. This helps not only to keep your body in good condition, but also to reduce the effects of stress. Also consider weight training to strengthen the muscle groups you rely on for your work. You may want to use a squeeze ball to strengthen hands, wrists and forearms.

## Introspection

Involve yourself in psychotherapy, or meditation, and have a support group you can turn to in times of need. This will help you release your emotions, help you stay healthy, and promote your own growth. One of the most important qualities a massage practitioner can bring to their work is being centered and not distracted by thoughts, worries and anxieties. Taking time to "clear out" your mind and emotions on a regular basis will enhance the quality of your massage.

## Diet

Eat a balanced diet and drink plenty of water. You depend on your body as you would on a professional tool. You put good gasoline in your car, and keep the oil changed. Treat your body at least as well.

## Attitude

Learn to let go. Life in the business world will bring you ups and downs, rewards and frustrations. Accept people and situations as they are, let your emotions flow, and move on.

Cultivate positive thinking. Face a problem by solving it instead of focusing on how the problem makes you feel. Successful business people naturally take this approach—the rest of us need to learn it and make it a habit.

## Receive Massage

Get massage on a regular basis. Three reasons: it promotes your overall health and well-being; you will learn techniques and awarenesses from receiving massage that will make you a better massage therapist; your credibility with your clients will be better if you "practice what you preach."

## Body Mechanics

Watch your body mechanics. Don't bend over when you work. Keep your wrists straight as much as possible while you work. Keep your spine straight and bend your knees. Let your force come from your hara, your abdominal center. Use the minimum number of muscles necessary for any particular motion. Avoid setting your table too high if you do deep work. Make your body mechanics your first priority, even above the quality of work you do on your clients.

## Specifics of Body Maintenance

Stretch your wrists before and after working. Use open fist or elbows to do deep work instead of fingers or thumbs.

If a nodule appears in a finger, try not to use that finger in your work for a week or two; apply pressure with the other fingers of that hand, but raise the finger with the nodule slightly so it is not used. If the nodule persists, work it with transverse friction to break it up. Consult a physician if the nodule will not recede.

Use a paraffin bath for sore hands, ice forearms or use liniment if inflamed.

Take a class in biomechanics, offered at many massage schools.

## The Sense of Isolation

In many ways, massage is a solitary occupation. That may seem strange, since massage cannot take place unless two people are together at the same time and place. However, in most settings, a massage practitioner typically has little verbal communication with clients during the session. When there is communication, it is not "socializing", since the relationship is a therapist/client relationship, and not a social meeting of peers. This can lead to a feeling of loneliness for the practitioner.

Those who practice chair massage may feel less of this effect, since conversation is more common during chair massage than table massage. However, in a clinic or office setting where you are practicing relaxation or therapeutic massage, most practitioners do not start conversations unless the client does, and usually limit conversation to topics related to the treatment or the client's concerns.

Some practitioners find that keeping a keen focus on the client's needs and the importance of each session helps to avoid a sense of isolation. Others find that entering a meditative state while working helps. Also important is to set aside quality time for yourself after work, whether that is social interactions, self-guided time, hobbies or, as is discussed below, vacations and days off.

## Vacations and Days Off

After working intensely to make your practice a busy one, you may find that success, when it finally comes, is a shock to your system. If you find yourself very busy, make time to take care of yourself physically and emotionally.

Sometimes it is difficult to switch from the "I need all the clients I can get" consciousness to that of "I need to take time for myself." In the beginning, you do not have enough clients, and you are doing everything you can think of to get more. The time will arrive, however, when the clients will be coming. Allow yourself at that point to step back from your practice and make sure you are not wearing yourself out trying to achieve more "success" than you can stand.

A goal to work toward is creating a regular weekly work schedule so you know in advance what days off you have and what hours you work each day. One therapist I know felt she had fully matured as a massage practitioner when she was able to make her schedule Monday through Friday and have every weekend for herself.

## Don't Lose Your Sense of Humor

Sometimes we can take our work so seriously that we lose our spontaneity or suppress our individuality. Charlotte M. Versagi, a professional journalist and massage therapist, wrote an essay that first appeared in Massage Magazine exploring this important aspect of staying healthy in a demanding field. "How Enya Stole My Sense of Humor" is about the art of balancing your professional demeanor with the need to be who you really are.

### How Enya Stole My Sense of Humor—And How I Got It Back Again
### By Charlotte M. Versagi

Somewhere in this process of becoming a massage therapist, I've lost my sense of humor. In the past, I listened to Broadway soundtracks; I whistled while I worked, said hello to strangers on elevators, smiled at my plants. Somehow, as I became focused on healing, I became morose.

We're not talking clinical depression here, folks; I'm getting out of bed in the morning and dressing myself. But I've lost part of myself—my joy—and as much as I love my profession, I'm quite sure it's a direct result of my immersion into this healing business.

I think this is how it happened: I'm a career changer, so when I started massage therapy school I worked full-time and attended school full-time. I hunkered down, determined to learn it all and prove to myself I hadn't lost the ability to succeed in academics. For two straight years I lost all social skills while I merely worked and studied.

I then became keenly aware of the beautiful responsibility of actually putting my hands on complete strangers who were naked under sheets on my table. *Wow*, I thought. *Awesome. Better take this seriously.* So again, I hunkered down, and studied energy work and the chakras so I could combine my spiritual knowledge with bodywork. Made me very successful, but again, very serious.

Then the music. Got to have that new-age sound. So instead of remembering the words to the *Mickey Mouse Club* theme song, I repeatedly listed to the music of dead, chanting monks or deader saintly nuns. Enya and Yanni were as light as I allowed myself to get.

People were leaving my table calm, all right. Feeling as if they had been given a haven, a safe place from the world. My candles, my hands and my music were really doing the job. And I became progressively more serious. No more hellos on the elevator; after all, I was looking for auras. No more singing Broadway musicals while I cleaned house. Tina Turner gathered dust.

Then one day I realized I had lost joy. I thought I was supposed to be a certain kind of person in order to be a massage therapist—calm, quiet, gentle, wise, somehow deeper and more perceptive than the rest. OK, fine, I may be some of those things—but I am also an Italian-American woman who occasionally raises a little hell; someone who has been known to stop traffic on a busy street just for the fun of it. And that's what I had lost—the fun of it.

It's time to loosen up, to rediscover my joy. But how? Baby steps.

Last night I dusted off Tina Turner and Gershwin. I blasted them so loud I thought my neighbors would come knocking. I ate a chocolate donut—taking the dreadful risk of upsetting my chakras—gasp! I dragged out all my rhinestone jewelry and put every piece on a purple sweatshirt and sat in my apartment, grinning. I packed up all my white cotton uniforms and made a note to purchase colorful, lively professional garb.

And today, when I saw a client who has multiple sclerosis—and who loves Broadway shows, I played Gershwin during the massage. You should have seen his smile. And the energy we exchanged during that massage—Wow! He left the table with a lift in his step I hadn't seen before

No, I'm not tossing all my Enya—but she's no longer the reigning queen.

I'm a complicated, joyful human being. My clients deserve better than a tightly wrapped massage therapist with a preconceived, canned concept of what it's like to be a healer.

With all due reverence to my beloved profession, I nailed a favorite picture of myself on my office wall—right next to my Reiki certificate. It's a picture of me at 3 years old. I'm running straight at the camera, hair flying, coat wide open, and a smile on my face that could warm the world. That picture is going to remind me to keep singing musicals and to give that smile to the world. Preconceived ideas of healers be damned—my hair's too busy flyin'!

# 15 Laundry and Linens

If you do Swedish massage, the issue of laundry is one you will face throughout your career. Unless you work in a setting where your employer takes care of laundry, you will have to make certain decisions about how to supply yourself with fresh linens to practice your trade.

## Hire a Laundry Service vs. Do It Yourself

Depending on the laundry service you choose and what type of draping you use, having your laundry done for you can cost between $1 and $2.50 per client. Doing it yourself will bring the cost down dramatically, to between 10 cents and 50 cents per client.

If you hire a service, you will have to choose between furnishing your own linens and using theirs. If you use theirs, the cost will be higher. If you furnish your own, you will need twice as many as if you did your own wash, because at any given time, half your sheets and towels will be at the laundry.

Hiring a service makes the most sense in these situations:

1. You do not have a washer and dryer in your home or office. Trips to the laundromat can be very wearing when you are taking several loads per week.

2. You have a busy massage practice. If you are seeing lots of clients, then you are making enough money to afford paying a service to launder for you. If you have a busy practice, you probably do not have the time or energy to be dealing with the large amount of laundry your practice generates.

## Choosing a Laundry Service

If you decide to use a laundry service, shop around. The prices charged by different services will vary quite a bit, as will the quality of their service.

Things to consider in hiring a service:

1. They may require you to use their sheets and towels, or they may be willing to sell you sheets and towels at wholesale prices.

2. If you use their linens, be sure this company will supply sheets and towels you will like. See and feel samples before making an agreement.

3. Some massage oils can be difficult to remove from linens unless the company has the proper chemicals. Be sure they have experience with massage therapists and they understand how to get these linens clean.

4. If you use a service, and they deliver a load of sheets and towels which are unsuitable in some way, you will be stuck with them unless the company is willing to make a special trip to remedy the problem. Find out how willing the company is to make sure problems will be taken care of and your needs will be met.

## Drop-off at a Laundromat

Another choice is to use your local laundromat as a cleaning service. Most laundromats offer the option of having their staff wash your clothes for a fixed price, usually 50 to 75 cents per pound. You may have to supply special detergent to make sure the oil residues are fully removed. (See pages 123–124.) However, having a laundromat launder your linens may be a cost-effective "in-between" solution that is cheaper than a service but easier than doing your own laundry.

## Finding Suppliers of Sheets and Towels

### Buying a few linens at a time

If your practice is a casual one, meaning that you work on just a few clients a week, you will need a relatively small amount of linens, and should therefore purchase sheets and towels in the same way you do for personal use.

One option to consider is buying twin sheet sets. These include one fitted sheet, one flat sheet and one pillowcase, and sometimes can be found on sale for not much more than the cost of a single sheet. The fitted sheet on the table covered by the matching flat sheet creates a pleasant appearance.

Some therapists are quite particular about the linens they use, and this can be a very sensible attitude. The sheets and towels come in contact with a client's body, and you may want to create a luxurious impression by using colorful linens with a lush texture.

### Buying in quantity

If you are most interested in presenting a clean (white) image, and keeping your costs to a minimum, consider purchasing sheets and towels through business channels. This is a decision to make when you begin to establish yourself in the field. It is not unlike a carpenter buying a set of tools—think toward the future and invest in a supply of sheets and towels you will be able to use for years to come.

Most companies that sell sheets and towels commercially are in the habit of selling at least 50 dozen at a time. The difficulty lies in finding a vendor who supplies linens commercially and is also willing to sell by the dozen. These are rare, but they do exist.

You will get some help looking in the yellow pages under "laundries." If your community has a Business-to-Business yellow pages, check under "linens." Occasionally, a commercial or institutional laundry will sell you one or two dozen odd or surplus sheets. These companies have large clients, and need to buy sheets by the gross for their own purposes. If they are willing to deal with you, you may be able to get a couple of dozen sheets from them at a discount price.

If you cannot locate any such businesses in your area, consider contacting someone who may have the connections you do not have. Your local hospital may be a wholesale purchaser of sheets and towels, and if you get in touch with the purchasing agent, she or he may be willing to resell a few dozen to you.

## Choosing Sheets and Towels

### Sheets

Whether you do your own laundry or use a service, you will still need to decide what size and quality sheets and towels to use. The thicker and more luxurious the linens, the more they will cost to buy and the more they will cost to launder.

*Composition of sheets.* The quality and comfort of sheets is determined by the "thread count." This is the number of threads used in a square inch of the fabric the sheet is made of. A higher thread count means a softer sheet. A thread count of 180 or higher usually signifies a good quality sheet. A thread count of 250 or more signifies a very luxurious sheet.

Also consider the fabric composition. The higher the percentage of cotton, the softer the sheet; the higher the percentage of polyester, the coarser the sheet.

*Size of sheets.* Keeping the size small helps a great deal in keeping the cost down at laundry time. Sheets come in a great variety of sizes, and the actual size of the sheets you receive may be a few inches smaller than the stated measurements.

The normal size of a massage table is between 72″ × 26″ and 72″ × 30″. Two standard sheet sizes to consider are 72″ × 42″ and 75″ × 54″.

The actual size of the sheets you buy will be slightly smaller than the size stated on the package. This is partly because the stated size is "before hemming," and partly because it is accepted practice in the industry to have minor variations in sheet sizes. Therefore, a sheet that is called 72″ long will actually be a few inches shorter than that, and will not quite cover the length of a massage table.

A 72″ × 42″ sheet is ideal for a table that has a face hole; it will cover the rest of the table and overlap a bit on all sides. It is also a good size to drape over a client, as it will cover most people from the neck down. A 75″ × 54″ sheet will cover the entire massage table, and will drape a few inches farther over the sides.

For a better looking image, you can leave a larger sheet draped over the table, concealing the legs. For each client, change the 72″ × 42″ or 75″ × 54″ sheet.

These smaller sheets are convenient to handle in laundry, and will take up a minimum of space in your washing machine. In fact, well over a dozen 72″ × 42″ sheets will fit into a normal washing machine at a time.

As you shop for sheets, you may hear a confusing mix of terms used to describe sheets—terms like "draw sheet," "twin sheet," "standard," and other terms. These names have general meanings, but they do not convey accurate information about the size of the sheets you will actually be buying. Keep in mind actual measurements only. Decide what size will be best for your style of draping and the image you want to create, and then shop with these requirements in mind.

### Towels

The same considerations apply to towels as apply to sheets. The larger and more luxurious a towel is, the costlier it will be to purchase and launder. Keeping the size down is a big help.

Many standard sizes are available to fit almost any need. The size I find most convenient is 20″ × 40″. This is the size of a small bath towel. I find it meets my needs for draping very well, while taking up a minimum of space in the cabinet and the washer.

The quality of towels is measured in "pounds per dozen." This means, simply, how much does a dozen of these towels weigh? For a given size towel, the "pounds per dozen" figure will give you an idea of how thick and fluffy the towel is.

For the size I use, 20″ × 40″, a normal weight might be 6 or 7 pounds per dozen. I use a towel that weighs 8.5 pounds per dozen, because I want a soft and hefty feel to my towels. Towels like these are available for around $2.50 each, plus shipping, when purchased wholesale. A wholesale order is usually 16 dozen towels. I purchased 16 dozen of these towels, and had no trouble selling my extras to local massage therapists, leaving me with a large supply of towels at a low cost.

If you are doing comparison shopping, remember that increasing thickness increases "pounds per dozen," and increasing size also increases "pounds per dozen." It helps to decide on the size you want, and then compare the different towels of that size based on the "pounds per dozen" figure. So long as you are comparing towels of the same size, the "pounds per dozen" figure will give you a good measure of the thickness of the towel.

## Tips for Do-It-Yourself Launderers

Doing your own laundry has advantages. First, you are in control of how many clean sheets and towels you have, and you know you will not run out unexpectedly, or have to rely on someone else to get your needs met.

Second, it is much cheaper to do your own laundry. Even factoring in the cost of a washer and dryer, in the long run doing your own laundry will probably cost only 10% to 20% as much as hiring a service.

### *Have the machines at your place*

The most important consideration, if you plan to do your own laundry, is to have your own washer and dryer, in your home or in your office—whichever will be most convenient to your practice.

When your washer and dryer are convenient to use, you can throw in a load and be busy working, reading or relaxing. Throwing in a load becomes a routine activity and not a tedious chore, as it is when you have to leave your home or office to go to a laundromat. In addition, if the washer and dryer are for the exclusive use of your business, their cost can be deducted for income tax purposes (see Chapter 19).

## *Water dispersible oils*

Most oil manufacturers now sell water-dispersible oils that reduce to oil buildup in sheets and towels. With water-dispersible oils, the oil removal process is now needed much less frequently than it was before this innovation. However, even with these "improved" products, oil will still accumulate in your linens, and you may need to purchase a product to remove oil residues.

## *Jojoba oil and fractionated coconut oil*

Practitioners recommend pure jojoba oil as a non-staining oil that reduces or eliminates oil buildup in sheets.

Another non-staining oil is fractionated coconut oil, which has the greasy components removed by a high-pressure process. If you purchase fractionated coconut oil, find a supplier you can trust, as some practitioners have reported quality issues with distributors of this product.

## *Beating oil residues*

The following common products are all recommended by practitioners as successfully removing oil residues from linens:

### Additives
½ cup baking soda added to each load
one cup vinegar plus ½ to one cup borax added to each load
one cup powdered bleach plus one cup borax added to each load
2 to 3 tablespoons of Dawn dishwashing liquid added to each load
Biz non-chlorine bleach (follow instructions on box)

### Pre-soaks
Citra-Solv – soak linens for 1 to 24 hours before laundering
Simple Green – soak linens for 1 to 24 hours before laundering

In addition to these "home remedies," several different products are marketed specifically to massage therapists for removing old residues from massage linens: Clean Again (formerly "Fresh Again"), Pure Pro Orange, and Totally Clean and Fresh. You can purchase these products from the following suppliers:

**Clean Again** is available from:

**Biotone**
1-800-445-6457
(619) 582-0027
**www.biotone.com**

**Pure Pro Orange** is available from:

> **Pure Pro**
> 1-800-900-7873
> (413) 775-9998
> www.purepro.com

**Totally Clean and Fresh** is available from:

> **Sheahan Enterprises**
> 1-877-679-0807
> (925) 679-0807
> www.totallycleanandfresh.com

## *Hints for success with Clean Again*

Clean Again is the oil removal product I tried first. I have been happy with it, so I have stayed with it. Through experience, I have learned the following:

You do not need to use Clean Again each time you wash. Use it to treat your sheets and towels when you notice a buildup of oil. You will notice either a rough texture, or the odor of cooked oil when the linens get hot in the dryer.

*Shake well* before pouring to mix the detergent fully. Use the hottest water you can. Use a larger amount of detergent for heavy oil stains. For persistent stains, soak the linens in hot wash water overnight and complete the wash in the morning.

If you have stubborn oil stains, you can use about 1/3 cup Clean Again to one or two gallons of water, and boil the linen in this mixture at a low boil for about five minutes. A remarkable amount of oil comes out of a soiled linen with this process.

# 16 Professional Associations

This chapter describes the major professional associations for practitioners of massage. The largest of these organizations are American Massage Therapy Association, Associated Bodywork and Massage Professionals, and IMA Group. These three associations are profiled first.

For many practitioners, the primary motivation for joining a professional association is to obtain liability insurance, also called malpractice insurance. If liability insurance is the only benefit of membership you are looking for, you have at least two options for purchasing such insurance without joining any association.

Insurance is available for $129.00 per year through Massage Magazine (**www. massagemag.com**)

Insurance is also available from Healthcare Providers Services Organization (1-800-982-9491 or **www.hpso.com**). Their policy is very good, and pricing varies depending on 1) what state you practice in, 2) whether you are employed or self-employed, and 3) whether you work full-time or part-time. In their preferred states, insurance may be cost between $84.00 and $168.00 per year. Rates in non-preferred states are much higher.

However, if you choose to obtain professional liability insurance by belonging to one of the three major professional associations, your association membership will include other benefits as well. Each of the "big three" professional associations has a referral program for its members, and provides members with practice-building materials. In addition, AMTA provides a bi-monthly magazine, a newsletter, chapters in all 50 states, and the opportunity to vote in association elections. ABMP provides a bi-monthly magazine and pre-paid legal consultation services.

Each of the associations has a different view of the issue of state regulation of massage. AMTA promotes standardized educational requirements and seeks to set the standard for massage education in the United States. ABMP has no official position for or against massage legislation, but tries to work for laws based upon consensus among the practitioners that will be affected by the laws. IMA Group has not been active in the legislative arena, but maintains divisions for many non-massage modalities such as movement, reiki, estheticians, and many others.

As is discussed in Chapter 3, politics often plays a major role in the interactions between these associations. Some people have strong feelings about the conflicting approaches of the associations, and sometimes have strong opinions about one or more of these associations. Your choice of which association to join may be a practical one, or it may be an emotional one. Below are some of the facts and figures you can use to help you make your choice.

# Association Profiles

## General Membership Organizations

### American Massage Therapy Association ® (AMTA®)

500 Davis St., Suite 900
Evanston, IL 60201
(877) 864-0123
www.amtamassage.org

The AMTA is the oldest professional association for massage. It was founded in Chicago in 1943.

Requirements for membership:

> *Professional Membership* is available to practitioners who are certified by NCTMB, or licensed by states that meet AMTA's 500-hour curriculum requirement, or who have graduated from a 500 in-class hour program. ($235 per year plus chapter fee of $0 to $30.)

All members receive professional and general liability insurance, optional health, life, business and disability insurance at group rates, member discounts on catalog products, listing in AMTA's *Membership Registry*, voice at AMTA meetings, *Massage Therapy Journal* and *HANDS ON Newsletter*, right to use ATMA logo in promotional materials, and the right to participate in state chapters and on state and national committees.

AMTA's spin-off accrediting agency, Commission on Massage Therapy Accreditation (COMTA) accredits massage therapy training programs. A list of accredited schools is maintained at **www.COMTA.org**. As of publication, the following schools were accredited by COMTA:

AK:  University of Alaska, Anchorage

AR:  Desert Institute of the Healing Arts

CA:  Mueller College of Holistic Studies

CO:  Massage Therapy Institute of Colorado

CT:  Connecticut Center for Massage Therapy

DE:  The National Massage Therapy Institute

DC:  Potomac Massage Training Institute

FL:  Core Institute
     Educating Hands School of Massage
     Florida College of Natural Health
     Florida School of Massage
     Sarasota School of Massage Therapy

IL:  Chicago School of Massage Therapy
     Kishwaukee College
     Morton College
     National University of Health Sciences

IN:  Alexandria School of Scientific Therapeutics

IA:  Carlson College of Massage Therapy

KS:  BMSI Institute

LA:  Massage Therapy College of Baton Rouge

ME:  Downeast School of Massage
     New Hampshire Institute for Therapeutic Arts (Bridgeton)

MD:  Allegany College of Maryland
     Baltimore School of Massage

MA:  Muscular Therapy Institute
     Springfield Technical Community College

MI:  Ann Arbor Institute of Massage Therapy
     Lakewood School of Massage Therapy

MO:  St. Charles School of Massage Therapy

MS:  Mississippi School of Therapeutic Massage

MT:  Health Works Institute

NH:  New Hampshire Institute for Therapeutic Arts

NJ:  Academy of Massage Therapy
     Healing Hands Institute for Massage Therapy
     Institute for Therapeutic Massage
     National Massage Therapy Institute
     Omega Institute
     Somerset School of Massage Therapy

NM:  Crystal Mountain School of Massage Therapy

NC:  Body Therapy Institute

OR:  East-West College of the Healing Arts

PA:  Baltimore School of Massage - York, PA
     National Massage Therapy Institute
     Pennsylvania School of Muscle Therapy

RI:  Community College of Rhode Island

TN:  Institute of Therapeutic Massage & Movement
     Roane State Community College
     Tennessee School of Massage

VA:   Cayce / Reilly School of Massotherapy
       Massage Therapy Program, The
       Virginia School of Massage

WA:  Brenneke School of Massage
       Brian Utting School of Massage

WV:  Mountain State School of Massage

WI:   Blue Sky School of Professional Massage
       Lakeside School of Massage Therapy

COMTA can be contacted at (847) 869-5039 or at **www.comta.org**.

AMTA has created the AMTA Foundation, a tax-exempt public charity which funds massage therapy related research, community outreach, educational scholarships and conferences (see Chapter 20).

Each year the association sponsors one national conference and one national convention. Chapters exist in all 50 states, the District of Columbia, and the Virgin Islands, and some chapters have regional meetings.

Of the professional associations for massage, AMTA is the most active in the legislative arena. AMTA helps chapters and members to promote legislation which it believes will assist the profession, and it funds selected efforts to keep or change laws governing massage. Some individuals within the AMTA work to have laws passed that require attendance at an AMTA-approved school, and some states have passed laws requiring AMTA-approved schooling, but the advocacy of such laws is not official AMTA policy.

### *Associated Bodywork And Massage Professionals (ABMP)*

28677 Buffalo Park Road
Evergreen, CO 80439-7347
1-800-458-2267
**www.abmp.com**

ABMP was founded in 1987. It attempts to be an effective, efficient, non-bureaucratic networking and services organization.

Requirements for membership:

*Certified* level requires at least 500 hours of training and 16 hours of continuing education each two years. Certified members receive enhanced listing on ABMP's MassageFinder referral service, a CD of photos and marketing materials and priority processing. Cost: $229.00 per year

*Professional* level requires at least 500 hours of training but does not require continuing education. Cost: $199 per year

*Practitioner* level requires at least 100 hours of training. Cost $199 per year.

Members at the Certified, Professional or Practitioner level all receive professional liability insurance, referral service, regulatory interaction, pin, decal and certificate, subscription to *Massage & Bodywork*, membership newsletter, Massage & Bodywork

Yellow Pages and Successful Business Handbook. Members are also eligible for group rates on business insurance and disability insurance. Members who join for longer than one year receive a discount on the second year dues.

ABMP sponsors IMSTAC, the International Massage & Somatic Therapies Accrediting Council, which accredits massage schools. As of publication time, the following schools had been accredited by IMSTAC:

AZ:   Rainstar University

CO:   Colorado Institute of Massage Therapy
      Colorado School of Healing Arts

GA:   Academy of Somatic Healing Arts
      Atlanta School of Massage
      Lake Lanier School of Massage

IL:   Central Illinois School of Massage Therapy
      Northern Prairie School of Therapeutic Massage

IA:   Carlson College of Massage Therapy

KS:   Massage Therapy Training Institute

ME:   Spa Tech Institute

MA:   Spa Tech Institute
      Healing Touch Institute

MI:   Kalamazoo Center of Healing Arts

MN:   Minneapolis School of Massage and Bodywork
      Sister Rosalind Gefre Schools

MO:   Massage Therapy Training Institute

NM:   New Mexico School of Natural Therapeutics

ND:   Sister Rosalind Gefre School - Fargo

OR:   Oregon School of Massage

PA:   Career Training Academy
      East-West School of Massage Therapy
      East-West School of Massage Therapy
      Pennsylvania School of Muscle Therapy

TX:   Lauterstein-Conway Massage School
      New Beginning School of Massage

ABMP sponsors research by Touch Research Institute and the Stanford Myofascial Institute.

ABMP attempts to foster a favorable legal climate for its membership, and has worked on a state-by-state basis to amend or defeat laws it considers biased.

### International Massage Association (IMA Group)

P.O. Drawer 421
Warrenton, VA 20188
(540) 351-0800
www.imagroup.com

IMA was founded in 1994. Its mission statement includes the goals of taking massage mainstream, uniting all natural health care professionals and gaining respect for their professions, providing members with liability insurance at the lowest possible cost, and giving members marketing tools to help their practices grow.

Requirements for membership: 100 hours of approved training for practicing members.

*Practicing membership* costs $149.00 per year and includes liability insurance.
*Associate membership* costs $89.00 per year.

Benefits of membership include free internet referral service, opportunity to establish merchant accounts to accept credit cards, opportunity for mortgage financing for home or office, and debt consolidation loans.

The IMA Group links the International Massage Association to its other divisions for movement therapies, aromatherapy, reflexology, yoga, caricaturists, colonic educators, kinesiology, personal trainers, aerobics instructors, and dance teachers.

## Specialized Membership Organizations

### Medical Massage: American Manual Medicine Association

1845 Lakeshore Dr., Ste. 7
Muskegon, MI 49441
(888) 375-7245
www.americanmedicalmassage.com

The American Manual Medicine Association was created to promote medical massage therapy as an allied health care profession and to differentiate it from other forms of massage. This goal is achieved through professional standards, education, and testing.

Membership is open to massage therapists with 600 hours of education including anatomy, physiology, kinesiology, medical massage, orthopedic assessment, pathology, business, ethics, and supervised clinical practicum. Annual membership costs $175.00 and includes insurance.

The AMMA endorses a 1200 hour training program in medical massage, with a goal of 2400 hours of education.

AMMA has selected three "model schools":
> Blue Hereon Academy, Grand Rapids, MI
> Galen Institute, Wethersfield, CT
> American Institute of Clinical Massage, Post Falls, ID

The association also maintains a list of approved CEU providers at its website.

### American Oriental Bodywork Therapy Association (AOBTA)

1010 Haddonfield-Berlin Rd., Ste. 408
Voorhees, NJ 08043
(856) 782-1616
**www.aobta.org**

The AOBTA is a non-profit membership organization for practitioners of oriental bodywork that was formed in 1989. It maintains a "Council of Schools and Programs" (COSP) which approves curricula that meet AOBTA educational standards. As of publication time, 16 schools and programs had been accepted into the Council and two schools' applications were pending.

Requirements for membership:

> *Certified Practitioner* level: 500 hours training, at COSP-approved school or taught by AOBTA-certified instructor. Application fee $30, dues $100 per year.

> *Associate* level: 150 hours training, taught by AOBTA-certified instructor or qualified certified practitioner. Application fee $30, dues $75 per year.

> *Student* level: Must be studying with AOBTA-certified instructor or practitioner. Application fee $10, annual dues $30.

Benefits of membership include the Organization's protection of the interests and rights and professional standards of Oriental Bodywork Therapy, high quality educational opportunities, legislative support and action-oriented representation, *Pulse* quarterly newsletter, member discount for advertising, optional insurance (professional liability, group health, disability), annual membership directory, practitioner referral service.

### American Polarity Therapy Association (APTA)

P.O. Box 19858
Boulder, CO 80308
(303) 545-2080
**www.polaritytherapy.org**

Established in 1985, The American Polarity Therapy Association sets standards in Polarity Therapy practice and ethics, promotes public awareness, and cooperates with public agencies and other professional groups.

The association hosts an annual conference, publishes a membership directory, and produces Energy, a quarterly newsletter.

Membership costs $66.00 per year. Student membership is $44.00

### American Holistic Nurses' Association (AHNA)

P.O. Box 2130
Flagstaff, AZ 86003
(800) 278-2462
**www.ahna.org**

An organization founded in 1981 to promote the inclusion of alternative healing modalities into the practice of nursing. Membership is open to nurses, and costs $125.00 per year, or $50.00 for student members.

### National Association of Nurse Massage Therapists (NANMT)

P.O. Box 24004
Huber Hts., OH 45424
(800) 262-4017
**www.nanmt.org**

The NANMT was formed in 1987. The NANMT is committed to bringing an increased awareness and acceptance of touch therapy to the mainstream medical and hospital community. It supports gaining insurance reimbursement for massage services, and also supports research into the health benefits of massage. Active membership costs $85.00 per year, student and senior memberships cost $50, corporate membership costs $125, and supporting membership costs $75. Benefits of membership include NANMT's bulletin and quarterly publication, listing in annual directory, copy of directory, discounts, CEUs and use of NANMT seal on promotional material.

### Hospital-Based Massage Network

**Hospital Based Massage Network**
Association Site Hosted by Information for People
**www.info4people.com**
**domain: www.hbmn.com**

A resource to promote and support the establishment of massage therapy in hospitals nationwide. (see page 32).

### Bodywork Modality Organizations

For additional specialized membership organizations see the Bodywork Directory that starts on page 221, as many individual forms of bodywork have guiding organizations that are catalogued under the particular bodywork modality listing.

## State and Local Organizations

Many states and regions have their own massage and bodywork associations. Since these are usually volunteer organizations, the contact information changes frequently as officers serve their terms of office and move on. The best sources of up-to-date information for state and local associations are massage schools and practitioners in your local area.

# 17 Insurance

This chapter is about the types of insurance you can buy to protect yourself against certain risks. This chapter does not discuss having your work paid for by your clients' insurance, which is covered in Chapter 21.

## Why Buy Insurance?

Insurance is risk protection. If you have no insurance, you bear all of life's financial risks alone.

The kinds of risks insurance covers are illustrated by the following examples:

- If you are sued by a client and lose, you are responsible to pay the amount awarded to your client by the court.

- If a client slips and falls in your office, you might be required to pay for that injury.

- If you are sued by a client for any reason, you will have to pay your own legal fees for defending the suit.

- If your office burns down or is vandalized, you absorb the loss.

- If you are injured and cannot work for a period of time, you will have no assistance in meeting your financial obligations.

- If you fall ill and need medical attention, you will have to pay the full amount of the medical expenses.

Each of the examples above illustrates one type of risk for which the self-employed bodyworker can purchase insurance. Each kind of insurance is profiled in the next part of this chapter.

## Kinds of Insurance Available to the Professional Bodyworker

### Professional Liability Insurance

This insurance defends you against claims by clients that you harmed them in the course of performing your professional services. The insurance company will provide a legal defense against a claim, and will pay any judgment against you, up to the policy limit.

These policies cover practically all claims of harm to a client during a massage. The major exception is for allegations of sexual misconduct by a practitioner. The insurance carriers used by AMTA, ABMP and IMA do not provide a defense to a charge of sexual misconduct, nor will they pay a judgment based on sexual misconduct. The insurance provided by HPSO (**www.hpso.com**) includes coverage if you are called before a professional licensing board for conduct arising out of a covered "medical or non-medical incident".

Professional liability insurance has become very expensive in other professions. Lawyers and doctors pay very large annual premiums for this type of coverage because of the large number of lawsuits that are filed and the large judgments that result. However, the average doctor is about 60 times more likely to be sued for malpractice than the average massage therapist—and the average amount paid to settle a malpractice suit against a doctor is about 35 times as much as the average to settle a malpractice suit against a massage therapist. Since the risk of harm to clients by massage practitioners is so low, professional liability insurance for massage is quite inexpensive.

### Sources of Professional Insurance

Professional liability insurance is a benefit of membership in the AMTA, ABMP and IMA. The associations purchase group insurance policies, and their per-member cost is very low. Discounted professional liability insurance is also available at an additional charge to members of the AOBTA, Rolf Institute, American Polarity Therapy Association, Trager Institute and Feldenkrais Guild.

Professional liability insurance is also available without joining an association. Insurance can be purchased for $129.00 per year through Massage Magazine (1-800-872-1282 or **www.massagemag.com**), or through Healthcare Providers Services Organization, (800) 982-9491 or **www.hpso.com**; rates vary depending on state, employer/employee status and full-time/part-time work.

### Types of Professional Insurance

Two general types of professional liability insurance are sold: "claims-made" insurance and "occurrence form" insurance.

A claims-made policy covers you for claims that are made while the policy is in force. "Claim" refers to the announcement by the client of their complaint against you. With this type of policy, you are covered if it was in force when the claim was filed.

An occurrence form policy covers you for incidents that "occur" while your policy is in force. The act occurs at the moment you allegedly caused harm to the client. With this type of policy, you are covered if it was in force when the alleged misconduct occurred.

The difference between these two types of policy comes up if you discontinue your insurance—for example, if you stop practicing massage. Say you began practicing in 1998 and purchased professional liability insurance at that time. On January 1, 2008, you retire from the practice of massage and discontinue your insurance coverage. A client comes forth on February 1, 2008 and claims you injured her during a massage you gave her in 2005.

An occurrence form policy would cover you in this case, because the alleged injury *occurred* while the policy was in force. A claims-made policy would not cover you, because the *claim* was made after your insurance had lapsed. For your protection, you should obtain "occurrence" form insurance, so that you are covered no matter when the client decides to bring a claim. Fortunately, all of the major professional associations for massage offer "occurrence form" policies.

### The need for professional insurance

If you plan to have a significant career in the massage or bodywork field, professional liability insurance is virtually a necessity. While you may think you do not need such insurance because you have no significant possessions to lose anyway, consider the broader question of how being uninsured might restrict your career.

Spa owners, chiropractors and other massage employers will usually not hire an uninsured massage therapist. If the therapist is uninsured, then any client with a claim against the therapist would likely sue the employer, who does have insurance. An uninsured therapist is seen as an unnecessary risk and most employers therefore will not hire an uninsured practitioner.

## Business Liability Insurance

Business Liability, or premises liability insurance, is "slip and fall" coverage. It protects you against suits that result from injuries people sustain on your business premises. The cause of these injuries might be icy steps, loose carpet, or any other cause of accidental injury.

Legally, you are liable for these injuries only if you do not keep your office in a reasonably safe condition for your clients. The legalities of how safe you need to keep it vary slightly from place to place. However, as a practical matter, any injury to a client is a potential problem, even if you are not ultimately legally responsible for it. If the client sues, you still will have to bear the expense of lawyer's fees to defend the action.

Business liability insurance covers both attorneys' fees to defend an action and any recovery that is ultimately awarded. It is included in the cost of membership in some professional associations (check with the association), and can be purchased on the open market through insurance agents and insurance companies.

If you practice in a home office, you can try to get a rider for your homeowner's policy to cover business liability. Some companies will issue these and others will not. You may need to change insurance carriers after setting up a home office because some companies will discontinue your coverage if they learn you operate a business in a home office. If available, a rider for your home office should cost between $100 and $250 per year.

## Business Insurance

Business insurance covers your business equipment and premises against losses such as fire and theft. These policies usually cover the replacement cost of your equipment and supplies, and perhaps even petty cash in the office. Many will also cover lost income while your office is closed and the cost of renting temporary office space if your office is destroyed. Policies are generally available through major insurance companies and independent agents. Prices usually range from $250 to $500 per year.

## *Disability Insurance or Business Interruption Insurance*

In the event you are unable to work due to accident or illness, disability insurance provides you with continued income. You usually must be disabled for several weeks (or several months) before the policy will pay you a weekly income, and you can usually collect payments under the policy up to a maximum of one year.

Disability insurance is not cheap; a policy to provide you with $300 to $400 per week in the event of disability may cost around $1,000 per year to purchase. It has also become increasingly difficult to find a company willing to write a disability insurance policy, especially for women. Decide whether or not to buy such insurance based on how strong your need is to be sure of continued income.

## *Medical Insurance / Group Medical Insurance*

Policies for medical insurance are available in many forms, from bare-bones to deluxe. The costs of such insurance range from high to exorbitant.

The least expensive coverage is referred to as "catastrophic illness insurance." This insurance will pay for most of the expense of a hospital stay, after a deductible of, for example, $2000. This is protection against being turned away from a hospital when you need care, and against being placed into bankruptcy by an illness. Such insurance may cost $500 to $2,000 per year, depending on your age and place of residence. It is not available in all states. It can be combined with a "medical savings account" which is a tax-saving way of putting money aside for routine medical expenses.

The most expensive coverage is major medical, which will cover a wide range of treatments, procedures and medications. The cost of this type of coverage has been rising dramatically for a number of years, much faster than the rate of inflation, and seems to just continue to become more and more expensive.

In-between are a wide range of compromise plans with varying price tags. AMTA and ABMP offer members opportunities to purchase discounted group health policies. Many other groups offer their members group health insurance of one sort or another. One good source is the local chamber of commerce or other non-profit civic group.

You can also check with National Association for the Self-Employed (1-800-232-6273 or **www.nase.org**) and the Home Office Association of America (212-588-9097 or 1-800-809-4622 or **www.hoaa.com**). Other options are farmers' cooperative organizations, and any organization that bands together large numbers of consumers to improve their bargaining power.

One more idea to consider is that most colleges and universities offer very cheap medical insurance to students—both full-time and part-time students. Consider enrolling for one or two classes at a local college and purchasing discounted student health insurance. You may be able to purchase insurance *and* college courses substantially cheaper than you could purchase just insurance outside the university setting.

# 18 Laws You Should Know About and State Regulation of Massage

The first section of this chapter, "Laws you should know about", summarizes basic laws and legal principles. This section will provide you with background information you should understand before entering the business world as a massage practitioner.

For example, you will learn about the different functions of local, state and federal governments; zoning laws that relate to massage offices; types of businesses you can form for your practice, and rules that govern contractual relationships such as leases and employment contracts.

The second section, "State Laws Regulating Massage", has a directory of the licensing laws in the 35 states (plus the District of Columbia) that regulate the practice of massage, including contact information for all of the regulatory boards. In addition, there is information about related laws and legislative activity in some states that do not have state-wide massage regulation.

A directory of all municipal and county licensing requirements in California appears on pages 144–145.

A quick-review chart summarizing all 35 state laws regulating massage is on page 151.

## Laws you should know about

*Federal, State, County and Local governments.* Most Americans live under the authority of four different governments. Each one has its own areas of major influence, in terms of what it offers you and what it requires of you.

The *Federal* government requires you to pay federal taxes on all the money you earn. The federal government also authorizes certain organizations to accredit massage schools, paving the way for the granting of financial aid for massage education. (See pages 243–244 for further information on financial aid.)

*State* governments sometimes enact laws regulating the practice of massage in the state. These laws are described in the second part of this chapter, and summarized on page 151. State governments sometimes require the payment of income taxes on the money you earn.

*County* governments occasionally pass laws concerning the practice of massage in the county. Such laws apply only in unincorporated areas of the county—that is, in areas which are not within the borders of a town or city that has a municipal government. The county government may also take over zoning and health requirements in unincorporated areas within the county, and has the power to levy some taxes.

County governments also keep records of business names ("assumed names" or "fictitious names") and issue certificates to businesses allowing them to use business names.

*City* (or township or village) governments, also called *municipal* governments, regulate zoning, parking, health concerns, and the operation of businesses within the city limits. They have the power to decide what businesses can and cannot operate in the city, and what locations within the city are permissible locations for different types of businesses. Some cities have regulations for the practice of massage within the city limits, and some even prohibit the practice of massage. Many cities also have some form of municipal taxation.

If there is ever a conflict between the laws of different governments, the power structure works as follows: Federal law always has priority; state laws have priority over county and local laws; municipal laws control within the borders of the city, town or village; in unincorporated areas of the county, county law applies unless it is in conflict with state or Federal law.

***County and Municipal Professional Licensing Laws.*** As mentioned above, laws specifically regulating the practice of massage can be enacted by state, county or local governments. In many areas, no regulatory law applies to the practice of massage, as neither the state, county nor city has enacted one.

Many local laws regulating the practice of massage require the applicant for a massage license to submit items like fingerprints, recent photo, recent employment history, references, and physician's certificate that he or she has no communicable disease. In addition, some have educational requirements.

Some representative municipal educational requirements are listed below: Ames, IA 750 hours at AMTA-approved school; Cedar Rapids, IA 500 hours; Colorado Springs, CO 1000 hours; Davenport, IA 500 hours over a period of at least one year; Des Moines, IA 1000 hours; Las Vegas, NV 500 hours; Pueblo, CO 70 hours; St. Louis, MO 70 hours; St. Paul, MN, 40 hours; Tempe, AZ 600 hours; Tucson, AZ 1000 hours (500 in-class hours), Newport Beach, CA 500 hours plus background check, dress code, $342 annual fee (see also the list of California municipal laws on pages 144–145).

As you can see, the range of 40 hours to 1000 hours is quite a broad one, and this reflects the situation within the nation as a whole concerning massage licensing.

***Other Local Requirements.*** If your local government has a law regulating massage establishments, the law may have requirements for bathrooms, lighting, signs and other specifics. If there is no such law, consider contacting the health department, fire department and the police department to see if there are any requirements you should know about before committing to a particular office space.

Sometimes local laws require large licensing fees, background checks, fingerprinting, or medical examinations. Some locations have severe zoning restrictions, dress codes for massage therapists, or other restrictive ordinances. Before establishing an office in a particular location it is prudent to investigate the local laws affecting massage businesses.

*Business License.* Business licenses are usually required by city governments. Occasionally a county requires a business license, and the state of Alaska requires such a license. It is used by the city government to keep track of who is performing what business activity, to generate money for the municipal treasury, and to make sure that zoning laws are being followed. The license fee may be a fixed annual fee, or it may be a percentage of your annual income.

*Zoning Laws.* Most cities have a special map of the city that divides every location into one of several zones (see Sample Zoning Map, page 65). A key explains the meaning of each zone. The zones create different kinds of neighborhoods—business areas, residential areas, industrial areas, and areas of mixed usage.

When you open a massage or bodywork practice, you will need to be sure you are locating your office in an area that is zoned for your type of business. You may find there is a dispute about the type of business you have—some zoning agencies classify massage as a profession, others consider it a health service, others call it a personal service, and others classify it as adult entertainment. The zoning board's classification decision can affect permissible locations for your office.

While most states leave zoning issues to the local governments, Florida has a state-wide ban on home offices in residential zones. Other states, such as Vermont, take the opposite approach and have state-wide laws specifically protecting the right to operate a home-based business. The Home Office Association of America, **www.hoaa.com**, advocates for greater freedom for home offices in zoning laws.

*Local Taxes.* Some local governments charge businesses a tax on business property. That means that they decide the value of the business property you own, and tax you a fixed percentage of that value each year. Some local governments also charge a sewer tax, which may be based on water usage or number of plumbing units.

*Fictitious Name (or Assumed Name) Statement.* If you use a made-up name for your business that does not include your own name, you should register that name with the county government. There is a fee, usually around $20, and you may be required to search through the county's record books to make sure that no one has already taken the name you are choosing. You may also be required to advertise the name in the legal classifieds of your local newspaper. Registering your fictitious name is a requirement for opening a checking account in the name of the business.

*Taxpayer Identification Number.* If you are a sole proprietor (see below) and do not have any employees, you can use your social security number on all tax documents. If you have employees, or if you incorporate or form a partnership, you will need to apply for a taxpayer identification number. Obtain form SS-4 from the Internal Revenue Service. For information on how to get the form, see the end of Chapter 19.

*Business identity.* In the eyes of the law, there are several possible "identities" for your business. The main ones are corporation, partnership and sole proprietor.

Corporations have a separate legal identity apart from the shareholders and employees. They can have tax advantages in some sophisticated situations, but if you are a self-employed bodyworker, it is not an advantage to incorporate.

Partnership is a special legal relationship in which the two or more partners can speak and act for each other. A promise by one binds the other, so if your partner makes a business deal and then fails to follow through, you can be held responsible for it. Partners usually share the partnership income, without regard to who actually did the work that generated the money.

Sole Proprietor means you, and you alone, run your business. In legal terms, there is no difference between you and your business. Your business is treated legally just as it is in fact—as an extension of your life and a part of yourself.

Practically every bodyworker operates as a sole proprietor, and unless you have some good reason not to, you should too. Becoming a corporation or a partnership will not benefit you unless you are involved in some complicated or sophisticated business dealings. If you become involved in a group practice, the group may choose to incorporate. This is something the group will decide in consultation with a lawyer or accountant.

*Contractual relationship.* A contract can be oral or written. It is simply an exchange of promises in which each party agrees to do or give something of value to the other party. Once made, a contract is legally enforceable until it is ended by the parties who made it.

Written contracts are easier to enforce, because the exact terms of the agreement are on paper for all to see. Oral contracts can also be enforced, but the specifics must be proven by testimony about the agreement.

Even something as simple as opening a checking account involves making a contract. The bank agrees to hold your money and give it to you or the people you write checks to, according to certain rules the bank establishes. You agree to pay a set fee per check written, or keep a minimum monthly balance, and to pay prescribed penalties for writing checks that your account cannot cover.

As a massage therapist, contracts you are likely to enter into include agreements to work for others or to have others work for you, rental agreements for office space, contracts with the phone company for business phone service, and contracts for performance of services like printing, laundry and cleaning.

## Does a law regulating "massage" include "bodywork"?

As state regulation of massage practitioners becomes more and more common in the United States, practitioners of various forms of bodywork may find themselves required to obtain massage licenses to practice, even though their work is very different from massage.

Licensing laws are enacted by legislators, and implemented by Boards or Commissions, such as the Board of Massage. When a state law specifies which forms of bodywork are included in its regulation and which are excluded, there is no room for confusion and no need for the Board to make an interpretation. However, most of the massage laws in the 35 states regulating massages give only a "definition" of massage, leaving it up to the Board to determine which therapies fit under that definition.

In Florida, the Board of Massage has ruled that Reiki practitioners must be licensed as massage therapists. Under this ruling, one who works only with Reiki energy must devote thousands of dollars and many months to learning all the subjects necessary for the practice of Swedish massage.

Following is a sampling of some of the current rulings and controversies about the licensing of bodywork practitioners in states that license massage therapists.

> Maryland enacted in 2000 an exemption from massage licensing for therapies directed at the "energetic field of the human body." Therefore, practitioners of Reiki, polarity, and other energy-based forms of bodywork do not have to obtain massage licenses.

> Mississippi's licensing law *includes* "shiatsu, acupressure, oriental, eastern or Asian massage, spa, rub, and therapeutic touch" and *excludes* "allied modalities that are certified by a nationally accredited organization recognized by the board."

> New York includes shiatsu, polarity, reflexology, Alexander, Trager, and other bodywork modalities in massage regulation, by ruling of the Board, but exempts Reiki.

> North Carolina exempts Trager, Reiki, Healing Touch, Bowen, Jin Shin, Polarity, Therapeutic Touch, Body Mind Centering, Feldenkrais and Alexander from its massage licensing law.

> North Dakota exempts reflexology from massage licensing but includes Reiki as massage.

> Tennessee's Board originally ruled that reflexology should be regulated as massage, but reflexologists subsequently obtained an exemption from the law.

> Utah's Department of Occupational and Professional Licensing previously regulated Reiki as massage, but reviewed their position and ruled that Reiki is a "spiritual healing art" and therefore not subject to the massage licensing laws.

As the field of massage and bodywork continues to evolve, some forms of bodywork will establish strong independent certifications that may allow them to be regulated independently from massage. At the moment, there are no generalities that give any useful guidance on this topic. It is a question that is addressed state by state, and even within states, a specific bodywork modality may be regulated as massage one year but not the next.

If you belong to a professional organization for the form of bodywork you practice, that organization is probably the best source for current information about licensing issues. Another source for such information is any of the massage schools in the state in which you practice.

## The unique status of animal massage

The regulation of animal massage may become the next political battleground, as there are indications that veterinarians may be attempting to exert control over the field through legislation.

In the last few years, the American Veterinary Medicine Association has sponsored legislative efforts in many states aimed at restricting animal massage to veterinarians or those under direct supervision of a veterinarian.

In 1996, when Maryland adopted massage licensing, a lobbyist for the state veterinary association worked to ensure that massage therapists would be authorized to work on human patients only.

In 1997, a Maine law added massage therapy (and other complementary therapies) to the veterinary practice act, which made veterinarians the only practitioners authorized to perform animal massage.

At the time of publication, there were actions pending to enact restrictive legislation in Florida and Texas. Individuals and grass-roots organizations are attempting to take counter-measures.

Washington state has a law recognizing animal massage as a professional service, and establishing the right of non-veterinarians to practice animal massage with a 100-hour credential.

In Utah, the definition of massage under the state licensing law includes massage done on animals

A practitioner who wishes to practice massage in a given state should contact the state veterinary board to make inquiry. Another source of information is the International Alliance for Animal Therapy and Healing (**www.iaath.com**).

The most common animal massage is equine sports massage, since sports massage for high-performance horses is in demand and is well-paid work. For further information and resources about equine sports massage, see pages 227–228.

## State Laws Regulating Massage as of June, 2005

State laws regulating the practice of massage are described below, along with contact information for the boards that license or otherwise regulate massage practitioners.

### Moving from state to state

Moving from state to state is complicated by the fact that the various state educational requirements range from 300 hours (Texas) to 1,000 hours (Nebraska and New York), and Maryland requires 500 hours plus 60 college credits. However, one recent trend that has made it easier to move from state to state is the *National Certification Exam*.

The *National Certification Exam* is now either required or accepted in 32 of the 35 states that regulate massage, plus the District of Columbia. Once you pass the *National Certification Exam* in any location, your passing test score will satisfy the written test requirement in all 32 of those states.

Remember, though, that individual states have other licensing requirements that must be met to qualify for a license, such as hours of education, required courses, practical exam, health certificate, fees, and continuing education requirements. These are not listed in this book. For these details you should visit the State Board's website, or contact the Board directly to obtain guidance about your exact situation.

## Obtaining updated information on state licensing laws

Information of this nature necessarily goes out of date, since legislation regarding massage is continually evolving. Fortunately, there are sources you can turn to that will provide periodic updates to this information.

For up-to-date information on massage laws, a good resource is *Massage Magazine*, which prints a summary of current licensing laws near the back of each issue. Another good source is any of the massage schools located in the state you are interested in. In addition, numerous websites maintain updated information about nationwide licensing laws, including this book's website. The site's home page, **www.CareerAtYourFingertips.com**, has a link to "State Laws Regulating Massage" which is updated whenever significant changes in massage laws take place. Another good list is at **www.massagetherapy.com/careers**.

For quick and easy reference, all of the current state licensing laws are summarized in the State Licensing Chart on page 151.

### Alabama

State licensing, 650 hours from an institution approved by the Board, *National Certification Exam*

> **Alabama Massage Licensing Board**
> **610 S. McDonough St.**
> **Montgomery, AL 36104**
> **(334) 269-9990**
> **almtbd@aol.com**
> **www.almtbd.state.al.us**

### Arizona

State licensing, 500 hours, *National Certification Exam*

> **Board of Massage Therapy**
> **1400 West Washington, #230**
> **Phoenix, AZ 85007**
> **Tel: (602) 542-8604**
> **info@massageboard.state.az.us**
> **www.massageboard.az.gov**

### Arkansas

State licensing, 500 hours required. Reciprocity is on a case-by-case basis and requires education in an accredited school

> **Arkansas Massage Board**
> **P.O. Box 20739**
> **Hot Springs, AR 71903**
> **(501) 623-0444**
> **info@arkansasmassagetherapy.com**
> **www.arkansasmassagetherapy.com**

### California

See pages 144–145.

### Colorado

In 1989, representatives of AMTA and ABMP, school owners, and several unaffiliated massage therapists came together to form a coalition to represent massage practitioners on licensing issues. These efforts resulted in a law defining "Massage Therapist" as a graduate of a state-approved school with at least 500 hours of education. One who meets this definition is exempted from the "massage parlor" law.

Massage regulation in Colorado is done by city and county governments, and approximately 15 county and municipal governments have laws regulating the practice of massage. At present, there is no plan to pursue state regulation of massage or bodywork.

### Connecticut

State licensing, 500 hours at a school approved by COMTA *and* by an accrediting agency recognized by the U.S. Department of Education. Reciprocity is available if school is on CT's approved list—contact the department. *National Certification Exam*

> **Ct. Dept. of Public Health**
> **Massage Therapy Licensure**
> **410 Capitol Avenue, MS# 12APP**
> **PO Box 340308, Hartford, CT 06134**
> **(860) 509-7603    www.dph.state.ct.us**

# California Regulations

California does not have statewide massage regulation. Massage schools are regulated by the Bureau of Private Post-Secondary and Vocational Education (BPPVE), and licensing of massage practitioners is done only by city and county governments.

A State of California law (Chapter 6, sections 51030 through 51034) gives authority to cities and counties to regulate massage. The law states what aspects of the practice may and may not be regulated. Section 51034 states that local laws may not restrict the practice of massage to same-sex massage only.

Some southern California jurisdictions exempt "Holistic Health Practitioners" from their massage regulation laws. This type of local law originated in San Diego and has been adopted in several other locations. A Holistic Health Practitioner is usually defined as someone with demonstrable training and experience in massage.

The following table of municipal and county licensing requirements was originally compiled in 1991 for the first edition of this book, and was updated in 2005 with information from the "Sunrise Survey for Regulation of Massage Therapy by the State of California" prepared by ABMP April 30, 2004.

The amount charged for business or professional licenses varies tremendously from place to place, from a few dollars to over two thousand dollars. Some towns require a business license but no professional credentials. The world-renowned massage program at Esalen Institute in Big Sur still functions by authorization of the local sheriff's department.

For updated information about local laws, inquire at the town hall or city hall for municipal laws, or the county government building in the county seat for county laws.

## Required Educational Hours

**Variable hours:** Bakersfield (200/500); Cathedral City (300/500); Desert Hot Springs (100/500); Hermosa Beach (100/500); Indian Wells (300/500); La Quinta (300/500); Mission Viejo (100/500); Palm Desert (300/500); Rancho Mirage (300/500); San Diego, city (500/1000); San Francisco, city (100/200); San Juan Capistrano (200/500)

**1,000 hours:** Indio, San Clemente, San Diego (see variable hours), Santa Ana, Thousand Oaks, Tustin, Vista

**600 hours:** Fontana, Rialto

**500 hours:** Orange County, San Francisco County, Santa Cruz County, Aliso Viejo, Anaheim, Apple Valley, Arcadia, Bell Gardens, Belmont, Berkeley, Brea, Carpenteria, Carson, Corona, Costa Mesa, Cupertino, Dana Point, Downey, El Monte, Encinitas, Fountain Valley, Fullerton, Glendora, Huntington Beach, Irvine, La Verne, Laguna Hills, Lake Forest, Lawndale, Long Beach, Los Banos, Modesto, Monrovia, Montclair, Moreno Valley, National City, Newark, Newport Beach, Ontario, Palmdale, Pittsburg, Pleasanton, Rancho Cucamonga, Redlands, Riverside, San Diego (see variable hours), Seal Beach, Stanton, Sunnyvale, Torrance, Victorville, Walnut, Westminster, Yorba Linda

**400 hours:** Hesperia

**300 hours:** Alameda County, San Joaquin County, Santa Clara County, Alameda, Castro Valley, Chino Hills, Hacienda, Los Altos, Los Angeles (city), Norco, San Dimas, Saratoga

**250 hours:** Orange (city), Sacramento (city)

**200 hours:** Kern County, San Bernardino County, Ventura County, Yuba County, Alhambra, Auburn, Barstow, Camarillo, Carlsbad, Chino, Chula Vista, Cudahy, Daly City, Duarte, El Cajon, El Centro, El Segundo, Gardena, Gilroy, Grover City, Hayward, Hercules, Huntington Park,

# California Regulations

Imperial Beach, Laguna Beach, Laguna Niguel, La Mesa, Lancaster, Lodi, Loma Linda, Marysville, Maywood, Milpitas, Montebello, Monterey Park, Mountain View, Oxnard, Ridgecrest, San Bernardino (city), San Buenaventura, San Luis Obispo, San Mateo, Santa Barbara, Santa Clara, Signal Hill, Simi Valley, Solano Beach, South Pasadena, South San Francisco, Twentynine Palms, Union City, West Sacramento, Whittier.

**180 hours**: Atwater, Livingston, Merced

**160 hours**: Inglewood

**150 hours**: Foster City, Glendale, Santa Monica

**130 hours**: Citrus Heights, Woodland

**125 hours**: Orangevale, Roseville

**100 hours**: Los Angeles County, Sacramento County, San Diego County, Arcade, Arden, Coronado, Corte Madera, Culver City, Cypres, Del Mar, Dublin, Escondido, Fairoaks, Fremont, Hollister, Manhattan Beach, Marina, Monterey, Morgan Hill, Novato, Oakland, Palo Alto, Pleasant Hill, Rancho Cordova, Richmond, Salinas, San Jose, San Leandro, San Rafael, Santa Rosa, Taft, Temecula, West Hollywood

**70 hours**: Contra Costa County, Solano County, Danville, Half Moon Bay, Lakewood, Livermore, Manteca, Pacifica, San Bruno, San Pablo, San Ramon, Selma.

## No Educational Requirement

**Counties:** Alpine County, Amador County, Butte County, Calaveras County, Colusa County, Del Norte County, Fresno County, Glenn County, Humboldt, County, Imperial County, Inyo County, Kings County, Lake County, Lassen County, Madera County, Marin county, Mariposa county, Mendocino County, Merced County, Modoc County, Mono County, Monterey County, Napa County, Nevada County, Placer County, Plumas County, Riverside County, San Benito County, San Luis Obispo County, Shasta County, Sierra county, Siskiyou County,

Sonoma County, Stanislaus County, Sutter County, Tehama County, Trinity County, Tulare County, Yolo County

**Municipalities:** Agora Hills, Albany, Altadena, Antioch, Arroyo Grande, Atascadero, Azusa, Baldwin Park, Blythe, Burbank, Burlingame, Calabasas. Campbell, Carmichael, Ceres, Cerritos, Chico, Chowchilla, Claremont, Clovis, Colton, Compton, Concord, Cotati, Covina, Davis, Delano, East Palo Alto, Elk Grove, Emeryville, Eureka, Folsom, Fresno, Garden Grove, Hanford, Hawthorne, Hemet, King City, La Habra, La Mirada, La Puente, Lemon Grove, Loomis, Los Alamitos, Los Altos Hills, Los Gatos, Lynwood, Madera, Malibu, Mammoth Lakes, Martinez, Mendocino, Menlo Park, Monte Sereno, Moorpark, Napa, Oceanside, Ojai, Orinda, Palm Springs, Paradise, Pasa Robles, Pasadena, Patterson, Perris, Petaluma, Pismo Beach, Placentia, Porterville, Poway, Rancho Palos Verdes, Redding, Redondo Beach, Redwood City, Rocklin, Rohnert, Rosemead, Rowland Heights, San Anselmo, San Carlos, San Fernando, San Gabriel, San Joaquin, San Marcus, Santa Cruz, Santa Paula, Santee, Scotts Valley, South Gate, Spring Valley, St. Helena, Stockton, Suisun City, Temple City, Tiburon, Tracy, Tulare, Turlock, Upland, Vacaville, Vallejo, Villa Park, Visalia, Walnut Creek, West Covina, Westlake Village, Willowbrook, Windsor, Yuba City

## Special Restrictions

**Regulated as Adult Entertainment:** El Dorado County, Santa Barbara County, Bellflower, Beverly Hills, Brentwood, Buena Park, El Cerrito, Fairfield, Fillmore, Goleta, Lompoc, Murrieta, Norwalk, Oakley, Oroville, Paso Robles, Pico Rivera, Portola, Santa Clarita, Seaside, Shasta Lake

**Restricted to Chiropractic offices:** Paramount

**Prohibited:** Buelton, Highland, La Canada Flingtridge, Pomona

## Delaware

Massage Therapist: 500 hours, *National Certification Exam*

Certified Technician: 100 hours

**Delaware of Massage and Bodywork**
**Cannon Building, Ste. 203**
**861 Silver Lake Blvd.**
**Dover, DE 19904**
**(302) 739-4522, ext. 205    www.dpr.delaware.gov**

Only licensed massage and bodywork therapists may work by prescription of physicians. Certified technicians may work in any other massage setting. To practice massage in Delaware, one must be either licensed or certified.

## District of Columbia

State Licensing, 500 hours, *National Certification Exam*

**Board of Massage Therapy**
**717 14th St., NW**
**Washington, DC 20005**
**(877) 672-2174**
**www.dchealth.dc.gov**

## Florida

State licensing, 500 hours required, *National Certification Exam.* Reciprocity (called Endorsement in Florida) for graduates of a school or apprenticeship approved by the Board.

**Florida Department of Health**
**Board of Massage Therapy**
**4052 Bald Cypress Way, Bin #C06**
**Tallahassee, FL 32399**
**(850) 245-4161**
**www.doh.state.fl.us/mqa/massage/ma_home.html**

## Georgia

**GEORGIA** State licensing, 500 hours required, *National Certification Exam*

Georgia's law was signed into law May 10, 2005, and as of publication date for this edition, the members of the Board of Massage had not been chosen.

## Hawaii

State licensing, 570 hours required; or apprenticeship of 150 in-class hours and 420 hours practical.

Educational institution must be approved or licensed by a state department of education or approved by an accredited community college, college or university or approved by the AMTA or approved by the Rolf Institute.

**Dept. of Commerce & Consumer Affairs**
**State Board of Massage**
**P.O. Box 3469 / 1010 Richards Street**
**Honolulu, HI 96801**
**(808) 586-3000**
**www.hawaii.gov/dcca/areas/pvl/boards/massage/**

## Illinois

500 hours, *National Certification Exam*

**Division of Professional Regulation**
**320 West Washington St**
**Springfield, IL 62786**
**(217) 785-0800**

**Chicago Office:**
**James R. Thompson Ctr**
**100 W. Randolph St, Suite 9-300**
**Chicago, IL 60601**
**(312) 814-4500**
**www.ildpr.com/who/masst.asp**

## Iowa

State licensing, 500 hours, *National Certification Exam*

**Iowa Department of Public Health**
**Massage Therapy Board**
**321 E. 12th St.**
**Lucas State Office Building**
**Des Moines, IA 50319**
**(515) 281-6959**
**www.idph.state.ia.us/licensure**

## Kentucky

**Kentucky Board of Licensure for Massage Therapy**
**PO Box 1360**
**Frankfort, KY 40602**
**(502) 564-3296 ext 240**
**http://finance.ky.gov/ourcabinet/caboff/OAS/op**

## Louisiana

State licensing, 500 hours, *National Certification Exam* (optional)

Louisiana Board of Massage Therapy
12022 Plank Road
Baton Rouge, LA 70811
(225) 771-4090
Email: admin@lsbmt.org
www.lsbmt.org

*National Certification Exam* may be used to substitute for the written portion of State Exam.

## Maine

State Licensing, 500 hours from a Department-approved school (no exam) or *National Certification Exam* in lieu of approved education

Maine Department of Professional and Financial Regulation, Division of Licensing and Enforcement—Massage Therapists
State House Station #35
Augusta, ME 04333
(207) 624-8603    www.state.me.us/pfr/olr

Maine's law does not prohibit the practice of massage by non-licensed persons, but it prohibits the use of the terms "massage therapist" or "massage practitioner" by unlicensed persons.

## Maryland

State Certification / State Registration, 500 hours massage education and 60 college credit hours, *National Certification Exam*

Maryland Board of Chiropractic Examiners
4201 Patterson Avenue
Baltimore, MD 21215
(410) 764-4738    www.mdmassage.org

Maryland was a battleground between the professions of Physical Therapy and Massage in the 1990s. The Physical Therapy Board made a serious attempt to prohibit the practice of massage by anyone except physical therapists during the 1990s. This battle raged in Maryland for about a decade, and it ended with the enactment of massage licensing legislation in 1998.

Effective 2002, Maryland adopted a two-tier licensing scheme. Certified Massage Therapists (CMTs) must have 500 hours of education, NCE and 60 college credit hours (in any subjects). CMTs may give and receive referrals from other health-care practitioners and may practice in health-care settings, such as hospitals, medical offices, clinics and nursing homes.

Registered Massage Practitioners (RMPs) must have 500 hours training and pass the NCE, but are not required to have 60 college credits. RMPs may practice in spas, health clubs, or private practices. RMPs cannot practice in health-care settings and cannot receive or give referrals to health-care practitioners.

## Michigan

A statewide massage licensure law was adopted in 1974 and modified in 1980, but it is legally defective and has never been implemented. Even though there is a licensing law "on the books," there is no license available in Michigan to those who practice massage or bodywork.

## Minnesota

In 1999, a bill to license massage was defeated in the Minnesota legislature. The bill had the backing of the local AMTA chapter and many of the state's massage schools, but was opposed by an independent coalition of massage therapists who mounted a campaign in the state legislature to defeat the bill.

Then, in 2000, Minnesota sent shock waves throughout legislative circles by enacting the first of its kind "Freedom of Access" act for alternative health care. Rather than establishing requirements for *licensure* of alternative medical practitioners, the legislature chose to protect consumers by requiring practitioners to *disclose* certain facts to their clients.

Under the Minnesota freedom of access law, practitioners are required to (1) tell their clients that the state has not established educational requirements for unlicensed practitioners, (2) reveal their academic and professional credentials, (3) inform clients of their right to confidentiality and right to choice of services, and (4) advise clients about the procedure for filing complaints.

This law gives consumers the right to know what services are being provided and what qualifications the provider has. This is "true free-market capitalism" applied to alternative health care.

The law applies to any unlicensed health care modality and it specifically mentions massage, as well as acupressure, naturopathy, aromatherapy, ayurveda, craniosacral therapy, energetic healing, homeopathy, meditation, and other therapies involving foods, supplements, and applications of heat, cold, water, touch and light.

Other states have citizen groups pursuing similar legislation.

## Mississippi

State Registration, 700 hours, *National Certification Exam*

Massage
)
9326
7
director@msbmt.state.ms.us
www.msbmt.state.ms.us

## Missouri

State Licensing, 500 hours, *National Certification Exam*

Division of Professional Registration
Massage Therapy Board
P.O. Box 1335
Jefferson City, MO 65102
(573) 522-6277
massagether@pr.mo.gov
http://pr.mo.gov/massage.asp

## Nebraska

State licensing, 1000 hours, *National Certification Exam*, Reciprocity for those attending a school approved by the Board, or upon review of school transcript.

Department of Health, Credentialing Division
301 Centennial Mall South
P.O. Box 94986
Lincoln, NE 68509
(402) 471-2115
rita.watson@hhss.ne.gov
www.hhs.state.ne.us/reg/regindex.htm

## New Hampshire

State licensing, 750 hours, *National Certification Exam*

NH Dept. of Health and Human Services
Licensing and Regulative Services
129 Pleasant Street
Concord, NH 03301
(603) 271-4594
www.dhhs.state.nh.us/DHHS/LRS

## New Jersey

State Licensing, 500 hours, *National Certification Exam*

Board of Nursing
PO Box 45010
Newark, NJ 07101
(973) 504-6430
www.state.nj.us/lps/ca/medical/nursing.htm#massage

## New Mexico

State licensing, 650 hours (may be 300 hours plus 350 hours Alternative Qualifying Experience) *National Certification Exam* plus Jurisprudence Exam. Reciprocity on a case-by-case basis (referred to as "by credentials")

New Mexico Board of Massage Therapy
2550 Cerrillos Rd.
Santa Fe, NM 87505
(505) 476-4870
www.rld.state.nm.us/b&c/massage

## New York

State licensing, 1,000 hours, *National Certification Exam*. Reciprocity is case-by-case and requires proof of practice for two years

New York State Education Department
Office of the Professions, Massage Therapy Unit
89 Washington Ave.
Albany, NY 12234
(518) 474-3817
http://www.op.nysed.gov/massage.htm

## North Carolina

State Licensing, 500 hours from a school approved by the Board, *National Certification Exam*

North Carolina Board of Massage
and Bodywork Therapy
P.O. Box 2539
Raleigh, NC 27602
(919) 546-0050
admin@bmbt.org
www.bmbt.org

## North Dakota

State certificate of registration, 750 hours, state exam. Requires attendance at COMTA-approved school

North Dakota State Board of Massage
PO Box 218
Beach, ND 58621
701-872-4895
www.ndboardofmassage.com

## Ohio

State licensing, 600 hours (during at least 12 months), state exam. Reciprocity is on a case-by-case basis, but an exam is still required.

**Ohio State Medical Board**
**77 South High St., 17th floor**
**Columbus, OH 43266**
**(614) 466-3934   www.med.ohio.gov**

In Ohio, a massage license is required for use of the title "licensed massage therapist". A massage license is required to practice therapeutic massage, but is not required to practice relaxation massage. Unlicensed practitioners probably cannot receive reimbursement from insurance companies.

## Oregon

State licensing, 500 hours, *National Certification Exam*

**Oregon Board of Massage Technicians**
**748 Hawthorne Ave. NE**
**Salem, OR 97301**
**(503) 365-8657   www.oregonmassage.org/**

## Rhode Island

State licensing, 500 hours at a COMTA-approved school, *National Certification Exam*

**Rhode Island Department of Health**
**Three Capitol Hill, Rm. 105**
**Providence, RI 02908**
**(401) 222-2827**
**www.health.ri.gov/hsr/professions/massage.php**

## South Carolina

State licensing, 500 hours, *National Certification Exam*

**Division of Professional Licensing**
**110 Center View / P.O. Box 11329**
**Columbia, SC 29210**
**(803) 896-4490**
**jonese@mail.llr.state.sc.us**
**www.llr.state.sc.us/POL/MassageTherapy**

## Tennessee

State Licensing, 500 hours from State-accredited school (no exam) or *National Certification Exam* in lieu of accredited schooling

**Board of Massage Therapy**
**First Floor, Cordell Hull Building**
**425 5th Ave North,**
**Nashville, TN 37247-1010**
**(615) 532-5135**
**www2.state.tn.us/health/Boards/Massage/index. htm**

Students who attend a school on the state's list of accredited schools do not need to take a written test. Anyone who has passed the *National Certification Exam* and submits proof of passing may be licensed, regardless of what school they attended. In addition, those licensed in states with equivalent educational requirements may be admitted by reciprocity.

## Texas

State registration, 250 hours plus 50 hours internship, state exam

**Texas Massage Therapy Registration**
**Texas Department of Health**
**1100 W. 49th St.**
**Austin, TX 78756**
**(512) 834-6616**
**www.tdh.state.tx.us/hcqs/plc/massage.htm**

Registration is required to practice massage in Texas.

## Utah

State licensing, Board-approved massage education or apprenticeship of 1000 hours, state exam or *National Certification Exam*. Reciprocity is available to licensed out-of-state therapists whether or not their training was at board-approved school.

**Utah Department of Commerce**
**Division of Occupational and Professional Licensing**
**Herbert M. Wells Building**
**160 East 300 South**
**Salt Lake City, UT 84145**
**(801) 530-6628**
**www.dopl.utah.gov/licensing/massage.html**

## Virginia

State certification, 500 hours, *National Certification Exam*. Certification required for the use of the term "therapeutic massage" or "certified massage therapist"

**Virginia Board of Nursing**
**6603 West Broad St., 4th floor**
**Richmond, VA 23230**
**(804) 662-7636**
**www.dhp.virginia.gov/nursing**

## Washington

State licensing, 500 hours, *National Certification Exam*

**Washington Department of Health**
**Massage Licensing Program**
**P.O. Box 47865**
**Olympia, WA 98504**
**(360) 236-4700**
**www.doh.wa.gov/Massage**

## West Virginia

State licensing, 500 hours from a massage therapy school approved in its home state (no exam) or *National Certification Exam* in lieu of approved education

**Massage Therapy Licensure Board**
**200 Davis Street, #1**
**Princeton, WV 24740**
**(304) 487-1400**
**ms325c@wvdhhr.org**
**www.wvmassage.org**

As originally enacted, the law required attendance at a COMTA-approved school (even though there were none in the state). Before long, a coalition of members of all the major massage associations worked together to amend the law to its current form.

## Wisconsin

State licensing, 600 hours, *National Certification Exam*

**Department of Regulation and Licensing**
**1400 E. Washington Ave. / P.O. Box 8935**
**Madison, WI 53708**
**(608) 266-2811**
**www.drl.wi.gov/prof/mass/def.htm**

# State Licensing Chart as of July, 2005

| State | Education Required | NCE | Year Begun |
|---|---|---|---|
| Alabama | 650 hours | yes | 1996 |
| Arizona | 500 hours | yes | 2004 |
| Arkansas | 500 hours | yes | 1951 |
| Connecticut | 500 hours COMTA | yes | 1993 |
| Delaware | 500 (therapist) 300 (technician) | yes | 1993 |
| Dist. of Columbia | 500 hours | yes | 1999 |
| Florida | 500 hours | yes | 1943 |
| Georgia | 500 hours | yes | 2005 |
| Hawaii | 570 hours or 150 plus 420 apprenticeship | no | 1947 |
| Illinois | 500 hours | yes | 2004 |
| Iowa | 500 hours | yes | 1992 |
| Kentucky | 600 hours | yes | 2003 |
| Louisiana | 500 hours | yes | 1992 |
| Maine | 500 hours | yes | 1991 |
| Maryland | 500 hours / 60 credits | yes | 1998 |
| Mississippi | 700 hours | yes | 2001 |
| Missouri | 500 hours | yes | 1998 |
| Nebraska | 1000 hours | yes | 1958 |
| New Hampshire | 750 hours | yes | 1980 |
| New Jersey | 500 hours | yes | 1999 |
| New Mexico | 650 hours or 300 plus 350 experience | yes | 1991 |
| New York | 1,000 hours | yes | 1967 |
| North Carolina | 500 hours Board-approved | yes | 1999 |
| North Dakota | 750 hours | yes | 1959 |
| Ohio | 600 hours | no | 1916 |
| Oregon | 500 hours | yes | 1999 |
| Rhode Island | 500 hours | yes | 1980 |
| South Carolina | 500 hours | yes | 1997 |
| South Dakota | 500 hours | yes | 2005 |
| Tennessee | 500 hours | yes | 1995 |
| Texas | 300 hours | no | 1985 |
| Utah | 600 hours | yes | 1981 |
| Virginia | 500 hours | yes | 1996 |
| Washington | 500 hours | yes | 1976 |
| West Virginia | 500 hours | yes | 1998 |
| Wisconsin | 600 hours | yes | 1999 |

# 19 Income Taxes

This chapter cannot give you all the information and advice you will need to prepare your income tax return. Instead, this chapter will:

1. Familiarize you with all of the key facts and ideas you need to understand Federal income tax;

2. Explain what records you should keep for tax purposes, why you need them and how to keep them;

3. Guide you to all the resources you will need to do your own taxes, or to hire a professional to do your taxes for you.

## The Big Picture

The following discussion gives you the basis of the federal tax laws that determine how much money you give the government at the end of the year.

This information is presented in condensed form, and on the first reading it may seem difficult to understand. This is only because the words are strange, not because the ideas are difficult.

Really try to "get" this big picture in your mind. Everything else in this chapter relates to this overall picture.

Some of the statements in this "big picture" would need additional explanation to be 100% accurate, so just use this information to understand the concepts at this point.

### 1. Employment income only

If you are an employee, and have no income from self-employment, your taxes will be very simple. You employer will give you a W-2 form showing income and withholding, and the forms the IRS sends you to fill out your taxes should be sufficient.

### 2. Self-employment income

Almost all massage therapists and bodyworkers are at least partially self-employed. When you are self-employed, your business activity is reported on a separate IRS form, called Schedule C (see page 156). In reporting your business activity on your

Schedule C, you add up all of the money you received during the year in your business, and you subtract your business deductions. (What you can subtract as business deductions will be discussed later).

If the money you *received* is a larger amount than your allowable *deductions*, you have a *profit*. We will call this your "business profit." You have to pay a percentage of your business profit as self-employment tax, and you also have to pay a percentage of your business profit as income tax.

### *3. Self-employment tax*

Business profit is subject to a "self-employment tax" as well as income tax. This is the self-employed person's equivalent of Social Security Tax. This tax rate for 2004 was 15.3 percent on self-employment profit up to $87,900.

### *4. Income tax*

Business profit is also subject to income tax, which is separate from self-employment tax. In 2004, income tax rates were between 10% and 35%, depending on your income and your marital and family status. As a rough rule of thumb for planning purposes, you may want to estimate that about 15% of your income will be taken as income taxes.

Your income from non-business sources is called "Personal Income". Examples are interest and dividend income. Personal income is subject to the income tax only, *not* the self-employment tax.

If you have been following along this far, see if the following chart makes it a little clearer for you:

| Business earnings | Personal income |
|:---:|:---:|
| *minus* | *minus* |
| Business deductions | Personal deductions |
| *equals* | *equals* |
| Business profit | Personal income |
| | |
| Pay self-employment tax on business profit (approximately 15%) | Pay income tax on personal income (approximately 15%) |
| *and* | |
| Pay Income tax on business profit (approximately 15%) | |

Notice that you pay both self-employment tax and income tax on your business profit, or a total of about 30% of your earnings. Personal (non-business) income is subject only to the income tax of about 15%.

## Deductions are Beautiful

Once you grasp the overall picture of how taxes are figured, it becomes apparent that business deductions and personal deductions put money in your pocket. Since they reduce the total amount subject to taxes, they reduce the total taxes you have to pay.

*Business deductions* are especially helpful, since they reduce both the self-employment tax and the income tax.

If you earn $40,000.00 in business income and have no deductions, your overall tax burden would be about $12,000.00 (approximately $6,000.00 for social security tax and $6,000.00 for income tax).

However, if you earn $40,000.00 in business income and have $10,000.00 in deductions, you pay taxes on $30,000.00 ($40,000.00 minus deductions of $10,000.00), and you overall tax burden would be about $9,000.00 (approximately $4,500.00 for social security tax and $4,500.00 for income tax). Your $10,000.00 in deductions would save you about $3,000.00 in taxes.

In other words, since your overall tax rate is about 30%, whenever you can "deduct" a business expense, you save about 30% of the cost of that item in the form of reduced taxes.

Personal deductions reduce only the income tax. Personal deductions include items such as charitable contributions, certain medical expenses, and the like.

Business deductions are discussed in some detail below. Become familiar with this information so that you have a clear understanding of what is deductible, and what records you need to keep to support your deductions.

You will list your deductions on "Schedule C" which is the form self-employed persons file with their income tax returns. If your total deductions for the year were $5,000.00 or less and you do not report a loss for the year, you can use Schedule C-EZ (see page 157). Otherwise, you must use the slightly more complicated Schedule C.

## What Can I Deduct?

In general, if it's a business expense, it's deductible. The expense must be for something "appropriate and helpful in developing and maintaining your trade or business" and the cost must be reasonable. This allows for a broad range of business deductions.

The following list demonstrates the most common deductible items.

- Business use of your automobile
- Office rental expense
- Massage table and other equipment for treatment room
- Music system and music for treatment room
- Painting or repair costs for office
- Advertising
- Long-distance business phone calls

- Business travel expenses (cost of lodging plus 80% of cost of meals)
- Entertainment expenses (50% is deductible)
- Gifts to clients (up to $25 per client per year)
- Professional convention fees (and travel expenses)
- Continuing education expenses, including books
- Professional association dues
- Licensing fees
- Laundry expenses
- Your appointment book
- Business cards and any other business printing jobs
- Costs of oil and other supplies

### Education

You can deduct the cost of education, plus travel and meals expenses, if the education maintains or improves your professional skills, or is required by law for keeping your professional status.

Educational expenses are *not* deductible for training in a new field, or to meet minimum professional requirements, because that is considered a "start-up" cost, and start-up costs are not deductible. The only exception to that is the new "HOPE" Credit or Lifetime Education Credit, which are available only if you attend a degree-granting institution. Your accountant can tell you if these apply to you.

Once you are a practicing massage therapist, the expenses of continuing education are deductible, even if they are for education that "improves" your professional skills. Therefore, you can probably deduct even a major educational expense, as long as you are already a practicing massage therapist.

This is one advantage of taking a small amount of training and practicing massage on the side (in states where this is permissible) before making a commitment to a more serious educational program.

### Gifts

You can deduct the cost of gifts you give as part of doing business, up to a maximum of $25 worth of gifts to any one individual in one year. If there is a question whether something is a gift or entertainment (such as football tickets) it will be considered entertainment.

### Handicap Accessibility Costs

If you have a disabled client, the cost of making your office disabled accessible is subsidized by a special tax credit. The maximum tax credit is $5,000.00

Assume, for example, that you spend $8,000.00 on ramps and a hydraulic lift table for handicapped access. First you deduct $250.00 (the amount specified by the law), leaving $7,750.00 that qualifies for a credit.

**SCHEDULE C**
**(Form 1040)**

Department of the Treasury
Internal Revenue Service

**Profit or Loss From Business**
(Sole Proprietorship)
▶ Partnerships, joint ventures, etc., must file Form 1065 or 1065-B.
▶ Attach to Form 1040 or 1041.   ▶ See Instructions for Schedule C (Form 1040).

OMB No. 1545-0074

**2004**

Attachment
Sequence No. **09**

Name of proprietor

Social security number (SSN)

| A | Principal business or profession, including product or service (see page C-2 of the instructions) | B Enter code from pages C-7, 8, & 9 ▶ |
| C | Business name. If no separate business name, leave blank. | D Employer ID number (EIN), if any |

E   Business address (including suite or room no.) ▶
City, town or post office, state, and ZIP code

F   Accounting method:   (1) ☐ Cash   (2) ☐ Accrual   (3) ☐ Other (specify) ▶

G   Did you "materially participate" in the operation of this business during 2004? If "No," see page C-3 for limit on losses   ☐ Yes   ☐ No

H   If you started or acquired this business during 2004, check here   ▶ ☐

**Part I   Income**

| 1 | Gross receipts or sales. **Caution.** If this income was reported to you on Form W-2 and the "Statutory employee" box on that form was checked, see page C-3 and check here ▶ ☐ | 1 | |
| 2 | Returns and allowances | 2 | |
| 3 | Subtract line 2 from line 1 | 3 | |
| 4 | Cost of goods sold (from line 42 on page 2) | 4 | |
| 5 | **Gross profit.** Subtract line 4 from line 3 | 5 | |
| 6 | Other income, including Federal and state gasoline or fuel tax credit or refund (see page C-3) | 6 | |
| 7 | **Gross income.** Add lines 5 and 6 ▶ | 7 | |

**Part II   Expenses.** Enter expenses for business use of your home **only** on line 30.

| 8 | Advertising | 8 | | 19 | Pension and profit-sharing plans | 19 | |
| 9 | Car and truck expenses (see page C-3) | 9 | | 20 | Rent or lease (see page C-5): | | |
| 10 | Commissions and fees | 10 | | a | Vehicles, machinery, and equipment | 20a | |
| 11 | Contract labor (see page C-4) | 11 | | b | Other business property | 20b | |
| 12 | Depletion | 12 | | 21 | Repairs and maintenance | 21 | |
| 13 | Depreciation and section 179 expense deduction (not included in Part III) (see page C-4) | 13 | | 22 | Supplies (not included in Part III) | 22 | |
| | | | | 23 | Taxes and licenses | 23 | |
| | | | | 24 | Travel, meals, and entertainment: | | |
| 14 | Employee benefit programs (other than on line 19) | 14 | | a | Travel | 24a | |
| 15 | Insurance (other than health) | 15 | | b | Meals and entertainment | | |
| 16 | Interest: | | | c | Enter nondeductible amount included on line 24b (see page C-5) | | |
| a | Mortgage (paid to banks, etc.) | 16a | | d | Subtract line 24c from line 24b | 24d | |
| b | Other | 16b | | 25 | Utilities | 25 | |
| 17 | Legal and professional services | 17 | | 26 | Wages (less employment credits) | 26 | |
| 18 | Office expense | 18 | | 27 | Other expenses (from line 48 on page 2) | 27 | |

28   **Total expenses** before expenses for business use of home. Add lines

29   Tentative profit (loss). Subtract line 28 from line 7

30   Expenses for business use of your home. Attach **Form 8829**

31   **Net profit or (loss).** Subtract line 30 from line 29.

   • If a profit, enter on **Form 1040, line 12,** and **also** on **Schedule SE, li** see page C-6). Estates and trusts, enter on Form 1041, line 3.

   • If a loss, you **must** go to line 32.

32   If you have a loss, check the box that describes your investment in this

   • If you checked 32a, enter the loss on **Form 1040, line 12,** and **als** (statutory employees, see page C-6). Estates and trusts, enter on Form

   • If you checked 32b, you **must** attach **Form 6198.**

For Paperwork Reduction Act Notice, see Form 1040 instructions.

**IRS form 1040
Schedule C,
page 1**

Schedule C (Form 1040) 2004                                                                 Page **2**

**Part III   Cost of Goods Sold** (see page C-6)

| 33 | Method(s) used to value closing inventory:   a ☐ Cost   b ☐ Lower of cost or market   c ☐ Other (attach explanation) | | |
| 34 | Was there any change in determining quantities, costs, or valuations between opening and closing inventory? If "Yes," attach explanation | ☐ Yes | ☐ No |
| 35 | Inventory at beginning of year. If different from last year's closing inventory, attach explanation | 35 | |
| 36 | Purchases less cost of items withdrawn for personal use | 36 | |
| 37 | Cost of labor. Do not include any amounts paid to yourself | 37 | |
| 38 | Materials and supplies | 38 | |
| 39 | Other costs | 39 | |
| 40 | Add lines 35 through 39 | 40 | |
| 41 | Inventory at end of year | 41 | |
| 42 | **Cost of goods sold.** Subtract line 41 from line 40. Enter the result here and on page 1, line 4 | 42 | |

**Part IV   Information on Your Vehicle.** Complete this part **only** if you are claiming car or truck expenses on line 9 and are not required to file Form 4562 for this business. See the instructions for line 13 on page C-4 to find out if you must file Form 4562.

43   When did you place your vehicle in service for business purposes? (month, day, year) ▶ ...../...../.....

44   Of the total number of miles you drove your vehicle during 2004, enter the number of miles you used your vehicle for:

   a   Business ...................   b   Commuting ...................   c   Other ...................

45   Do you (or your spouse) have another vehicle available for personal use?   ☐ Yes   ☐ No

46   Was your vehicle available for personal use during off-duty hours?   ☐ Yes   ☐ No

47a   Do you have evidence to support your deduction?   ☐ Yes   ☐ No

   b   If "Yes," is the evidence written?   ☐ Yes   ☐ No

**Part V   Other Expenses.** List below business expenses not included on lines 8–26 or line 30.

| | | |
| | | |
| | | |
| | | |
| | | |
| | | |
| | | |
| | | |
| | | |
| | | |

48   **Total other expenses.** Enter here and on page 1, line 27 | 48 | |

Schedule C (Form 1040) 2004

**IRS form 1040
Schedule C,
page 2**

SCHEDULE C-EZ
(Form 1040)

Department of the Treasury
Internal Revenue Service

**Net Profit From Business**
(Sole Proprietorship)

▶ **Partnerships, joint ventures, etc., must file Form 1065 or 1065-B.**

▶ **Attach to Form 1040 or 1041.** ▶ **See instructions on back.**

OMB No. 1545-0074

20**04**

Attachment
Sequence No. **09A**

Name of proprietor

Social securit  number (SSN)

**Part I** General Information

**You Ma  Use Schedule C-EZ Instead of Schedule C Onl  If You:**

- Had business expenses of $5,000 or less.
- Use the cash method of accounting.
- Did not have an inventory at any time during the year.
- Did not have a net loss from your business.
- Had only one business as a sole proprietor.

**And You:**

- Had no employees during the year.
- Are not required to file **Form 4562,** Depreciation and Amortization, for this business. See the instructions for Schedule C, line 13, on page C-4 to find out if you must file.
- Do not deduct expenses for business use of your home.
- Do not have prior year unallowed passive activity losses from this business.

**A** Principal business or profession, including product or service

**B** Enter code from pages C-7, 8, & 9
▶

**C** Business name. If no separate business name, leave blank.

**D** Employer ID number (EIN), if any

**E** Business address (including suite or room no.). Address not required if same as on Form 1040, page 1.

City, town or post office, state, and ZIP code

**Part II** Figure Your Net Profit

**1** Gross receipts. **Caution.** If this income was reported to you on Form W-2 and the "Statutory employee" box on that form was checked, see **Statutor  Emplo ees** in the instructions for Schedule C, line 1, on page C-3 and check here . . . . . . . . . ▶ ☐

**1**

**2** Total expenses (see instructions). If more than $5,000, you **must** use Schedule C. . . . . .

**2**

**3** Net profit. Subtract line 2 from line 1. If less than zero, you **must** use Schedule C. Enter on **Form 1040, line 12,** and **also** on **Schedule SE, line 2.** (Statutory employees **do not** report this amount on Schedule SE, line 2. Estates and trusts, enter on Form 1041, line 3.) . . . . .

**3**

**Part III** Information on Your Vehicle. Complete this part onl  if you are claiming car or truck expenses on line 2.

**4** When did you place your vehicle in service for business purposes? (month, day, year) ▶ ...... / ...... / ...... .

**5** Of the total number of miles you drove your vehicle during 2004, enter the number of miles you used your vehicle for:

**a** Business .................... **b** Commuting .................... **c** Other ....................

**6** Do you (or your spouse) have another vehicle available for personal use? . . . . . . . . . . ☐ Yes ☐ No

**7** Was your vehicle available for personal use during off-duty hours? . . . . . . . . . . . . ☐ Yes ☐ No

**8a** Do you have evidence to support your deduction? . . . . . . . . . . . . . . . ☐ Yes ☐ No

**b** If "Yes," is the evidence written? . . . . . . . . . . . . . . . . . . . . . ☐ Yes ☐ No

For Paperwork Reduction Act Notice, see Form 1040 instructions. Cat. No. 14374D Schedule C-EZ (Form 1040) 2004

# IRS form 1040 Schedule C–EZ

Then you multiply that amount by 50% because the law provides a tax credit of 50% of the allowable expenses. Therefore, you get a tax credit of $3,875.00 (50% of $4,750.00). Unlike a deduction, this $3,875.00 *credit* reduces your income taxes by $3,875.00 – as if you had already paid that amount to the IRS.

Now your out-of-pocket expense for making your office accessible is only $4,125.00 (the $8,000.00 you spent minus the $3,875.00 the government gave you back as a tax credit) and this $4,125.00 expense qualifies as a business deduction, further reducing your taxes.

### Home office expenses

Rent and other costs for an office in your home are deductible if:

1. You use a part of your home as your principal place of business, *or*

2. You use a part of your home as a place to meet and deal with clients in the normal course of your practice, *or*

3. You use a separate building in your business, such as a cottage or detached garage, *or*

4. You use a part of your home as a place to do necessary activities such as billing and phone calls, and you do not have any outside office available to you to do these tasks.

To qualify as a home office, the room or part of your house needs to be used "regularly" and "exclusively" in your practice. That means you have to use it for your business on a regular basis—not just on rare occasions. It also means you cannot use it for any other purpose, such as a den or guest bedroom.

Additionally, your home office must qualify under number 1, number 2 number 3, or number 4, above. Most home offices for massage therapists qualify under number 2. You give massages to clients there, so obviously, you meet and deal with clients there in the normal course of your practice. You qualify for the home office deduction.

The same applies if your office is in a separate building on your property. (An office in a separate building is deductible even if you only do your bookwork there, as long as you use it only for business). And if you have another business, such as selling products to your clients, the office where you store your inventory or where you do your bookkeeping for that business also qualifies as a home office under number 1, as long as you use it exclusively for business.

If you qualify for a home office deduction, you can deduct a proportionate share of all household expenses. Such expenses include real estate taxes, mortgage interest, rent, utility bills, insurance, repairs, security systems and depreciation. *Not* included are repairs or improvements that increase the value of a home you own.

To determine the percentage of your home expenses that is deductible as a business expense, calculate the total square footage of your home, and the square footage of your home office. Divide the square footage of the office by the total square footage of the home, and you will get a decimal, for example .23. You then multiply your home expenses (or your rent if you are a renter) by .23 (or whatever number applies) to find the amount of your deduction for your home office.

If the rooms in your home are roughly the same size, and you use one room as an office, you can use a fraction instead of doing the square-foot computation. For example, if you have six equal-sized rooms and use one as an office, deduct one sixth of your household expenses (or rent) as your home office expense.

The home office deduction cannot be larger than the amount of business income generated in the home office. In other words, the deduction cannot be used to create a business loss, only to offset income that you actually earned using that office.

### Meal and Entertainment Expense

If you purchase meals or entertainment as a means of conducting business, you can deduct 50% of the cost of the meals and entertainment, including tips (as long as the costs are reasonable). You can also deduct 100% of your automobile costs for driving to the meal or entertainment. An example of meal and entertainment expense would be taking a chiropractor to lunch to discuss the possibility of cross-referrals.

### Rent and other office expenses

Rental payments for your business office are fully deductible, as are other costs such as heat, electricity, insurance and the like.

### Self-employed health insurance

If you are self-employed, 100% of your payments for health insurance coverage are deductible.

### Self-employment tax

You can deduct one-half of your self-employment tax from your gross income when you figure your income tax.

### Start-up costs

If you are already a practicing massage therapist, and open a new office, or expand an exiting office, the costs involved in doing so are ordinary and necessary business expenses, and are fully deductible.

However, when you first begin your business as a massage therapist, the costs involved in starting your business are "start-up costs" and these are *not* deductible.

This issue generally will not arise for a massage therapist or bodyworker, since opening an office without prior professional experience is not usually a realistic approach. It does, however, become an issue when you want to deduct education expenses. Continuing education is deductible, but your initial educational expense is a non-deductible "start-up" cost.

### Travel

When you travel away from home for business, most of your expenses are deductible. Travel away from home means going for more than just a day's work, and must include going away long enough to need sleep or rest before coming home.

### Deductible items

When traveling away from home on business, your deductible expenses include airplane, rail or bus tickets, automobile expenses, taxi fares, baggage costs, meals, lodging costs, cleaning and laundry expenses, telephone, fax, internet access costs, tips, and other similar expenses related to travel.

### Travel receipts

Keep receipts during your trip. If you travel by car, keep an envelope in the glove compartment, and put all receipts in the envelope. When you get home, staple them together and put them in the place where you collect all business receipts. At the end of the year, they will be together and easy to handle when you are totaling your deductions.

### Optional methods for deducting meal costs when traveling

Meals can be deducted two ways—(1) you may deduct amount you actually spend or (2) you may deduct the "standard meal allowance" which varies between $31 and $46 per day, depending on location. For detailed information on the standard meal allowance, request Publication 463 free from the IRS.

When using the standard meal allowance, you do not need to produce receipts for your meals. For all other expenses, however, you need to have receipts to document your travel expenditures.

### Mixed business and personal travel

If a trip is mainly business but partly personal, you can deduct the round trip travel expenses to get to your business destination, and the meals, lodging and incidental expenses that relate to the business portion of your trip. Any personal side trips, or expenses on days that were vacation days, are not tax-deductible.

If your trip was primarily for vacation and partly for business, no part of the expense is tax-deductible.

## Business use vs. Personal use

If a particular expense has aspects of business and personal activity mixed together, remember that the test is whether it is "appropriate and helpful in promoting your business." If it meets this test, the fact that it also helps you personally is irrelevant; it is still deductible.

Some activities are personal and not business-related. For example, if you go to a bar on Saturday night hoping to meet someone who will become a bodywork client, you will not convince the IRS that your expenses are business-related.

However, if you go to the hardware store to get a wing nut to repair your massage table, that is a business trip, and it remains a business trip even if you also pick up a surge protector for your home computer while you are there.

If you pay attention to all the things you do for your business, you will see that much of your lifestyle actually is deductible. The cost of professional books, phone calls, entertainment, uniforms, and business laundry are all deductible expenses. You can also deduct the cost of traveling to shop for items for the business and to do errands for the business. You are entitled to proper business deductions, so plan for them, document them and take them.

## Documenting deductions

The key to documenting deductions is keeping receipts, canceled checks, and in the case of automobile mileage, a log of business miles driven in your car.

### *What is documentation?*

The IRS can demand a paper record of any transaction you are claiming as a deduction. If you pay a bill for a business expense, keep the bill. When you get your canceled checks from your bank, save the ones that relate to business expenses.

### *Where to keep your documents*

Create a space in your office or your home where you regularly keep a whole year's bills, receipts and canceled checks. It can be a drawer, a filing cabinet, a sturdy box, or any space that you can regularly keep these records. At the end of the year, you will take them out and organize them so they can be totaled and figured into your tax return.

### *What to document*

Keep all records of money spent on goods or services that relate to your business. These are items listed above under the heading "What Can I Deduct?", and any other items which are related to the operation of your business.

### *At the end of the year*

When you go through your year's receipts and canceled checks, gather them into categories of deductions. This will make it easier for you or your accountant to make a final presentation of your business activity on your schedule C.

Schedule C contains a partial list of business deductions. These include: advertising, bad debts, car and truck expenses, depreciation, insurance, legal and professional services, office expenses, supplies, travel, meals, and entertainment. In addition, the form provides space for other categories than the ones listed.

Use this list as a basis for organizing your receipts. Other categories you might use for organization purposes are printing and photocopying, telephone expense, and gifts to clients. Receipts which do not fit into any other category can be labeled "miscellaneous."

## Business use of your car

### *Are you a commuter?*

Business use of your car is deductible, with one important exception: Commuting expense is not deductible. For tax purposes, commuting means traveling between your home and your main or regular place of work. The trip to your work and the trip home again are both considered non-deductible commuting.

If you leave your *office* to do a house call, that mileage is deductible business travel. However, if you leave your *home* to do a house call, that is not deductible.

The "gray area" comes when you have an office in your home; in that case, you are leaving a *home* and an *office* at the same time when you leave for business travel.

If you have a home office, step into your home office just before you leave on any other business trip. Then you are going from one place of business to another. When you return, step into your home office before doing anything else. Thus your return trip is from one office to another. In this way, none of your business driving is considered commuting. While this may sound a little shady, it is apparently entirely legal, at least at the present moment.

It is possible the IRS would question this deduction if you were audited. If you wish to be more conservative, then deduct mileage expenses only on days when you see clients in your home office. If you are actually working in your home office on a particular day, there can be no question that travel from that office to some other business destination is business travel.

### *Two methods of computing automobile deduction*

You may choose either of two methods to compute your deduction for business use of your car.

The methods are to use the standard deduction (37.5 cents in tax year 2004) for each mile driven for business, or to calculate actual expenses of operating your car for the year and to figure mathematically the amount of your deduction.

If you have a car that is not very expensive and costs little to operate, such as a Honda Civic, you will come out ahead using the 37.5 cents per mile computation. If you have an expensive new car or one that required lots of expensive repairs this year, you may come out ahead using the actual computation method.

The standard per mile method is quite simple to use, and the actual cost method can become quite involved. I use the per mile method on my tax return, because I don't enjoy keeping all the records necessary to use the actual cost method. Even if I am paying a few dollars more in taxes, for me it is worth it to simplify my record-keeping.

A brief explanation of both methods follows.

### *Standard deduction method—37.5 cents per mile (tax year 2004)*

Keep a daily log of the use of your car. You should record business and personal use.

The best kind of record to keep is a list of the starting and ending odometer mileage for each business trip. This type of record shows each business trip individually. It is also acceptable to list only the destination and the number of miles driven for each trip.

At the end of the year, total all the business miles and multiply the total by .345 to get the deduction for business use of your car.

Example: Your total business miles turn out to be 3,000.

$$\begin{array}{r} 3000 \\ \times\ \underline{.375} \\ \$\ \overline{1,125} \end{array}$$

Your deduction for business use of your car is $1,125.00. This figure is included on your Schedule C as your mileage deduction.

## *Actual cost method*

Keep itemized records of all expenses related to operating your car. These include gasoline, oil, tires, lubrication, repairs and maintenance, insurance, license and registration fees and automobile club membership dues.

These actual costs will be added up at the end of the year. Another actual cost that can be included is the depreciation in value of your car during the year. The IRS has guidelines for computing depreciation.

Keep a log of business and personal miles, since you will need to figure the percentage of business use. At the end of the year, divide the year's total business miles by the year's total miles to arrive at the percentage of business use. Multiply the total of actual expenses by percentage of business use to determine your deduction.

For example, your total costs of operating your car for the year were $1,758. In addition, your depreciation allowance was $3,500. The total of these figures is $5,258.

If your business use of the car was 20% of the year's total use, your calculation would be:

$$\begin{array}{r} 5258 \\ \times\,.20 \\ \hline \$1,051.60 \end{array}$$

Your deduction for business use of your car is $1,051.60. This figure is included on your Schedule C as your mileage deduction.

## Depreciation

Depreciation is one of the most complex concepts facing someone trying to understand income taxes. Fortunately, you can get along just fine without ever conquering this particular challenge.

In a nutshell, depreciation refers to spreading out the cost of a large expense over a period of years, and deducting part of the expense each year. This usually applies to heavy equipment which costs a great deal and lasts for many years. During each tax year, the owner takes a portion of the total cost as a deduction. A small business person, such as a massage therapist, usually does not have to worry about depreciation, unless you purchase something with a large value that will last many years. The rules for spreading out the deduction over many years get extremely complicated and difficult to apply.

The government has given small businesses the option of avoiding the whole problem, by using what is called a "section 179 deduction". By using this option, you can deduct the entire cost of business items up to $100,000 entirely during the year you purchase the deductible item. Therefore, even if you purchase ten massage tables this year, you can take the whole deduction as a business expense during the year in which you spend the money. Consult a professional tax preparer if you are planning to use this type of deduction.

In some cases, there can be tax advantages to using depreciation instead of taking the whole deduction in one year. For example, if you make a large expenditure this year, and earn very little, the expenditure would be "wasted" if you took the whole deduction this year, because you would pay no taxes whether or not you take the deduction. Next year, when you have more income, you would like to be able to use part of the deduction to reduce you income taxes.

If you think that using depreciation could help you, send for IRS publication 946, How to Depreciate Property, or buy *Small-Time Operator*. See pages 165–166 for information on obtaining these items.

## Estimated tax payments

If you will owe at least $1,000 in tax next year, you are required to pay estimated tax payments four times a year, on April 15, June 15, September 15 and January 15. You can also be penalized if you make your estimated tax payments late.

Estimated taxes are paid on IRS form 1040-ES, and the form includes a worksheet for you to use to calculate the amount of your estimated tax payments. It is based on the previous year's income, and if you follow the instructions in the worksheet, you are guaranteed not to be assessed a penalty for underpayment. To avoid penalties, you must pay either 90% of the tax you owed in the previous year, or 100% of the tax you owe for the current year.

Consider this: Your estimated tax payments are based on last year's income. If you make exactly the same income this year, your estimated payments will exactly pay your tax bill. However, what if you make more this year than last year? Your estimated tax payments cover the amount you earned last year, but on April 15, you will owe tax on any amount more than that. If you had a really good year, this additional amount could be several thousand dollars.

Consider also that April 15 is the date you must pay your first estimated tax payment for the coming year. In addition to paying the excess tax for last year, you must now make the first installment on next year's taxes. This "double whammy" can make April 15 a very expensive day for the self-employed bodyworker. Remember this if your practice is increasing, and find the discipline to put some money away all year so you will have enough to pay your taxes in April.

## Hiring an accountant

Accountants are not cheap, but often they can pay for themselves in tax savings they find that you might miss. If you are motivated to do your own taxes, there is no reason you cannot do so. The resources listed below will give you all the information you need. With some time and study, you can learn what you need to know.

However, it can get complex, and unless you enjoy this sort of thing, consider hiring professional help. Non-CPA tax preparers may know just as much as an accountant, and may charge a little less.

Ask other therapists for recommendations for an accountant. When they recommend someone, ask why they like him or her, or why they think he is a good accountant. If the reasons they give refer to things that matter to you in an accountant, consider using that person.

Consider finding an accountant who will trade accounting services for massage. Use the yellow pages, and call accountants. Explain that you are just getting established, have a simple return, and would like to find an accountant who appreciates massage. You may catch someone in the proper mood to make an arrangement to trade services.

Consider, also, hiring an accountant to get you started with bookkeeping and tax systems you can understand, so that you can do your own taxes in future years. An accountant may be able to explain everything you need to know, and set you up with forms you will be able to use in future years.

If you hire an accountant or tax preparer, keep your records clear and organized. If possible, keep them in categories that will make it easy to sort out at tax time. This will make the accountant's job easier, and may encourage him to keep his fees reasonable.

## How long to keep tax records

Keep your records and receipts for four to six years after filing. The normal time limit on an IRS audit is three years, but for serious reporting misstatements, they can go back six years, and for "fraud" there is no time limit.

While you can discard your supporting papers after time has passed, it is good practice to keep your actual tax returns "forever"—or as long as you can. After four years, the government will not demand to see all your receipts and records to defend your returns, but you should always have your tax returns available to prove what you filed in case there is ever a controversy about your taxes.

## Getting further information

If you want help doing your own taxes, there are several good resources you can turn to.

1. One is a book, written by an accountant, for the purpose of helping small business owners take care of bookkeeping and taxes. It is well-organized, well written and inexpensive. It goes into more detail about depreciation, and a few other minor subjects, than this chapter, and has practical advice about book-keeping. The book is called *Small-Time Operator* and is available from:

   **Bell Springs Publishing**
   Box 640 Bell Springs Road
   Laytonville, CA 95454
   (707) 984-6746

2. Also good is Nolo Press: Tax Savvy for Small Business, written by lawyers and directed at sole practitioners and owners of small companies. It is available from **www.nolo.com** and in bookstores.

3. Check out your local bookstore as tax season approaches. All major bookstores carry a selection of Do-It-Yourself tax guides. They are usually several hundred pages, and cost around $15.00. They cover in detail any subject you would need to know about in order to do your tax return. When April 15 rolls around and you are up against

a deadline, book like this can be a comforting resource to have with you.

4. The final source of information is the IRS, and its information is available at no charge. The IRS will send you booklets explaining various aspects of your taxes, and is also available to answer questions by phone.

IRS publications can be ordered by calling

1-800-829-3676 (1-800-TAX-FORM) or at **www.irs.gov**

The first publication to order is Tax Guide for Small Businesses, Publication 334. This contains the basics of record-keeping and taxes for small businesses, including filled-in sample forms.

The second publication to order is "Guide to Free Tax Services." This lists all the other IRS publications. Once you have this booklet, you can leaf through it to see what else is available and what you need.

Some of the subjects covered in these IRS publications are listed below. The IRS publication number is listed after each name. These can be ordered from the toll-free number listed above.

Travel, Entertainment and Gift Expense 463
Tax Withholding and Estimated Tax 505
Educational Expenses 508
Moving Expenses 521
Reporting Income from Tips 531
Self-Employment Tax 533
Business Expense 535
Retirement Plans for the Self-employed 560
Taxpayers Starting a Business 583
Business Use of Your Home 587
Alternative Minimum Tax for Individuals 909
How to Depreciate Property 946

All of these publications provide good detail, and are written in clear and readable fashion. However, they are written by the IRS, and will not necessarily tip you off to the best ways of getting the most out of your deductions.

To reach an IRS representative by phone, check your local phone book blue pages under Federal Government, Internal Revenue Service. Major cities have local offices. To find your local office, visit **www.irs.gov** and use the "site map" link located at the top of the home page. From the site map, choose "contact my local office" If you do not have internet access, call the IRS toll-free at 1-800-829-1040.

# **20** Scientific Research on the Benefits of Massage

Although massage has been practiced for thousands of years, helping billions of people, little scientific documentation of the health benefits of massage has existed until very recently. The massage profession was attempting to be taken seriously by the health care establishment with virtually no scientific evidence of the health benefits of massage.

All that has changed in the last fifteen years. Recent scientific research has produced tremendous amounts of verifiable data showing the efficacy of massage for a large variety of health problems. This documentation will be useful in promoting hospital-based massage, in securing reimbursement for massage from insurance companies, in gaining physician referrals and collaborations, and in convincing the general population of the benefits of massage as a health modality.

The best sources of information about scientific evidence on the efficacy of massage are summarized below. Touch Research Institute publishes abstracts of all of its research on its website, and the extensive excerpts reproduced below summarize the most interesting studies conducted by the Institute.

## Massage Therapy Foundation

The foundation was created by AMTA in 1990. It maintains a searchable database of over 2,500 articles on massage. It also keeps a "Library" on its website, with a link to "Articles of Interest" containing articles that are especially useful in demonstrating the medical efficacy of massage and related modalities.

**Massage Therapy Foundation**
500 Davis Street, Suite 900
Evanston, IL 60201
(847) 869-5019
info@massagetherapyfoundation.org
www.massagetherapyfoundation.org

## Touch Research Institute

TRI was established in 1992 at the University of Miami School of Medicine. Under the direction of Tiffany Field, Ph.D., the institute has been conducting numerous studies to document the health benefits of massage. Some of their studies use licensed massage therapists, and others use college students or parents or grandparents who are given some training in how to give a massage.

Most of this chapter consists of a summary of the studies that have been conducted at TRI about the benefits of massage. Information about these studies and library references for all of them can be found at the Institute's website, **www. miami.edu/touch-research**.

## Scientific Research on Massage in Book Form

An excellent volume of scientific research on massage is *Massage Therapy: The Evidence for Practice* by Grant Jewell Rich. It is a well-organized and medically sound analysis of the current evidence for the efficacy of massage. It is written in the language of a medical researcher and presents reviews of scientific data about massage in scientific terms. It could be something a massage practitioner might give or loan to a physician to convince him or her of the medical efficacy of massage, and may be useful to convince a mainstream physician to refer to massage practitioners. It sells for $36.95 and is available through all bookstores. Further information is at **www.intl.elsevierhealth.com**.

## Studies Conducted by Touch Research Institute

### Adolescents

Massaged adolescents had lower anxiety after the first and last sessions. By the end of the study, they also reported feeling less hostile and they were perceived by their parents as being less aggressive.

### Alzheimer's

Verbal displays of agitation, the most frequently cited form of agitation in community-dwelling individuals with AD, were not diffused by slow-stroke massage. However, more physical expressions of agitation such as pacing, wandering, and resisting were decreased when slow-stroke massage was applied.

### Anorexia

Massaged anorexia patients reported lower stress and anxiety levels and showed lower cortisol levels immediately following the massage. Over the five-week treatment period, they also reported decreased body dissatisfaction.

### Anxiety

1. Hospitalized depressed and adjustment disorder children and adolescents received massage. Compared with a control group who viewed relaxing videotapes, the massage subjects were less depressed and anxious and had lower saliva cortisol levels after the massage. In addition, nurses rated the subjects as being less anxious and more cooperative on the last day of the study, and nighttime sleep increased over this period.

2. An on-site chair massage therapy program provided to 18 employees in a down-sizing organization revealed significant reductions in anxiety levels for the massaged group.

*Aromatherapy*

1. The therapeutic effect of two different species of lavender appeared to be different: one was almost twice as effective as the other, thereby disproving the hypothesis that aromatherapy, using topical application of essential oils, is effective purely because of touch, massage or placebo.

2. Lavender and rosemary applications were compared. The lavender group showed increased drowsiness, less depressed mood, and reported feeling more relaxed. They performed math computations faster and more accurately following aromatherapy. The rosemary group showed increased alertness, lower anxiety, and reported feeling more relaxed and alert. They were faster, but not more accurate, at math computations after the aromatherapy session.

*Arthritis*

Children with juvenile rheumatoid arthritis were massaged by their parents. The children's anxiety and stress hormone (cortisol) levels immediately decreased and over a 30-day period pain decreased on self-reports, parent reports, and their physician's assessments.

*Asthma*

Children with asthma received either massage therapy from parents or relaxation therapy. Their anxiety levels were reduced immediately after massage, and their attitude toward asthma and their pulmonary functions improved over the course of the study.

*Attention Deficit Hyperactivity Disorder*

1. Adolescents with attention deficit hyperactivity disorder received either massage therapy or relaxation therapy. The massage therapy group, but not the relaxation therapy group, rated themselves as happier and observers rated them as fidgeting less following the sessions. After the 2-week period, their teachers reported more time on task and assigned them lower hyperactivity scores based on classroom behavior.

2. Adolescents with Attention Deficit Hyperactivity Disorder participated in Tai Chi classes twice a week for 5 weeks. After the 10 Tai Chi sessions the adolescents displayed less anxiety, improved conduct, less daydreaming, fewer inappropriate emotions, and less hyperactivity. These improved scores persisted during the two weeks following classes.

3. Children and adolescents with attention-deficit/hyperactivity disorder received massage therapy for 20 minutes twice per week over the course of one month. Mood

state improved based on smiley face and thermometer scales. Classroom behavior also improved in the areas of anxiety, daydreaming and hyperactivity.

*Autism*

1. Orienting to irrelevant sounds decreased more in the massage group than the control group and stereotypic behaviors decreased more in the massage group than the control group.

2. Parents gave massage to autistic children prior to bedtime every night for one month. A control group read stories to their children. The children in the massage group exhibited less stereotypic behavior and showed more on-task and social relatedness behavior during play observations at school, and they experienced fewer sleep problems at home.

*Back Pain*

1. Patients with lumbar-sacral disc hernia received three treatments of reflexology massage for a week. 62.5% reported a reduction in pain.

2. Patients with chronic low back pain who received massage reported experiencing less pain, depression, anxiety and improved sleep. They also showed improved trunk and pain flexion performance, and their serotonin and dopamine levels were higher.

3. Four random clinical trials were located in which massage was tested as a therapy for low back pain. One of these studies suggests that massage is superior to no treatment. Two trials imply that it is equally effective as spinal manipulation or transcutaneous electrical stimulation. One study suggests that it is less effective than spinal manipulation. It is concluded that too few trials of massage therapy exist for a reliable evaluation of its efficacy. Massage seems to have some potential as a therapy for low back pain.

4. Patients with chronic low back pain who were treated with massage reported reduced pain, depression and anxiety and improved sleep. They also showed improved trunk and pain flexion performance, and serotonin and dopamine levels were higher.

5. Patients admitted for a diagnostic cardiac catheterization were given a 20-minute massage. There was a significant reduction in systolic blood pressure in the treatment group.

*Behavior Problems*

Preschool children with behavior problems received massage for 15-minutes twice a week for a month. The children who received massage were more drowsy, less active, less talkative and had lower anxiety levels after the sessions; and they were less anxious and more cooperative by the end of the study.

*Blood Flow*

1. Infant massage improved the weight, length, and midarm and midleg circumferences as compared to infants without massage. The femoral artery blood velocity, diameter and flow also improved as did their sleep.

2. Skeletal muscle blood flow was measured before, during and after short application of different forms of massage. Tapotement increased blood flow comparable to exercise. Petrissage did not cause a significant change.

3. A certified massage therapist administered effleurage, petrissage, and tapotement treatments to the forearm flexors (small muscle mass) and quadriceps (large muscle mass) muscle groups. The mean blood volume and blood flows for brachial and femoral arteries, respectively, were not altered by any of the massage treatments in either the forearm or quadriceps muscle groups. The results indicated that manual massage did not elevate muscle blood flow irrespective of massage type or the muscle mass receiving the treatment.

*Blood Pressure*

Massage-like stroking of the abdomen of rats under anesthesia caused a marked decrease in arterial blood pressure. After cessation of the stimulation blood pressure returned to the control level within 1 min. Stroking only the lateral sides of the abdomen elicited a significantly smaller decrease in blood pressure than stroking the ventral side.

*Breast Cancer*

Women with breast cancer received 30-minute massages three times per week for 5 weeks. The immediate massage therapy effects included reduced anxiety, depressed mood, and anger. The longer-term massage effects included reduced depression and hostility, increased urinary dopamine, serotonin values, natural killer cell number and lymphocytes.

*Bulimia*

Female adolescent bulimic inpatients were randomly assigned to a massage therapy or a standard treatment (control) group. RESULTS: The massaged patients showed immediate reductions in anxiety and depression (both self-report and behavior observation). In addition, by the last day of the therapy, they had lower depression scores, lower cortisol (stress) levels, higher dopamine levels, and showed improvement on several other psychological and behavioral measures.

*Burn*

1. Adult patients with burns received massage therapy. Anxiety and cortisol levels decreased, and behavior ratings improved after the massage therapy sessions. Longer-term effects included decreases in depression, anger and pain.

2. Patients with burn injuries received massage during the remodeling phase of wound healing. Massaged patients reported reduced itching, pain, and anxiety and improved mood.

3. Young children hospitalized for severe burns received standard dressing care or massage therapy in addition to standard dressing care. The massage therapy was conducted to body parts that were not burned. During the dressing change, the children who received massage therapy showed minimal distress behaviors and no increase in movement other than torso movement. In contrast, the children who did not receive massage therapy responded to the dressing change procedure with increased facial grimacing, torso movement, crying, leg movement and reaching out. Nurses also reported greater ease in completing the dressing change procedure for the children in the massage therapy group.

*Cancer*

1. Following foot reflexology, patients with breast and lung cancer experienced a significant decrease in anxiety. One of three pain measures showed that patients with breast cancer experienced a significant decrease in pain.

2. Foot massage was found to have a significant immediate effect on cancer patients' perceptions of pain, nausea, and relaxation when measured with a visual analog scale.

3. Hospitalized patients experiencing significant cancer pain received thirty minutes of therapeutic massage on two consecutive evenings. Massage therapy significantly reduced the subjects' level of pain and anxiety and enhanced their feelings of relaxation. Physiological measures (heart rate, respiratory rate, and blood pressure) tended to decrease from baseline, providing further indication of relaxation.

4. Hospice patients with terminal cancer received four massages, twice-weekly for two weeks. Pulse rate and respiratory rate were significantly reduced immediately after the massages.

5. Caregivers of stem cell transplant patients received massage. They showed significant declines in anxiety scores, depression, general fatigue, and emotional fatigue.

*Cardiovascular*

Healthy subjects received myofascial trigger-point massage therapy. There was a resulting decrease in heart rate, systolic blood pressure and diastolic blood pressure. Analysis also revealed a significant increase in parasympathetic activity following myofascial trigger-point massage therapy. Additionally both muscle tension and emotional state, showed significant improvement.

*Carpal Tunnel Syndrome*

Adults with CTS symptoms were taught a self-massage routine that was done daily at home. They were also massaged once a week by a therapist. Their progress was compared to a control group. Participants in the massage therapy group had improved grip strength. They also experienced lower levels of perceived pain, anxiety, and depressed mood.

### Cerebral Palsy

Twenty young children with Cerebral Palsy received 30-minutes of massage or reading twice weekly for 12 weeks. The children receiving massage therapy showed fewer physical symptoms, including reduced spasticity, less rigid muscle tone overall and in the arms and improved fine and gross motor functioning. The massage group also had improved cognition, social and dressing scores and they showed more positive facial expressions.

### Chronic Fatigue Syndrome

Twenty chronic fatigue syndrome subjects received either massage therapy or SHAM TENS (transcutaneous electrical stimulation): Immediately following the massage therapy patients had lower depression and anxiety scores and lower cortisol levels. Longer-term effects (last day versus first day) suggested that the massage therapy group had lower depression, emotional distress and somatic symptom scores, more hours of sleep and lower epinephrine and cortisol levels.

### Cocaine

Cocaine-exposed preterm neonates received massage therapy over a 10-day period. The massaged infants 28% greater weight gain and showed significantly fewer postnatal complications and stress behaviors than the control infants, and demonstrated more mature motor behaviors on the Brazelton examination at the end of the 10-day study period.

### Cognition (Learning)

Preschoolers were given tests, including Block Design, Animal Pegs and Mazes, before and after receiving a 15-minute massage or spending 15-minutes reading stories with an experimenter. Performance on the Block Design improved following massage and accuracy was greater on the Animal Pegs in the massage group.

### Cystic Fibrosis

Parents of children with cystic fibrosis gave their children 20-minute massage every night at bedtime for one month. Parents in the control group read to their children for 20 minutes. The massage group reported reduced anxiety, improved mood and improved peak air flow readings.

### Dancers

Female university dancers received either massage therapy or relaxation therapy twice a week for five weeks. Both groups reported less depressed mood and lowered anxiety levels. However, saliva cortisol (stress hormones) decreased only for the massage therapy group. Both groups reported less neck, shoulder, and back pain after the treatment sessions and reduced back pain across the study. However, only the massage therapy group showed increased range of motion across the study, including neck extension and shoulder abduction.

## Depression

1. Depressed mothers at 4 weeks postpartum were assigned to 1) infant massage class and a support group (massage group) or 2) support group (control group). Depression scores fell in both groups, but improvement of mother-infant interactions was seen only in the massage group.

2. A 30-minute back massage was given daily for a 5-day period to hospitalized depressed and adjustment disorder children and adolescents. Compared with a control group who viewed relaxing videotapes, the massaged subjects were less depressed and anxious and had lower saliva cortisol levels after the massage. In addition, nurses rated the subjects as being less anxious and more cooperative on the last day of the study, and nighttime sleep increased over this period.

3. Depressed adolescent mothers received ten 30-minute sessions of massage therapy or relaxation therapy over a five-week period. Although both groups reported lower anxiety following their first and last therapy sessions, only the massage therapy group showed behavioral and stress hormone changes including a decrease in anxious behavior, pulse, and salivary cortisol levels. A decrease in urine cortisol levels suggested lower stress following the five-week period for the massage therapy group.

## Dermatitis

Young children with atopic dermatitis were treated with standard topical care and massage by their parents for 20 minutes daily for a 1 month period. A control group received standard topical care only. Massaged children's affect and activity level significantly improved, and their parents' anxiety decreased immediately after the massage therapy sessions. Parents also reported lower anxiety levels in their children, and the children improved significantly on measures of redness, scaling, lichenification, excoriation, and pruritus.

## Diabetes

Diabetic children received touch therapy or relaxation therapy from their parents. The immediate effects of the touch therapy were reduced parent anxiety and depressed mood and reduced child anxiety, fidgetiness and depressed affect. Over the 30 day period compliance on insulin and food regulation improved and blood glucose levels decreased from 159 to within the normal range (121).

## Down Syndrome

Young children with Down syndrome receiving early intervention also were given two half-hour massage therapy or reading sessions (control group) per week for two months. Children in the massage therapy group experienced developmental gains in fine and gross motor functioning and showed less severe hypotonicity in their limbs.

## Endorphins

Massage did not change the measured serum levels of beta-endorphin or beta-lipotropin in these healthy subjects without pain. A follow-up study using patients experiencing acute or chronic back pain is recommended. Massage is used routinely in the treatment of such patients, and endogenous opiates are recognized as a possible mechanism for pain relief

## Extremities

There is no consistent or significant average increase in total blood flow after deep stroking and kneading massage of the extremities, in normal subjects, in those with rheumatoid arthritis or in those with spastic paralysis of the extremities. There is a moderate, consistent and definite increase in circulation after deep stroking and kneading massage to the extremities of subjects who have flaccid paralysis. Vigorous, stimulating massage results in consistent and significant increases in the average blood flow of the massaged extremity. Neither deep stroking and kneading massage nor vigorous, stimulating massage of the extremities results in consistent or significant changes in the blood flow of the contralateral unmassaged extremities.

## Fibromyalgia

1. Adult fibromyalgia syndrome subjects received massage therapy, transcutaneous electrical stimulation (TENS), or a transcutaneous electrical stimulation no-current group (Sham TENS) for 30-minute treatment sessions two times per week for 5 weeks. The massage therapy subjects reported lower anxiety and depression, and their cortisol levels were lower immediately after the therapy sessions on the first and last days of the study. The TENS group showed similar changes, but only after therapy on the last day of the study. The massage therapy group improved on the dolorimeter measure of pain. They also reported less pain the last week, less stiffness and fatigue, and fewer nights of difficult sleeping. Thus, massage therapy was the most effective therapy with these fibromyalgia patients.

2. Adult fibromyalgia patients received either massage therapy or relaxation therapy, twice a week for five weeks. Both groups showed a decrease in anxiety and depressed mood immediately after the first and last therapy sessions. However, across the course of the study only the massage therapy group reported an increase in the number of sleep hours and a decrease in their sleep movements. In addition, substance P levels decreased and the patients' physicians assigned lower disease and pain ratings and rated fewer tenderpoints in the massage therapy group.

## Headache

1. Adults with migraine headaches received twice-weekly 30-minute massages for five consecutive weeks. Patients reported fewer distress symptoms, less pain,

more headache free days, fewer sleep disturbances and taking fewer analgesics. They also showed increased serotonin levels.

2. Chronic tension headache sufferers received structured massage therapy treatment directed toward the neck and shoulder muscles during a 4-wk period. Massage therapy was effective in reducing the number of weekly headaches. A trend toward reduction in average duration of each headache was also observed. Headache intensity was unaffected by massage treatment.

### HIV

1. Neonates born to HIV-positive mothers were given three 15-minute massages daily for 10 days. They showed superior performance on almost every Brazelton newborn cluster score and had a greater daily weight gain at the end of the treatment period unlike the control group who showed declining performance.

2. 29 Gay men (20 HIV+, 9 HIV-) received daily massages for one month. Major immune findings included a significant increase in Natural Killer Cell number, Natural Killer Cell Cytotoxicity, soluble CD8, and the cytotoxic subset of CD8 cells. No changes occurred in HIV disease progression markers (CD4, CD4/CD8 ratio, Beta-2 microglobulin, neopterin). Major neuroendocrine findings included a significant decrease in cortisol. Decreased anxiety and increased relaxation were significantly correlated with increased NK cell number.

### HIV in Adolescents

HIV positive adolescents received massage therapy or muscle relaxation two times per week for 12 weeks. Adolescents who received massage therapy reported feeling less anxious and they were less depressed and showed enhanced immune function by the end of the 12 week study.

### Hospice

Slow stroke back massage was provided for 30 hospice patients. The massage was associated with decreases in systolic BP, diastolic BP, and heart rate and with an increase in skin temperature.

### Hospitalized Patients

Patients in acute care setting received 1 to 4 massages during the course of their hospital stay. The most frequently identified outcomes were increased relaxation (98%), a sense of well-being (93%), and positive mood change (88%). More than two thirds of patients attributed enhanced mobility, greater energy, increased participation in treatment, and faster recovery to massage therapy. Thirty-five percent stated that benefits lasted more than 1 day.

### Hypertension

Adults diagnosed with hypertension received ten 30-minute massage sessions over five weeks. Sitting diastolic blood pressure decreased after the first and last massage therapy sessions and reclining diastolic blood pressure decreased from the first to the last day of the study. Patients also reported less depression and hostility.

## Immunology

Healthy female medical students received a 1-hr full body massage 1 day before an anxiety-provoking academic examination. A significant decrease in respiratory rate occurred from pre- to post-massage. Mean anxiety scores decreased from 52.8 to 26.7 and mean scores on the visual analogue scale decreased from 75.6 to 34.6 from pre- to post-massage.

## Infants

1. Infants born to depressed adolescent mothers were given 15 minutes of either massage or rocking for 2 days per week for a 6-week period. Massaged infants spent more time in active alert and active awake states, cried less, and had lower salivary cortisol levels, suggesting lower stress. After the massage versus the rocking sessions, the infants spent less time in an active awake state, suggesting that massage may be more effective than rocking for inducing sleep. Over the 6-week period, the massage-therapy infants gained more weight, showed greater improvement on emotionality, sociability, and soothability.

2. Infants and toddlers with sleep onset problems were given daily massages by their parents prior to bedtime for one month. The massaged children showed fewer sleep delay behaviors and had a shorter latency to sleep onset by the end of the study. Forty-five minute behavior observations by an independent observer also revealed more time awake, alert and active and more positive affect in the massaged children by the end of the study.

3. Fathers gave their infants daily massages 15 minutes prior to bedtime for one month. By the end of the study, the fathers were more expressive and showed more enjoyment and more warmth during floor-play interactions with their infants.

4. Studies from several labs have documented a 31 to 47% greater weight gain in preterm newborns receiving massage therapy compared with standard medical treatment. In addition, functional magnetic resonance imaging studies are being conducted to assess the effects of touch therapy on brain development. Further behavioral, physiological, and genetic research is needed to understand these effects of massage therapy on growth and development.

## Intensive Care

122 patients admitted to a general intensive care unit were randomly assigned to either massage, aromatherapy using lavender, or a period of rest. Those patients who received aromatherapy reported significantly greater improvement in their mood and perceived levels of anxiety. They also felt less anxious and more positive immediately following the therapy.

### Labor Pain

Twenty-eight women were recruited from prenatal classes and randomly assigned to receive massage in addition coaching during labor. The massaged mothers reported a decrease in depressed mood, anxiety and more positive affect following the first massage during labor. In addition, the massaged mothers had significantly shorter labor, a shorter hospital stay and less postpartum depression.

### Leukemia

Twenty children with leukemia were provided with daily massage therapy by their parents and were compared to a standard treatment control group. Following a month of massage therapy, depressed mood decreased in the children's parents, and the children's white blood cell and neutrophil counts decreased.

### Lower Back Pain

1. 262 patients who had persistent back pain received Traditional Chinese Medical acupuncture, therapeutic massage, or self-care educational materials for up to 10 massage or acupuncture visits over 10 weeks. At 10 weeks, massage was superior to self-care on the symptom scale and the disability scale. Massage was also superior to acupuncture on the disability scale. The massage group used the least medications and had the lowest costs of subsequent care.

2. A study tested the effect of expectation on outcome. 135 patients with chronic low back pain who received acupuncture or massage were studied. Improved function was observed for 86% of the participants with higher expectations for the treatment they received, as compared with 68% of those with lower expectations. Patients who expected greater benefit from massage than from acupuncture were more likely to experience better outcomes with massage than with acupuncture, and vice versa.

### Multiple Sclerosis

Twenty-four adults with multiple sclerosis were randomly assigned to a standard medical treatment control group or a massage therapy group. The massage group had lower anxiety and less depressed mood immediately following the massage sessions and by the end of the study they had improved self-esteem, better body image and image of disease progression, and enhanced social functioning

### Pain

1. Tactile stimulation was used with 50 emergency department patients to relieve pain. Following stimulation, subjects reported significantly reduced pain, and demonstrated reduced heart rate, and blood pressure readings.

2. A treatment group of 19 patients and a control group of 20 patients were compared on the impact of massage therapy on patients' perceptions of post-operative pain. Results indicated that massage produced a significant reduction in patients' perceptions of pain over a 24 hour period.

3. Twelve hospital staff (10 registered nurses and 2 nonmedical ward staff) working in a large tertiary care center received workplace-based, 15-minute Swedish massage treatments provided by registered massage therapists. Pain intensity and tension levels were significantly lower after massage, and relaxation levels and overall mood state improved significantly after treatments.

## Parkinson's

Sixteen adults diagnosed with idiopathic Parkinson's Disease received 30-minute massage therapy or progressive muscle relaxation sessions twice a week for five weeks (10 sessions total). Physicians rated massage therapy participants as improved in daily living activities by the end of the study. Participants also rated themselves as improved in daily functioning, having more effective and less disturbed sleep.

## Physicians' Perspectives

The purpose of this study was to examine the knowledge, opinions, and referral behavior of family physicians with respect to massage therapy and to explore factors associated with referral. Three hundred family physicians were mailed a survey containing questions about sociodemographic and practice characteristics, perceived knowledge of massage therapy, opinions about the usefulness and legislation (government regulations) of massage therapy, and referral behavior. Sixty-eight percent of respondents indicated they had minimal or no knowledge. Of the remaining most (83%) believed massage therapy was a useful adjunct to their own practice. Moreover, 71% had referred patients to massage therapists and most (72%) perceived increasing demand from their patients for massage therapy. Approximately half of the physicians surveyed supported government regulation of massage therapy. Physicians who referred patients to massage therapists generally held more positive opinions and had more knowledge of the discipline.

## Posttraumatic Stress

Massage therapy was evaluated for children experiencing severe posttraumatic stress disorder after Hurricane Andrew. Sixty 1st-5th graders demonstrating classroom behavior problems either received massage therapy or viewed videos. Subjects who received massage reported being happier and less anxious and had lower salivary cortisol levels after the therapy than the video subjects. The massage group showed more sustained changes as manifested by lower scores for anxiety, depression, and self-drawings. The massage therapy subjects were also observed to be more relaxed.

## Pregnancy

Twenty-six pregnant women were assigned to a massage therapy or a relaxation therapy group for 5 weeks. Both groups reported feeling less anxious after the first session and less leg pain after the first and last session. Only the massage therapy group, however, reported reduced anxiety, improved mood, better sleep and less back pain by the last day of the study. In addition, women in the massage therapy group had fewer complications during labor and their infants had fewer postnatal complications (e.g., less prematurity).

*Premenstrual Syndrome*

Twenty-four women with premenstrual syndrome were randomly assigned to a massage therapy or a relaxation therapy group. The massage group showed decreases in anxiety, depressed mood and pain immediately after the massage sessions. In addition, by the last day of the study the massage therapy group reported a reduction in menstrual distress symptoms including pain and water retention.

*Preterm Infants*

1. Ninety-three preterm infants were randomly assigned to a massage therapy group or a control group once they were considered medically stable. The treatment group received three daily 15-minute massages for 10 days. The massage therapy infants gained more weight per day than the control infants.

2. Tactile/kinesthetic stimulation was given to 20 preterm neonates, who were compared with a group of 20 control neonates. The stimulated neonates averaged a 47% greater weight gain per day, were more active and alert during sleep/wake behavior observations, and showed more mature habituation, orientation, motor, and range of state behavior on the Brazelton scale than control infants. Finally, their hospital stay was 6 days shorter, yielding a cost savings of approximately $3,000 per infant.

*Sexual Abuse*

Women who had experienced sexual abuse were given a 30-minute massage twice a week for 1 month. Immediately after the massage the women reported being less depressed and less anxious and their salivary cortisol levels decreased following the session. Over the 1-month treatment period the massage therapy group experienced a decrease in depression and in life event stress. The relaxation therapy control group also reported a decrease in anxiety and depression. However, their stress hormones did not change, and they reported an increasingly negative attitude toward touch.

*Spinal Cord Injuries*

The study assessed the effects of massage therapy on depression, functionality and upper body muscle strength and range of motion on spinal cord injury patients. Although both the massage and exercise group appeared to benefit from treatment, only the massage group showed lower anxiety and depression scores and significantly increased their muscle strength and wrist range of motion.

*Surgery*

1. This study comprised 59 patients having cataract surgery. The patients were divided into those having a hand massage 5 minutes before surgery and those not receiving a hand massage. After the hand massage, the psychological anxiety levels, systolic and diastolic blood pressures, and pulse rate were significantly lower than before the massage. The hand massage significantly decreased epi-

nephrine and norepinephrine levels in the experimental group while epineph-rine, norepinephrine, and cortisol levels increased in the control group.

2. This study investigated the impact of foot massage and guided relaxation on the well-being of patients who had undergone coronary artery bypass graft surgery. Increased calm scores occurred for the massage group. There was a clear (non-significant) trend across all psychological variables for both foot massage and, to a lesser extent, guided relaxation to improve psychological well-being. Both interventions were well received by the subjects.

### Transplants

This study investigated the effects of Therapeutic Touch and massage therapy on the outcomes of engraftment time, complications, and perceived benefits of therapy during bone marrow transplant. A significantly lower score for central nervous system or neurological complications was noted for subjects who received massage therapy compared with the control group; however, no differences were found among the 3 groups with respect to the other 10 complication categories or in the total mean score for complications. Patients' perception of the benefits of therapy was significantly higher for those who received massage therapy compared with the friendly visit control group. The mean scores on the comfort subscale were significantly higher for patients receiving both massage therapy and therapeutic touch with the friendly visit control group.

### Voice Disorders

Subjects were recorded while reading a 3-min passage of prose text. Then, a 30-min session of massage was administered. Sixteen subjects were given the massage, while 15 controls rested, lying in silence for the same amount of time. The subjects were then recorded reading the same passage again. In the post-massage recordings, subjects had lowered their fundamental frequency and sound pressure level.

# 21 Reimbursement For Your Service by Insurance Companies

## The Current Status of Insurance Reimbursement for Massage

The issue of insurance reimbursement is a source of confusion for many in the massage industry. The question "is your work covered by insurance" sounds like a simple question, but when you try to answer it, it can become quite complicated.

Consider, for example:

- Some health insurance policies cover massage, some do not.

- Some cover massage only if it is performed in a doctor's office.

- Some states license massage, and being in a non-licensed state may affect reimbursement.

- Automobile accident victims are under auto insurance, which has a different set of rules than health insurance.

- Within the automobile insurance industry, there are different rules in different states.

The variations in insurance policies, in types of insurance cases, and in state laws, combine to make the subject of insurance reimbursement for massage a difficult one to explain. However, it is not so difficult that it cannot be understood, and this chapter will give you the basics for understanding the insurance reimbursement system as it applies to massage therapy.

## How big a part of the profession are we talking about?

In 1990, the AMTA surveyed its members about insurance reimbursement. Of those who answered the survey, 27% never participate in insurance billing. 9% have tried without success for insurance reimbursement. 34% report that they some-times receive insurance reimbursement, and 20% receive reimbursement whenever they submit a claim. These results are from AMTA members, who are probably more oriented toward medical massage than the average massage therapist. The national averages for the entire massage community would undoubtedly show a smaller percentage of the total pursuing insurance reimbursement than is reflected by that study.

Some massage therapists do exclusively medical massage, and have mastered the skills required for insurance billing. These therapists routinely receive compensation for their services from insurance companies. Others, who may not do much insurance billing, and may not understand the correct procedures, become frustrated by what they perceive as roadblocks or red tape in the insurance billing field. They tend to shy away from insurance reimbursement clients. Still other therapists decline to undertake the extra work involved in obtaining pre-approval, charting each client's progress, reporting to insurance companies, tracking billings and payments, and following up on unpaid cases. These therapists choose not to participate at all in insurance billing.

Some of the political issues discussed in Chapter 3 have their effect in the insurance billing field. The issues of credentialing, certification, and standardization of educational requirements all have relevance in this field. However, even with the national picture unsettled at this time, you as a practitioner can still learn what is necessary to successfully do insurance billing and make this a part of your practice if you choose to do so.

Before exploring "how to" do insurance billing, we will consider the advantages and disadvantages of this type of practice.

## Advantages and disadvantages

Insurance reimbursement for massage is a two-edged sword. On one side, people who could not otherwise afford massage, or who otherwise would not choose to pay for massage, become clients, and often repeat clients over a period of time. On the other side, your control over what you do as a massage therapist can be compromised, and each massage session you bill to insurance companies brings added paperwork for you.

These are the days of managed care. Doctors complain that managed care has ruined the practice of medicine. Insurance companies, eager to keep costs to a minimum, have become aggressive in telling doctors, psychotherapists and chiropractors what treatments will be paid for, at what rate, and under what conditions. Professionals who rely on insurance reimbursement are losing much of their freedom to practice as they see fit because they must conform to insurance company guidelines.

Another consideration is that you should expect at least some resistance by insurance companies to which you submit your claims for reimbursement. Insurance companies, like any other companies, make a profit by paying out less money than they take in. Most companies will pay legitimate claims, but they may require substantial paperwork to demonstrate that the claims are legitimate. Some companies resist even legitimate claims, requiring duplicative or excessive paperwork from the therapist.

Another hurdle some therapists have noticed in recent years is "bundling"— meaning that the insurance company that receives multiple claims on one client—for example chiropractic adjustment, massage therapy, and hot packs—may "bundle" them all under the chiropractic adjustment code and pay only for that service. This can cause the massage therapist to be denied compensation. One solution is to have the patient receive massage and adjustment on different days. In that situation, the treatments cannot be "bundled".

The big advantages of working for insurance compensation are higher compensation and a stable client base. The billable hourly rate for clinical massage is usually between $60 and $130. (It is often closer to the high end in licensed states and closer to the low end in non-licensed states). The possibility of insurance compensation will also bring you clients who otherwise could not afford to use your services. These can be substantial advantages to an individual who is committed to the full-time practice of massage therapy.

It is up to you to decide whether the advantages to you outweigh the disadvantages, and you may not really know until you try it.

## Your Role in the Health Care System

Massage therapists are not primary providers of health-care like physicians are. Massage therapists are "adjunct" therapists who work by prescription from a primary provider. Therefore, the doctor must provide a diagnosis and a prescription in order to initiate the process. Your therapy becomes part of the treatment plan of the referring doctor. He or she prescribes your services much the same as prescribing physical therapy or psychiatric care.

Some massage therapists have the knowledge and confidence to independently decide what a client needs and to make the insurance system work to reimburse them for what they do. Others work in a practice that can cast them more in the role of a technician, being told to work certain muscles only, or warm up an area for chiropractic adjustment. The kind of therapy you specialize in and your level of professional experience can make a large difference in this regard.

### *Relaxation Massage*

Occasionally, a doctor will prescribe massage solely for its benefits in relaxing the client. Relaxation massage may or may not be reimbursable, depending on the patient's diagnosis and treatment plan.

Some chiropractors prescribe massage for patients who are too rigid to adjust, in hopes that the massage therapist will be able to help the patient release muscle tension, thus facilitating chiropractic care. A few medical doctors also prescribe massage for patients who are overly tense, as relaxation can help with a variety of medical problems that result from anxiety.

### *Medical Massage*

Most prescriptions, however, are of a different sort, and involve what is commonly called "medical massage" or "clinical massage." This includes understanding of certain pathologies and knowledge of specific techniques that will be helpful in recovery from specific conditions and injuries. Some massage schools specialize in medical massage, and others offer some training in medical massage as part of their curriculum.

The American Manual Medicine Association, or AMMA (see page 130) has established a standardized credential for medical massage, and is attempting to have that credential widely accepted by the massage and medical professions.

No *legal* requirement exists that you take a training in medical massage before working from a doctor's prescription. However, to attempt to do medical massage without proper training would be ill-advised, and would lead to frustration for you and for the doctor. Unless you have substantial training, you will not be able to understand the doctor's orders, and you will not know what to do to carry them out. Most doctors do not understand what massage therapists know and don't know, and therefore the responsibility to keep communication clear rests with you. Unless you are familiar with the terminology and procedures to be used in medical massage, problems will arise.

A medical massage training will usually include courses in pathology, medical terminology, and neuromuscular therapy. Course work in trigger point therapy, cranio-sacral therapy, myofascial release, postural evaluation and deep tissue massage are useful. Also consider programs that include rehabilitative exercises and treatments for specific injuries and conditions.

## Professional arrangements

A variety of professional arrangements are available to a massage therapist or bodyworker who wants to work with clients for insurance reimbursement.

1. The client pays the therapist at the time of service, and the client then submits the therapist's bill to the insurance company for reimbursement.

2. The therapist works by prescription of a physician, and the therapist deals directly with the insurance company for reimbursement.

3. The therapist works closely with the prescribing physician (or physical therapist) and the physician's office handles insurance reimbursement. The physician or physical therapist pays the therapist by the hour or by sub-contract. This arrangement is most common in non-licensed states, and is especially common when massage therapists work in chiropractors' offices.

No matter which of these arrangements you participate in, you should have a good understanding of insurance guidelines and the billing process. Even if the doctor's office does your billing, you should be able to supervise and assist the process, since the doctor's office person may not understand how to classify and bill for your services.

### *Procedures for Insurance Reimbursement*

Assuming you have made the choice to work for insurance reimbursement, what follows is a nuts-and-bolts approach to the procedures you should follow. Note that there are entire manuals devoted to this topic, and the brief discussion in this chapter is meant to get you started, but cannot answer every question or cover every issue.

### Step One—Preapproval

When a new client comes to you for insurance reimbursed work, your first task is to make sure they have a doctor's referral or prescription. It is possible to receive insurance reimbursement without a referral letter in some locations, but it is a safer practice to always have a referral letter.

A sample Physician's Prescription Letter of Referral is on page 192. You should create your own Letter of Referral on your own letterhead. In the space titled "Treatment to include" create a list of the treatments you are able to do so the physician can check them off. Use accepted orthopedic language in this section so the physician will be comfortable with it.

Try to obtain a completed Letter of Referral for each client you will be working with. It establishes medical necessity, and it also lets the physician know what you do.

At your initial meeting with a client, in addition to reviewing the letter of referral, obtain the following information:
Patient's name
Date of birth
Social Security Number
Address and Phone Numbers
Date of Injury
Patient's Employer
Insurance Company's Name, Address, Telephone Number
Policy Number and Name of Insured Party

From the physician's referral or prescription note the following information:
Diagnosis codes
Frequency of Treatments
Total Number of Treatments
Name and UPIN# (Doctor's ID#) of Referring Physician
Statement That Massage Therapy is Medically Necessary

Once you have the above information, contact the client's insurance company and ask for preapproval. State that you are a massage therapist, and that the treatment has been declared "medically necessary" by a physician. You may want to seek preapproval for "soft tissue mobilization" or "myofascial release" rather than "massage". Find out how many visits will be paid for, how much the company will pay per visit, what CPT code procedures are acceptable, and whether there are any restrictions on who performs the service or where it is performed.

Write down the name of the person you spoke with and the date. Make note of the answers to all of the above questions, and make sure you have the correct phone number and extension in case you need to reach this person again to follow up. Place the note in the client's file for future reference.

### Step Two—Documentation

The first session should be documented in a separate report titled "Report of First Massage Therapy". Detail your objective findings, the client's symptoms, and any postural or range of motion measurements you made. This report will serve as a baseline from which you can measure future progress.

Each session should be individually documented. The customary format is the SOAP format. This stands for Subjective, Objective, Assessment, Plan/Prognosis.

> *Subjective* refers to the complaints and symptoms as the client expresses them. What pain is she having, and how often?

> *Objective* refers to postural distortions, gait pattern, and range of motion evaluation, and all measurable limitations.

> *Assessment* refers to the improvement resulting from this session. Did pain levels drop? Are there structural improvements? What aspects of the treatment plan are working ?

> *Plan/Prognosis* refers to the future treatment plans. Note goals for this client, including which muscles or regions of the body need treatment and what techniques are to be used.

Some therapists have modified the SOAP format to SOTAP format. The added "T" is for *Treatment,* and in this category they list the therapeutic procedures used in the session, such as massage (Mass), neuromuscular therapy (NMT), myofascial release (MFR), therapeutic exercise (Ther-X) for example. These prefixes are matched with insurance CPT codes for use on the HCFA insurance form.

After several visits, a "Progress Report" may be required to show the status of the client's treatment. This report compares all the objective client information to date with the measurements made at the initial visit, and reports on the change (if any) in the client's conditions and any circumstances that may be interfering with the client's progress.

### Step Three—Billing the Company

Submit your bill for insurance reimbursement on HCFA Form 1500. This form must include the CPT codes used by practitioners of physical medicine, and should be filled out in the language used by health care providers nationally. The CPT code book is updated annually and is available from the American Medical Association.

The following codes listed in the 2005 CPT code book are the ones most commonly used by massage therapists and bodyworkers:

97124 Massage
97140 Manual Therapy

The following codes are less commonly used by massage therapists and bodyworkers, but may be appropriate for your work.

97010 Application of hot or cold packs
97039 Unlisted Modality
97139 Unlisted Therapeutic Procedure
97110 Therapeutic Exercises (may require advanced training)
97530 Therapeutic Activities (may require advanced training)

Consult the current edition of the *CPT Manual* to determine which codes are currently in use, and to find out the exact definitions of each code so you can assure you are using a code that correctly describes your work.

Most insurance companies base their allowable fees on a national or regional average, and will furnish you with their schedule of fees upon request.

Note that if you are providing services under a Worker's Compensation claim, lower fees are paid, different CPT codes are used, and different rules apply to insurance billing. An explanation of how to do Worker's compensation billing is beyond the scope of this chapter.

### Step Four—Follow-up

If you do not receive payment within 45 days after you submit your bill, contact the representative at the insurance company (see the note you made when you called for preapproval). Make sure the bill has been received, and find out if there is any reason it has not been paid, or when you can expect payment. If forms have been incorrectly completed, your claim could be substantially delayed. Finding out about the error can help you clear it up.

Other times, simply drawing attention to your claim can help the wheels of bureaucracy turn a little faster; sometimes the "squeaky wheel" gets the oil. Send a written follow up or "tracer" stating "Tracer: please send payment or reason for non-payment".

If the company asks you to reduce your fee, you can send a "rebuttal" explaining in detail why your fees are appropriate. If your claim goes unpaid after you have sent two tracers, you have the option of filing a complaint with the state insurance commission. If the company is contacted by the state insurance commission, you can expect your claim to receive significant attention. Take this step only if diligent and reasonable collection efforts have failed.

### Avoid Billing Pitfalls

Some common reasons that claims are rejected or delayed and how to avoid them:

*Untimely billing.* Send out bills every two to four weeks.

*Incorrect dates.* Carefully verify all dates on your billing forms.

*Incomplete or unusual diagnosis.* Doctor's diagnosis must be clear and follow coding books.

*Diagnosis and treatment codes mismatched.* Make sure your treatment codes are compatible with the Doctor's diagnosis codes and are appropriate for that condition.

*Blank spaces on billing form.* Fill in all spaces, indicating "N/A" or "none" when necessary.

*Multiple same-day visits.* Avoid submitting bills for different services of the same date. Schedule doctor visits and massage sessions on different days.

*Unclear or excessive charges.* Your fees must be itemized, and you total of your fees for each claim. Know the prevailing fees in yc kind of work.

*Medical necessity.* Send prescription or doctor's referral letter with your claim form.

*Use standard forms.* While the HCFA 1500 "superbill" is not required, and technically any form can be used to submit a claim for reimbursement, use the HCFA 1500 to avoid missing any required items and to avoid having your claim singled out for "special" attention.

*Describe your work correctly.* When speaking with insurance representatives, use the terms "soft tissue mobilization" or "neuromuscular re-education," since "massage" is often interpreted as relaxation massage and excluded from coverage.

## Kinds of Insurance

One complicating aspect of this field is that there are different kinds of insurance carriers you may be submitting to. What follows is a brief discussion of the kinds of insurance you may encounter in this field, and how they differ.

*Workers' Compensation.* Generally a reliable payer; stay strictly within the authorized number of treatments, and work only on the regions of the body that are diagnosed and approved by the adjuster.

*Automobile Insurance.* Each policy will have a PIP (Personal Injury Protection) limit. This is the total amount available to pay all health care claims. Inquire at the time of preapproval as to the amount of PIP coverage, and whether the remaining balance is sufficient to pay for your treatment. Generally a reliable payer; when benefits expire, client will be responsible for balance if Financial Responsibility Form has been signed (see below). It is also possible to file a lien against the client's recovery for the cost of your services.

*Liability Insurance.* In rare cases, liability insurance will be responsible for payment for massage, such as a slip-and-fall in a grocery store. When preapproved, these carriers are usually reliable in paying for treatment. Sometimes payment is withheld until the end of treatment.

*Group Health Insurance/Indemnity Policies.* These policies usually have an annual deductible that must be met before benefits are paid to the insured, as well as a client co-pay amount, such as 20% of your fee. You would then bill 80% of your fee to the insurance company, and if the deductible is not yet satisfied, your fee would go toward the deductible. Billing this type of insurance carrier involves more details and restrictions than the types described above. These carriers are usually reliable payers after proper preapproval.

## Financial Responsibility Form

Except as to Workers' Compensation, all clients may be made responsible to pay fees that insurance will not reimburse. This form should be signed at the first office visit. Many clients have never considered that they might be responsible for fees insurance will not pay, and some therapists choose not to use a Financial Responsibility Form, choosing instead to waive their fee if insurance will not pay.

If you choose to have a Financial Responsibility Form, either consult an attorney to have a form drawn up, or if you are comfortable with your ability to write clearly, create your own form by which your clients acknowledge that they are financially responsible to pay for your services if insurance reimbursement is denied for any reason.

### States With Licensure vs. States Without Licensure

Practitioners in Washington State benefit from a 1996 law that requires insurance companies to cover expenses for health care by *any* licensed health professionals, including massage therapists. Therefore, all health insurance policies in Washington State must reimburse for massage therapy.

In the other states, the right to reimbursement for massage is not as well established. However, when all the proper procedures are followed, insurance reimbursement for massage should be received in states with massage licensure (see State Licensing Chart on page 151) and may also be available in states that do not have statewide massage licensing.

### Litigation and the "Letter of Protection"

In a personal injury case, you may be asked to wait until the conclusion of the lawsuit to be paid for your work. Your client's attorney may offer you a Letter of Protection that guarantees you will be paid out of the settlement or judgment.

Be aware, however, that there is not always enough money available to pay everyone. Claims may be paid in the order they are received, and if the funds are exhausted before yours is paid, you can lose out. Some litigation cases guarantee 100% payment, but usually you must wait until massage therapy treatment is completed.

Most of these claims are paid eventually, and if you can do without the money at present, it can be a welcome surprise to finally receive a large check for work long since completed.

### Fees and rate structures—legal and practical issues

Legally, you are *not* permitted to charge different rates for cash clients and for insurance reimbursement clients. Doing so constitutes insurance fraud.

This creates the unfair situation that the record-keeping, progress notes, billing and follow-up needed for insurance reimbursement work all go unpaid. As a result, working for insurance reimbursement can result in a substantially lower hourly rate when all of the additional tasks are figured in.

There are a couple of things you can legitimately do about this. First, while it is fraudulent to bill different charges to cash and insurance clients for the *same* service, it is not fraudulent to bill different charges for *different* services. Therefore, if you offer "relaxation massage" to cash clients for $60.00 per hour and "injury treatment" to insurance clients for $105.00 per hour, there is no fraud involved, assuming the two kinds of sessions you offer really are different.

Another possible solution is to establish a co-pay policy for insurance clients. Choose an amount that reasonably compensates you for the extra work involved in insurance billing, and establish that amount as a co-pay from your client at the time of service. You will then secure your customary fee for all the time you spend. The client may actually benefit from having a personal investment in the outcome of the therapy, becoming more involved in the healing process as a result.

## A Few Words About HIPAA

In 2003, the federal law was amended to put in place privacy protections relating to the electronic transmission of patient information.

If you submit your claims to insurance companies on paper, the following does not apply to you. However, if you communicate with health plans or insurance companies by any electronic means (other than telephone), you may be subject to a new group of regulations.

To find out if your transactions fall under HIPAA, you can visit the government's official HIPAA website, www.hhs.gov/ocr/hipaa and follow the link "Am I a Covered Entity". This will guide you to a definition of "covered transactions" and you can assess whether the law applies to your practice.

A complete discussion of HIPAA requirements is beyond the scope of this chapter, but if you are subject to HIPAA, you need to take steps that will:

- Notify patients about their privacy rights and how their information can be used.

- Adopt and implement privacy procedures for your practice.

- Train employees so that they understand the privacy procedures.

- Designate an individual to be responsible for seeing that the privacy procedures are adopted and followed.

- Secure patient records containing individually identifiable health information so that they are not readily available to those who do not need them.

———————————————

This chapter has provided you with "the basics."

You may feel comfortable taking this information and beginning to bill insurance companies, or you may feel that you need additional information and guidance. See the resources on pages 212, 213 and 216 and consider also people in your community who have expertise in insurance billing who could give you some help or instruction as you get started.

# Myofascial Associates

*Specializing in Neuromuscular & CranioSacral Therapy Injury Rehabilitation*

123 Maple Street • Suite ABC • Local Medical Park • Smallville, New York12345
t. (555) 296-7566 • f. (555) 296-1657

PRESCRIPTION/LETTER OF REFERRAL

| Patient's Name | Address | | |
|---|---|---|---|
| | City | State | Zip |

| Date of Birth | Date of Accident | Sex:  Male ☐  Female ☐ | S.S.# |
|---|---|---|---|

| ICD-9-CM Principal Diagnosis | Date |
|---|---|

**Treatment to include:**

**Treatment for the following area(s)/Diagnosis Codes**

_____ 784.0 Headaches    _____ 847.0 Cervical Strain/Sprain    _____ 840.0 Shoulder Strain/Sprain 840.9 Unspecified Upper Extremities: R _____  L _____
B_____ 842.0 Wrist Strain/Sprain: R _____  L _____  B _____    _____ 847.1 Thoracic Strain/Sprain    _____ 847.2 Lumbar Strain/Sprain
_____ 846.0 Lumbosacral Strain/Sprain  _____ 724.3 Sciatica (pain in leg, no back pain)  _____ 844.9 Unspecified site of knee and leg (strain/sprain):R _____
L _____    _____ 848.5 Pelvic Strain/Sprain  _____ 723.4 Cervical Radiculitis  _____ 354.0 Carpal Tunnel Syndrome
_____ Other:_____
Safety Measures:_____

**Orders of Discipline and Treatment Plan**

Duration:  _____ 8 weeks  _____ 6 weeks  _____ 6 weeks  _____ Other_____
Frequency:  _____ Daily  _____ 3x/weekly  _____ 2x/weekly  _____ Weekly  _____ Biweekly  _____ Monthly

Medically Necessary:  _____ Yes  _____ No
Start of Care:_____

**Physician's Name, Address, and Telephone**

| Physician's Signature | Date |
|---|---|

**Physician's U.P.I.N.**

# 22 Keeping Client and Financial Records

There are three basic kinds of records to keep; records you need to file your taxes, records about the operation of your practice, and records about each individual client.

## Tax records

These are your records of all the money you earn and all the money you spend on deductible items. If you should be called on one day to demonstrate to the IRS the truth of all the entries in your tax return, you will need to produce accurate records of your income and deductions. These records should be kept four years after your return is filed in case the IRS chooses to audit your return at a later date.

## Business records

These are the records you keep to give you a better understanding of your own practice. Different practices have different slow and busy times. Your practice may slow down for three weeks every August, which would make that a perfect time for your vacation in the Colorado Rockies. If you don't keep accurate records, you might not see that pattern, and might wind up staying in town during your slow season and leaving when clients will miss you more.

## Client records

Client records allow you to better know and serve each client. Your records will let you know basic personal and medical information about each client, and will show you their history of receiving treatments from you. When appropriate, your records will give you an at-a-glance view of how your treatments affected specific problems or situations in your clients' lives.

This chapter discusses how to keep each of these three kinds of records, and suggests some ways to design your own record-keeping system that will make the whole process easier and more efficient. Sample forms appear at the end of the chapter. You may copy and use these forms, modify them to suit you, or create your own.

## *Record-keeping For Tax-Time*

The records you need to keep are those proving your *income* and your *deductions*. Chapter 19 explains income and deductions.

The main things you should do to support proper tax record-keeping are 1) write down every payment you receive for your work in some type of ledger, 2) keep track of your automobile business mileage in a ledger, and 3) keep bills, receipts and canceled checks in one container until the end of the year, when you can sort them into categories and tally them up.

**SHOE** by Jeff MacNelly

### Recording income and business mileage

There is no required form for these records. The only requirement is that they be *accurate* and *complete*. If your car has a trip odometer, you can easily compute miles for each business trip by resetting the trip odometer to zero when you begin, and reading the trip odometer when you finish. Keep your log in the car, and record the mileage when you finish each business trip.

No matter what system you decide to use, take the time *each day* to record all of the day's business activity. Record the day's business mileage, and all income you receive each day. Get in the habit of recording each day's business activity before you go to sleep.

## *Records of Business Activity*

Your records should show you your business activity for each day, each week, each month, and each year. It takes a minimum amount of effort to translate your business records into a useful chart, and the rewards can be substantial.

If you do not have a convenient source of graph paper, do a Google search for "printable graph paper" and you will locate several sites offering free printable graph paper you can use.

Charting your business activity gives you information about when you can expect seasonal ups and downs, it tells you whether your overall business activity is going up, going down, or staying about the same, and it can give you feedback about whether particular promotions produced results, and to what extent.

During some slow weeks, I could have become depressed or pessimistic about the progress of my practice. Instead, I glanced at my business activity chart, and I saw that last month I had a slow week and it was in-between two better weeks.

Instead of thinking my practice was going sour, I realized I was experiencing a normal fluctuation and nothing was going wrong. That insight did a lot for my emotional health.

Business Activity          Year_____

## Keeping Client Records

If you or your clients are going to bill insurance companies for your services, you need to keep detailed records for each treatment you perform. See Chapter 21 dealing with billing insurance companies, and see pages 212–213 for resources to help with record-keeping for insurance clients.

Even if you are not dealing with insurance billing, you should keep client records. For each client, you should have a completed intake form that includes the following basic information:

- Date of first treatment

- Client's name, address, phone numbers and e-mail address

- Medical history (as much as you feel is necessary)

- Previous experience with massage or bodywork

- Current symptoms or problems

- Reason for seeking treatment

Date of first treatment will be useful to you later as you review your records on a particular client.

The address is necessary if you ever want to mail something to the client (such as a Christmas card, promotional flyer, or bill) or do a house call.

Client_____ Date of birth _____

Address_____

_____Phone (_____) _____

Date of first treatment_____

Occupation_____

Medical History:
Previous major Illnesses:



Previous broken bones or other
injuries:



Are you currently under a physician's
care?

    Physician _____

    For what condition? _____

    Are you taking any medications? _____

Current Condition:
Areas of pain or discomfort:



Reasons for seeking massage:



Have you previously had massage or
other bodywork? What type?



What do you do to manage your stress?



What is your routine of exercise?

Weekly Business Log

Week of _____

| Date | Client | fee | miles |
|------|--------|-----|-------|
|      |        |     |       |
|      |        |     |       |
|      |        |     |       |
|      |        |     |       |
|      |        |     |       |
|      |        |     |       |
|      |        |     |       |
|      |        |     |       |
|      |        |     |       |
|      |        |     |       |
|      |        |     |       |
|      |        |     |       |
|      |        |     |       |
|      |        |     |       |
|      |        |     |       |
|      |        |     |       |
|      |        |     |       |
|      |        |     |       |
|      |        |     |       |
|      |        |     |       |
|      |        |     |       |
|      |        |     |       |
|      |        |     |       |
|      |        |     |       |
|      |        |     |       |
|      |        |     |       |
|      |        |     |       |

The phone number is necessary in the event of cancellation or change of plans on short notice.

Medical history gives you a better sense of how your treatment can fit into this person's whole picture, and can be useful in discovering contraindications for part or all of the treatment you will give.

Whether the person has previously had bodywork helps you to know how to approach this session.

Current symptoms or problems, and reason for seeking treatment give you information about what this client wants from you. Failure to get this information can result in doing a session that does not satisfy a client. They will not usually spontaneously tell you what they expect from your work.

The sample intake form on the next page is one you can modify to suit your own needs. If you do remedial work, you may want substantially more medical information. Keep in mind that the intake form has two basic purposes. First, it provides you with contact information and essential data about your clients. Second, it serves to open a dialogue between you and your client, and thereby begin the therapeutic relationship. It is a tool for communication.

If the client's care does not involve insurance billing, you may not need to keep further records for this client, except those necessary for business activity and tax purposes. If you do need to keep further records, you can use the back of the client's intake form, or create a separate file for records about continuing care clients.

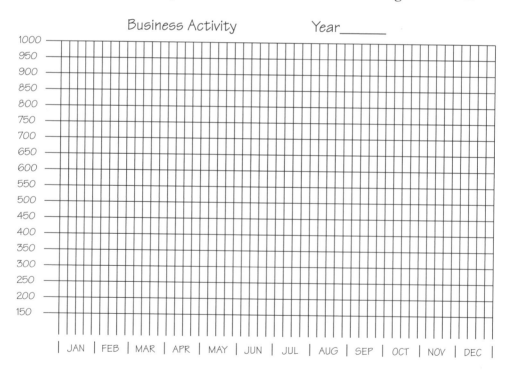

## *Complying with HIPAA*

Effective in 2003, congress amended the Health Insurance Portability and Accountability Act to require new privacy protections for patient information. Much of the Act relates to health care providers who transmit client information electronically. These provisions generally do not apply to massage therapists, especially if your practice does not include insurance billing.

If your practice involves any relationship between you and a third-party payor, such as a health plan or insurance company, you may be subject to the provisions of HIPAA. See the discussion of HIPAA at the end of Chapter 21 for further information.

# 23 Managing Your Money
## Some Ideas on
## Financial Planning

In the early years of your massage career, you will not have much money to manage. Spare dollars will go to necessities, and to improvements in your professional equipment.

In time, however, success will bring with it prosperity, and when it does, you will need to give at least a little thought to how to manage your money.

## Savings

One of the hardest things for a self-employed person to do is to put money into a savings account. However, it is a very important habit to get into. Consider the following expenses you will have:

1. Quarterly estimated tax payments

2. Health insurance, auto insurance

3. Professional association dues

These expenses come quarterly, semi-annually, or annually. They can put a strain on your budget if you are living from month to month. Having a reserve in your savings (or checking) account makes life easier when these expenses come due.

Open a savings account at your bank. Start it with at least $100, and add whatever amounts you can. Avoid making withdrawals unless absolutely necessary. The fact that you have a few hundred dollars, or a couple of thousand dollars, can be very comforting when the mechanic tells you that you need a transmission overhaul.

Beyond this issue of emergency reserves to meet unforeseen expenses, you will also want to consider the larger financial reserves you will need to meet the major expenses you can expect sooner or later:

4. Buying a new car

5. Buying a home

6. Rearing children

7. Retirement

These are the expenses that require you to make, and save, substantial sums of money, and to manage that money in a way that gives you the most advantage out of it.

## Long-range planning

As a rule of thumb, there are two critical points in the careers of many would-be massage therapists—two years into a career and five years into a career.

Many practitioners give up somewhere near the two-year mark. Either they failed to pursue any organized marketing approach, or they gave up before getting the benefit of the approach they were using.

Those who survive the two-year mark usually find some degree of success in the field. Another critical point often comes at the five-year mark, when the physical nature of the work may begin to take its toll, or the practitioner may decide to branch off into another kind of work.

Practitioners who stay with the work longer than five years can usually keep doing the work practically indefinitely. Some keep working into their seventies. If you are staying in the field longer than five years, you will do well to take up the study of estate planning and investment.

### *You can't live on Social Security*

Consider what you will have to live on when you retire.

Social security, once considered rock solid, now seems in danger of not surviving long enough to provide benefits for younger workers.

Even if it survives intact until you are ready to receive benefits, the benefits may be enough to keep a roof over your head, and bread on the table, but it is not enough money to *live* on.

Before you reach retirement age, you should have put aside enough to create your own retirement plan. The earlier you start, the easier it will be.

## Kinds of Savings Plans

Savings plans can take many forms.

1. You can stockpile cash, but if you do so you earn no interest, and can lose everything in a theft or fire.

2. You can keep your money in a savings account, certificate of deposit, or money market account. These will earn a small amount of interest, and your money will be as safe as possible.

3. You can choose a "tax shelter" keyed to retirement. While you must still pay self-employment tax on the money you put into your retirement plan, you do not pay federal income tax on this money. You pay income tax on the retirement money only when you receive it, at retirement. Tax breaks available to retired persons may help you pay lower taxes on your money at retirement time than you would now.

# Tax Shelter Retirement Plans

One major advantage of tax shelter retirement plans is that they force you to keep your money invested until you retire. Because of high penalties for withdrawing money prior to age 59½, you are forced to keep your "nest egg" safe for your future. You lose the flexibility to deal with your money on a whim; you have fewer options now, but more security later.

The government makes this appealing by giving you a slightly better tax treatment if you put your money into a retirement plan. Consider the following example:

It is April 14th, and you are preparing your tax return for the previous year. You do all your computations, find out you owe $2,104 in income tax (we are ignoring social security tax in this example, because retirement plans do not change your social security tax).

If you use some money you have saved to make a contribution of $2,000 to a qualified retirement plan, your income tax bill will be reduced to $1,804 (assuming you pay 15% income tax). You therefore reduce your tax by $300 by placing $2,000 in a retirement plan. As long as you make this contribution by April 15, it counts as a deduction for the preceding year's taxes.

# Save now, save later

To take the example a step further, consider the long-term effects of this decision. If you *do not* make the contribution to your retirement plan, you must spend $300 of the $2,000 on taxes. This leaves you with $1,700.

Assume that you keep this $1,700 invested at "average" interest rates for thirty years. Interest rates are always changing, but as a rule of thumb, you can figure that money well-invested will double itself every ten years. Therefore, in 30 years, an investment should grow to eight times the original amount. (After 10 years, the original investment will double; after 20 years it will double again, or be four times the original amount; after 30 years it will double a third time, and be eight times the original amount).

This rule of thumb tells us that $1,700 today will be $13,600 in 30 years.

Now consider the alternative where you put $2,000 in a retirement account. The same rule of thumb tells us that the $2,000 today will turn into $16,000 in 30 years. However, this $16,000 will be subject to income tax when you receive it at retirement. Current rates of income tax, 15%, would reduce that $16,000 to $13,600—exactly the same amount as if you had paid your $300 tax in the first place and left the $1,700 invested.

*However,* unless you are a person of incredible will power, you *will not* leave that $1,700 alone for 30 years to gain interest. What you will wind up with will be somewhat less than the $13,600 you know you can count on if you sock the money away in a retirement plan where you cannot reach it without substantial penalties.

In addition, tax breaks available to retired persons may make it possible for you to pay less than 15% tax on the money when you receive it at retirement. Any such breaks you get make it definitely advantageous to have your money in a retirement account.

## Kinds of Retirement Plans

There are three kinds of retirement plans available to you as a self-employed person: The IRA (Individual Retirement Account), the SEP (Simplified Employee Pension Plan, a form of IRA); and the Keogh.

### *IRA and ROTH IRA*

Easy to set up and widely available, an IRA allows you to shelter up to a maximum of $4,000 per year. IRAs are designed for people without large incomes. Roth IRAs, unlike the other retirement plans, do not shelter your income from taxes; the contributions to a Roth IRA come from after-tax dollars, and the withdrawals are tax-free so long as money is kept in at least five years, or you qualify as a first-time homebuyer or are disabled.

### *SEP*

Also easy to set up and widely available, the SEP allows you to shelter up to 15% of your earnings (to a maximum contribution of $30,000 in any one year)

### *Keogh*

Two types of plans exist, one which requires a set contribution each year, and one which does not. The maximum contribution is $40,000 per year. Keoghs are more complicated to set up, and can be more expensive to create and maintain than IRAs or SEPs.

IRAs and SEPs can be set up any time before April 15, and will still be valid for the previous year's taxes. Keoghs must be *set up* by December 31 in order to be valid for that tax year, although contributions can still be made until April 15 of the next year.

You also have the option of setting up a 401(k) as a self-employed individual. This allows almost unlimited contributions to your retirement account, but it is costly to set up and maintain. If you have very high income, consult with a financial professional about whether this might be the best option for you.

If you are interested in establishing a retirement account, start with your local bank, savings and loan, or insurance advisor. Chances are, they can advise you and set up an account for you, often at no charge. Also check with your accountant or financial advisor. Once established, these accounts cannot be modified, so be very careful that you understand how your account will fit into your future plans.

# V

# Equipment
# and Other
# Professional
# Resources

# Massage Tables and Chairs

All of the following companies ship their products nationwide. They will all send you brochures or information packets about their massage tables and other products at your request.

## Massage Table / Chair Manufacturers

**Astra Lite Tables**
120 Manfree Rd.
Watsonville, CA 95076
(800) 368-5483 or (831) 763-0397
www.astra-lite.com

Extremely lightweight, portable table; stationary table; fixed or push-button adjustable height, with recessed legs and cables and built-in face cradles; bolsters, carrying cases

**Colorado Healing Arts**
4635 Broadway
Boulder, CO 80304
(800) 728-2426 or (303) 449-2425
www.coloradohealingartsproducts.com

Portable and non-portable tables, oils, linens, bolsters, massage tools, charts, professional office forms and other items. Free brochure includes "How to select a massage table."

**Creative Touch**
P.O. Box 912
Lotus, CA 95651
(800) 441-6759 or (916) 441-6759
www.massageresources.com

Lightweight, adjustable height, oval massage tables and accessories

**Custom Craftworks**
P.O. Box 24621
Eugene, OR 97402
(800) 627-2387
www.customcraftworks.com

A selection of stationary and adjustable height portable tables; on-site chair, electric lift table, desktop portable support, bolsters, carrying cases,—and accessories. Lifetime warranty on all wood tables

**Earthlite**
3210 Executive Ridge Dr.
Vista, CA 92083
(800) 872-0560 or (760) 599-1112
www.earthlite.com

Full line of portable, stationary and electric lift massage tables; bolsters fleece pads, table skate, carry case, stools, headrest covers, flannel sheets

**Galaxy Enterprises, Inc.**
5411 Sheila St.
City of Commerce, CA 90040
(800) 876-4599
www.galaxymfg.com

Lightweight, portable, adjustable height massage table

**Golden Ratio Woodworks**
P.O Box 440
Emigrant, MT 59027
(800) 345-1129
www.goldenratio.com

Full line of stationary and portable tables, spa tables, on-site chair, 14-pound on-site chair, covers, oils, bolsters, charts, books and other accessories.

**Living Earth Crafts**
3210 Executive Ridge Dr.
Vista, CA 92081
(800) 358-8292 or (760) 597-2155
www.livingearthcrafts.com

Complete line of stationary and portable tables, including very inexpensive portable, on-site chair, desk-top face cradle, oils, linens, books, charts, music, videos, and more.

**Northern Touch, Inc**
(877) 948-6824 or (780) 921-2299
www.northerntouch.net

Massage tables with lifetime warranty on structure and foam

**Oakworks, Inc.**
**923 E. Wellspring Rd.**
New Freedom, PA 17349
(717) 235-6807 or (800) 558-8850
www.oakworks.net

Complete line of stationary and portable tables, on-site chair, carrying cases, bolsters and sheets

**Pisces Productions**
380 Morris St., Suite A
Sebastopol, CA 95472
(800) 822-5333 or (707) 829-1496
www.piscespro.com

Vertical to horizontal, adjusting on-site chair, portable tables ultra-light tables, and accessories

**Robert Hunter Bodywork Tables**
910 SE Stark St.
Portland, OR 97214
(800) 284-3988
www.RobertHunter.com

Stationary and portable adjustable height tables, sheets, massage oil, carrying cases, customization available

**Stronglite Massage Table Kits**
255 Davidson St.
Cottage Grove, OR 97424
(541) 942-0130
(800) BUY-KITS (800-289-5487)
www.stronglite.com

Portable, lightweight adjustable height, inexpensive tables, on-site partially assembled tables and kits at substantially lower cost. Stronglite also makes the ComforTable line of massage tables.

**Touch America**
P.O. Box 1304
Hillsborough, NC 27278
(919) 732-6968
(800) 678-6824
www.touchamerica.com

Complete line of stationary and portable tables, spa products, acoustic music table, on-site chair, stool, sheets, miscellaneous items workshop series, spa therapies, hydrokinetic Vichy.

# Powered Height Adjustment Tables

**Comfort Craft Bodywork Tables**
P.O. Box 520638
Longwood, FL 32752
(407) 830-7332 or (800) 858-2838
www.comfortcraft.com

**Custom Craftworks**
P.O. Box 24621
Eugene, OR 97402
(541) 345-2712 or (800) 627-2387
www.customcraftworks.com

**Earthlite**
3210 Executive Ridge Dr.
Vista, CA 92083
(800) 872-0560 or (760) 599-1112
www.earthlite.com

# Very Light Portable Tables (25 lbs. or less)

**Astra Lite Tables**
120 Manfree Rd.
Watsonville, CA 95076
(800) 368-5483 or (831) 763-0397
www.astra-lite.com

**Golden Ratio Woodworks**
P.O Box 440
Emigrant, MT 59027
(800) 345-1129
www.goldenratio.com

**Pisces Productions**
380 Morris St., Ste. A
Sebastopol, CA 95472
(800) 822-5333 or (707) 829-1496
www.piscespro.com

**Stronglite Massage Table Kits**
255 Davidson St.
Cottage Grove, OR 97424
(541) 942-0130 or (800) 289-5487
www.stronglite.com

**Ultra-Light Inc.**
4975 Crescent Technical Court
St. Augustine, FL 32086
(904) 749-7979 or (800) 999-1971
www.ultralightcorp.com

## Specialty Tables

**Somatron Corp.**
8503 N. 29th St.
Tampa, FL 33604
(800) 544-4294
www.somatron.com

Vibro-acoustic massage table that directs vibrations through the client's body during the massage

# Massage Supply Stores and Catalogue Services

**Alternative Essentials**
144 Western Ave.
Augusta, ME 04330
(207) 623-4551

Massage and physical therapy supplies, books, charts music, gift certificates, accessories, massage tables and chairs, aromatherapy supplies

**Advanced Health Products**
2263 Old Middlefield Way
Mountain View, CA 94043
(650) 969-4606 or 1-800 676 7976
www.massageproducts.com

Massage equipment and supplies, oils, linens, tables, chairs, aromatherapy supplies, yoga supplies. Showroom in Southern California, free shipping on most massage tables and massage chairs

**Banner Therapy Products**
891 Broadway St.
Asheville, NC 28804
(888) 277-1188 or (828) 277-1188
www.BannerTherapy.com

Aromatherapy, massage tools, oils, gels, lotions, vibrators, hot and cold packs, hydrocollators, pack chillers, paraffin baths, charts, supports, pillows, desktop portal, 30-day money back guarantee.

**Best of Nature**
10 River St.
Red Bank, NJ 07701
(800) 228-6457 or (732) 559-0022
www.bestofnature.com

Massage tables and chairs, oils, creams, lotions, liniments, essential oils, linens, self-massage tools, incense, books, videos, music, bottles and pillows

**BML (Basic Massage Lines)**
501 W. Kingshighway
Paragould, AR 72450
(800) 643-4751 or (870) 239-0993
www.bmlbasic.com

Oils, lotions, hydrocollators, vibrators, paraffin baths, hot and cold packs, massage tables and chairs, linens, bolsters, pillows, stools, other accessories

**The Body Shop**
2051 Hilltop Dr., suite A-5
Redding, CA 96002
(530) 221-1031 or (800) 736-6897

Massage Holster, aqua-relief pad, sunfresh soap, stronglite tables, aromatherapy supplies, oils, lotions, charts, face rest covers (fitted and flat).

**Buymassage.com**
Core Institute (FL)
(866) 830-0108 or (950) 222-8673
www.buymassage.com

Supplies, equipment, accessories, books, work-shops, large variety of products

**Gotyourback**
525 E. Hector St.
Conshohocken, PA 19428
(610) 834-3992
www.gotyourback.com

Massage tables and on-site chairs, accessories, oils & lotions. Large inventory, same-day shipping.

**Bodywork Central**
1533 Shattuck Ave.
Berkeley, CA 94709
orders: (888) 226-8500
www.bodyworkcentral.com

Variety of massage tables and on-site chairs, bolsters, Biotone oil & lotions, carry case, table skate, table carrier, spa supplies, body sup-port cushion, table selection assistance, yoga products.

**Bodywork Emporium**    www.bodyworkemporium.com    1-800-TABLE-4-U

338 North Coast Highway
Leucadia, CA 92024
(760) 942-9565

1451 Morena Blvd.
 San Diego, CA 92110
(619) 276-2608

414 Broadway
Santa Monica, CA 90401
(310) 394-4475

1804C Newport Blvd.
Costa Mesa, CA 92627
(949) 548-0220

4529 Sepulveda Blvd.
Sherman Oaks, CA 91403
(818) 990-6155

Large selection of massage tables and on-site chairs, massage oils and lotions, videos, books, charts, music and other supplies, on-site massage therapy.

**Edcat Enterprises**
P.O. Box 168
Daytona Beach, FL 32115
(386) 253-2385 or (800) 274-3566

Large selection of anatomical and other charts, self-massage tools, oils, lotions, tables, chairs, anatomy models, hydrocollators, hot & cold packs.

**Educating Hands School of Massage Bookstore Catalogue**
120 Southwest 8th Street
Miami, FL 33130
(800) 999-6991
www.educatinghands.com

Books, massage tables, massage oils charts, audio cassettes, videos, hot and cold application equip-ment, self-massage tools, linen and hand clean-ers, misc. items.

**Hands-on-supply**
Connecticut Center for MT Bookstore
(800) 842-9874
www.hands-on-supply.com

Oils, brochures, linens, pillows, videos, charts, books, music.

**The Health Touch**
261 Main St.
Royersford, PA 19468
(800) 890-6195 or (610) 948-5931
www.thehealthtouch.com

Oils, lotions, creams, aromatherapy supplies, mas-sage products, massage tools, massage tables. Free catalogue.

**Here's The Rub**
66 Evergreen Ave.
Warminster, PA 18974
(877) 484-3782
www.herestherub.net

Massage equipment, linens and pads, charts, oils, books, music, videos, aromatherapy, spa, hot and cold therapy

**Massage Central**
12235 Santa Monica Blvd.
Los Angeles, CA 90025
(888) 818-2040 or (310) 826-2209

Large display of massage tables and on-site chairs, and other supplies, spa and salon equipment.

| | |
|---|---|
| **Massage King**<br>(800) 290-3932<br>www.massageking.com | Tables, chairs, other supplies and specials |
| **MassageTableWarehouse**<br>(800) 224-5555<br>www.mtswarehouse.com | Massage tables and chairs from numerous makers, same-day shipping from Texas warehouse |
| **MassageWarehouse.com**<br>2775 Pacific Dr.<br>Norcross, GA 30071<br>(800) 507-3416 or (770) 582-9191<br>www.massagewarehouse.com | Large selection of tables, chairs, oils, books, and supplies for massage practitioners |
| **New England Massage Tables and Chairs**<br>20 Bridge St.<br>Manchester, NH 03101<br>(800) 545-8497<br>www.massagestore.com | Massage tables, massage chairs, oils, lotions, gels, essential oils, charts, books, self-massage tools, bolsters, hot and cold applications products, flash cards, other accessories |
| **Sunset Park Massage Supply**<br>4344 S. Manhattan Ave.<br>Tampa, FL 33611<br>(800) 344-7677 or (813) 835-7900<br>www.massagesupplies.com | Massage tables and chairs from 12 companies, accessories, charts, books, aromatherapy supplies, videos, hydrocollators, paraffin baths, lotions, oils, body & pregnancy cushions, CEU home study, etc. |

# Miscellaneous Massage Items

## Videos for Continuing Education

Many of the Catalogue and Internet sources listed above carry videos. However, two sources specialize in videos for continuing education and have a wide selection available:

**Massage Review Publications**
(954) 578-5042
www.massagereview.com

**Real Bodywork**
(888) 505-5511 or (805) 898-1539
www.realbodywork.com

## Table covers, sheets and related items:

| | |
|---|---|
| **Innerpeace**<br>P.O. Box 940<br>Walpole, NH 03608<br>1-800-949-7650<br>www.innerpeace.com | 100% cotton flannel sheets, face cradle covers, bolster slip covers and more |

## Printed items such as brochures about massage and gift certificates:

**Hemingway Massage Brochures**
(815) 877-5590
www.hemingwaymassageproducts.com

(Educational brochures about massage for display and client education)

**Information for people**
P.O. Box 1038
Olympia, WA 98507
(800) 754-9790 or (360) 754-9799
www.info4people.com

(Marketing materials, including brochures, selection of books and compassionate touch videos, display cases, gift certificates, greeting cards, post cards, sculptures)

**Sharper Communication Tools**
Sharper Cards
110 Pacific Ave., Suite 850
San Francisco, CA 94111
(800) 561-6677
www.sharpercards.com

(Business cards, appointment cars, post cards, magnets, gift certificates, bookmarks, calendars, coffee mugs, specifically designed for massage practices. Large selection of cover images. Free personalization, free stock logos, quick turn-around, satisfaction guarantee)

## *Practice Management Software:*

**Customer Pro-File**—Keeps track of clients, notes, scheduling, business records. Inexpensive program to computerize your practice.

**Land Software**
5138 Fulton St. NW
Washington, D.C. 20016
(202) 237-2733
www.landsw.com

**Easy Billing**—Produces SOAP notes and HCFA 1500 forms for insurance billing, prints letters and reports

**Marla Productions**
710 Colombia St.
Santa Fe, NM 87505
(800) 618-6136 or (505) 424-9263
www.easybillingsoftware.com

**Elite Software**—Keeps track of clients, sales, inventory, appointments, payroll, marketing.

**Elite Software**
3324 W. University Ave.
Gainesville, FL 32607
(800) 662-ELITE or (352) 335-3800
www.elite-usa.com

**MassageSOFT 5.1**—Daily appointment book, mailing lists, billing and follow-up, SOAP notes and HSCF forms.

**Get Physical! Software, Inc.**
(800) 622-0025 or (203) 622-0108
15 E. Putnam Ave., Ste. 376
Greenwich, CT
www.massageSOFT.com

**Massage Office 2.2**—Keeps track of clients, scheduling and records; will print SOAP notes onto anatomical chart and will print HCFA 1500 forms for insurance billing

> **Island Software**
> 717 Lingco Dr., Ste. 202
> Richardson, TX 75081
> (877) 384-0295 or (972) 241-0705
> www.islandsoftwareco.com

**MediSoft—The Medical Massage Office Billing System**—Keeps track of clients, scheduling and records, produces documentation and will print HCFA 1500 forms for insurance billing

> **ACTI Computer Systems**
> 1955 W. Downer Pl.
> Aurora, IL 60506
> (877) 476-1434
> www.ACTImedical.com

**TMOBS—The Massage Office Billing System**—Keeps track of clients, scheduling and records, produces documentation and will print HCFA 1500 forms for insurance billing

> **The Medical Massage Office & Associates**
> 5028 Randall Pkwy., Ste. 8
> Wilmington, NC 28403
> (888) 322-5520
> www.TMMO.biz

## *Assorted products and services:*

**My Receptionist**—The service provides you with a toll-free number, and you arrange call forwarding to have your appointment line ring in their offices. A professional receptionist answers your line with your business name, and can answer basic questions about your services, schedule your appointments, make reminder calls, take credit cards, and sell gift certificates. The service costs $29.95 per month plus a charge of seventy cents per minute for usage.

> **My Receptionist**
> 409 Main St.
> Eau Claire, WI 54701
> (800) 686-0162
> www.myreceptionist.com

**Khepra Foot Balm**—A preparation for use in massaging the feet, that creates a skin texture with a subtle resistance for better massage, eliminates foot odor, and conditions and refreshes the feet:

> **Khepra Skin Care, Inc.**
> 500 E. 36th St.
> Minneapolis, MN 55408
> (800) 367-9799
> www.khepracare.com

BodyCushion™—a contoured system of support that positions the body comfortably, prone, supine or laterally; useful for pregnancy, geriatric, disabled, on-site and seated massage:

**Body Support Systems, Inc.**
1040 Benson Way
Ashland, OR 97520
(800) 448-2400 or (541) 488-1172
www.bodysupport.com

# Magazines, Journals and Books

## Magazines

*Massage Magazine*, **www.massagemag.com**, covers a broad range of news and features of general interest to massage practitioners. Each issue also contains up-to-date nationwide licensing information. Published six times a year. Subscriptions (800) 533-4263

AMTA's *Massage Therapy Journal*, **www.amtamassage.org**, available by subscription to non-members, contains articles of interest to the general massage community, and items of special interest to AMTA members. Published four times a year. Subscriptions (877) 905-2700

ABMP's *Massage & Bodywork Magazine*, **www.abmp.com**, available by subscription to non-members, contains articles of interest to the general massage community, and items of special interest to ABMP members. Published four times a year. Subscriptions (800) 458-2267, ext. 603

## Journals

*Touch Research Abstracts—Touchpoints* This is the quarterly publication of the Touch Research Institute, Tiffany M. Field, Ph.D., director. The publication reports on the work of the Touch Research Institute in scientifically documenting the health benefits of touch, and also provides information on programs sponsored by the Institute. Subscriptions are $20.00 per year. Touchpoints/Touch Research Institute, Department of Pediatrics (D820), University of Miami School of Medicine, P.O. Box 016820, Miami, FL 33101, (305) 243-6781 or subscribe online at **www.miami.edu/touch-research**.

## On-line employment directory

**www.portablepractitioner.com** is an on-line service listing employment opportunities worldwide

## Books for Bodyworkers

The library of books for massage and bodywork seems to grow by the day. The books in the following list were selected because they can assist you with the career of massage.

## Self-Care Books

*Save Your Hands!* by Lauriann Greene. This book covers reasons for injury, common injuries, how to use your body, techniques to use or avoid, exercises, stretching and treatment. It retails for $19.95. Published by Guilded Age Press, (970) 493-3793, **www.saveyourhands.com**.

## National Certification Review Books

*Complete Review Guide for National & State Certification Examinations*, by Dr. Patrick Barron, $23.95. Publisher: Futurmed, available from **www.buymassage.com** or **www.pineislandpublishers.com**

*Massage Board Review Book*, by Don Newton, M.A., D.C., instruction on exam topics and sample questions, $26.95, available from **www.simran.com**

*Massage Therapy Exam Questions*, by Daphna Moore, Hughes Henshaw Publications, $39.00, available at **www.hugheshenshaw.com** or (321) 956-8885

*Questions & Answers*, by Daphna Moore, Hughes Henshaw Publications, $39.95, available at **www.hugheshenshaw.com** or (321) 956-8885

*Questions and Answers for Passing State and National Therapeutic Massage Examinations* and *More Questions and Answers for Passing State and National Therapeutic Massage Examination*, by Massage Review Publications, (954) 578-5055, **www.massagereview.com**. Spiral bound, 2-volume set $79.95, or $129.90 with CD Rom and Q & A set.

*Therapeutic Massage & Bodywork (Exam Review for the NCETMB)*, by Jane Garofano, Ph.D., Appleton & Lange $32.00, includes a computer diskette.

## Pathology for Massage and Bodywork

*Clinical Pathology for the Professional Bodyworker, 2nd edition*, by Don Newton, M.A., D.C., Simran Publications, $24.95. Each condition is discussed separately, along with suggestions for massage techniques and movements to assist with that malady. Available from **www.simran.com**

*Massage Therapist's Guide to Pathology*, by Ruth Werner, includes practice suggestions for each malady, $44.95, Lippincott Williams & Wilkins, available at **www.lww.com**

*Pathology A to Z, a Handbook for Massage Therapists, 2nd edition*, by Kalyani Premkumar, M.D. This book is arranged alphabetically. For each pathology, it discusses the cause, signs & symptoms, risk factors, cautions & recommendations, and notes. Optional CD-ROM. $42.95, Published by Lippincott Williams & Wilkins, **www.lww.com**

*Pocket Book of Pathology—a quick reference*, by Kalyani Premkumar, M.D., a brief version of *Pathology A to Z*, also available with a companion CD-ROM, Published by VanPub Books, 1640 16th Ave., suite 205 N.W., Calgary, AB, T2M0L6, Canada, 1-877-VANPUB-1, **www.meducational.com/vanpub**

*Recognizing Health and Illness, Pathology for Massage Therapists and Bodyworkers*, by Sharon Burch. This oversize textbook is well-organized, with each chapter covering a physiological system. It contains illustrations, study questions, references and chapter reviews. It is available from Health Positive! Publishing, P.O. Box 3818 Road, Lawrence, KS 66046, fax (888) 797-5594. $40.00 **www.healthpositive. com/schools.htm**

### Medical Massage / Clinical Massage

*The Medical Massage Office Manual, 2nd edition*, by Margery M. Callahan and David W. Luther, $59.95; to order (888) 322-5520, complete guidelines for insurance billing and reimbursement procedures, including sample forms and letters. Includes a diskette with printable forms. **www.TMMO.biz.**

*Hands Heal: Documentation for Massage Therapy: A Guide to SOAP Charting* by Diana L. Thompson, LMP. $32.95, Lippincott Williams & Wilkins, **www.lww.com.**

*Basic Clinical Massage: Integrating Anatomy and Treatment* by James H. Clay and David M. Pounds, $42.95 from Lippincott Williams & Wilkins, ISBN: 0683306537, published August, 2002

### Ethical issues for Massage and Bodywork

For those that wish to delve deeper into ethical issues than the information in Chapter 13 of this book, there are two comprehensive books dedicated to the ethics of massage and touch therapies:

*The Educated Heart*, by Nina McIntosh, MSW, Lippincott, Williams, Wilkins, **www.lww.com**, $29.95. A comprehensive volume on ethics for bodyworkers, emphasizing the need for strong boundaries and strict avoidance of dual relationships. Much of the advice in the book is most useful for bodyworkers who engage the client psychologically as well as physically, as this type of work requires stricter adherence to proper boundaries.

*Ethics of Touch*, by Ben E. Benjamin, Ph.D. and Cherie Sohnen-Moe, **www. sohnen-moe.com**, $28.00. Suitable for all types of wellness practitioners, offering many illustrative scenarios and suggestions. Reflective exercises and questions for each chapter.

### Massage for Cancer Patients and the Infirm

Findhorn Press, **www.findhornpress.com**, publishes two books about massage for cancer patients, the elderly and the infirm:

*Medicine Hands*, by Gayle MacDonald, M.S., LMT, The author reviews the medical literature and gives both a scientific and humanistic discussion of the benefits of using massage with cancer patients.

*From the Heart Through the Hands*, by Dawn Nelson. Written for the family member or caregiver who is working with cancer patients, Alzheimer's patients, the elderly and the ill who are being cared for at home.

A new book by Gayle MacDonald, M.S., LMT is *Massage for the Hospital Patient and the Medically Frail Client*, $29.95 from Lippincott, Williams and Wilkins, www.lww.com. Guidance for providing massage to patients in acute care settings and private practice clients who are medically frail.

See also **Oncology Massage**, in the Bodywork Modalities directory.

# VI

## Bodywork
## Organizations
## and
## Trainings

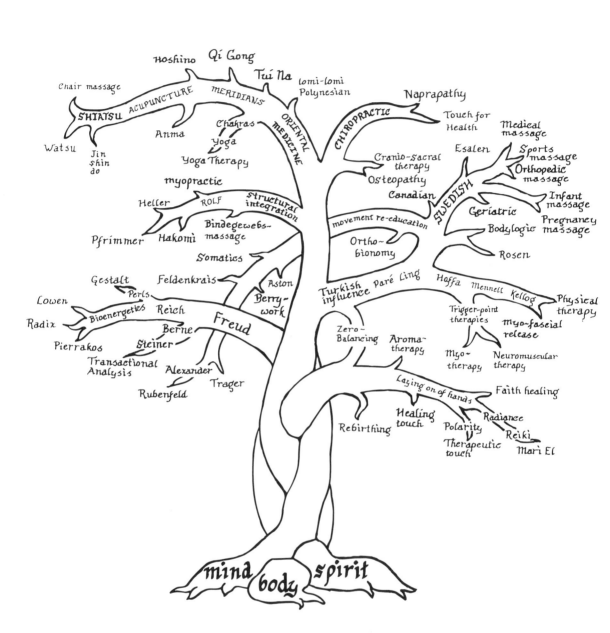

# The Bodywork Tree © 1999

Based on a concept by David Linton

# Bodywork Systems, Organizations and Trainings

For purposes of this Directory, "bodywork" refers to a body-centered therapy that is different from Swedish massage.

Some of the forms listed below are very similar to Swedish massage—for example, sports massage, Esalen, pregnancy massage. Some are entirely different from Swedish massage—for example, Alexander Technique, Reiki, Somatics Psychology.

For each form of bodywork, the listing includes a brief explanation of the nature of the work, the name and address of an official organization representing the form, if available, and in some cases, contact information for trainings and supplies.

New forms of bodywork are continually created as imaginative and dedicated bodyworkers explore their own unique gifts and systematize their work. Factors that go into the decision to include a form in this directory include how long the form has been in existence, how widely it is practiced, and whether it is taught in mainstream massage schools.

## Acupressure

See Shiatsu

## Alexander Technique

The Alexander technique is an educational method for improving coordination, and for developing awareness of unnecessary tensions in the body.

F. M. Alexander was an actor who had a problem with losing his voice. By studying his habitual movements in a mirror, he discovered ways he was using his body that created his vocal problem and was able to resolve the difficulty. He went on to create a system for enhancing balance, posture and the use of the body, which is called the Alexander technique. Practitioners refer to themselves as teachers of the Alexander method and refer to sessions as lessons.

Several websites that provide good resources concerning the Alexander technique are:

> www.alexandercenter.com
> www.alexandertech.com
> www.alexandertechnique.com
> www.ATI-net.com

## AMMA® Therapy (or ANMA)

AMMA therapy is a method of restoring the flow of life energy in the body, and is used to treat a wide range of medical conditions. It combines Oriental medical principles with a Western approach to organ dysfunction. AMMA therapy may include dietary plans, detoxification, herbs and vitamins, and therapeutic exercises.

## Applied Kinesiology (see also Touch for Health)

Applied Kinesiology is a technique used mainly by chiropractors to gain diagnostic information through muscle testing and to strengthen muscles to aid in structural correction. Muscles are related to specific organs or systems through the acupuncture meridian network. For information about muscle testing and applied kinesiology, you can explore:

www.kinesiology.net
www.touch4health.com
www.tfhka.org

## Aquatic Bodywork

See Watsu

## Aromatherapy

Aromatherapy involves working with aroma as a healing modality by using pure essential oils, each distilled from a single botanical source. Aromatherapy is often done in conjunction with massage, but not always. The major professional organizations for aromatherapy are:

National Association for
Holistic-Aromatherapy (NAHA)
3327 W. Indian Trail Rd., PMB 144
Spokane, WA 99208
(509) 325-3419   www.naha.org

International Aromatherapy
and Herb Association
3541 W. Acapulco Lane
Phoenix, AZ 85053
www.iaha.org

### Suppliers of essential oils

There are many suppliers of essential oils. The companies listed below have been recommended by practitioners as having a good reputation in the industry and supplying good quality oils:

Amrita Aromatherapy Inc.
1900 W. Stone
Fairfield, IA 52556
(800) 410-9651   www.amrita.net

Elizabeth Van Buren, Inc.
P.O. Box 7542
Santa Cruz, CA 95061
(800) 710-7759 or (831) 425-8218
www.evb-aromatherapy.com

Fragrant Earth
www.fragrant-earth.co.uk

Leydet Aromatics
P.O. Box 2345
Fair Oaks, CA 95628
(916) 965-7546
http://leydet.com

Nature's Gifts Custom Aromatherapy
314 Old Hickory Blvd. East
Madison, TN 37115
(615) 612-4270
www.naturesgift.com

Prima Fleur
1525 E. Francisco Blvd., Ste. 16
San Rafael, CA 94901
(415) 455-0957
www.primafleur.com

Samara Botane
P.O. Box 2483
Snohomish, WA 98291
(800) 782-4532
www.wingedseed.com

Snow Lotus Inc.
2430 Darla Dr.
Santa Rosa, CA 95401
(800) 628-8827
www.snowlotus.org

Time Laboratories
P.O. Box 3243
South Pasadena, CA 91031
(877)-TIMELABS (877-846-3522)
**www.timelabs.com**

Warren Botanicals
73-4689 Kahualani Rd.
Kailua-Kona, HI 96740
(888) 848-0642 or (808) 334-1112
**www.warrenbotanicals.com**

## Selected Aromatherapy trainings

Some massage schools teach aromatherapy as part of their curriculum. In addition, the following schools offer specialized instruction in aromatherapy:

CA: **Pacific Institute of Aromatherapy**
P.O. Box 6723, San Rafael, CA 94903, (415) 479-9120
www.pacificinstituteofaromatherapy.com

FL: **Atlantic Institute of Aromatherapy**
16018 Saddlestring Dr., Tampa, FL 33618, (813) 265-2222
www.atlanticinstitute.com

NY: **The American Institute for Aromatherapy and Herbal Studies**
P.O. Box 299, Eldred, New York 12732
www.aromatherpyinst.com

OR: **Australian College of Herbal Studies**
5940 SW Hood Ave., Portland, OR 97239, 1-800-48-STUDY (1-800-487-8839)
www.achs.edu

WA: **Institute of Dynamic Aromatherapy**
4925 6th Ave. NW, Marysville, WA 98271, (360) 651-9809
www.theida.com

## Asian Bodywork

A number of forms of Asian bodywork are described under separate headings, such as Jin Shin Do, Jin Shin Jyutsu, Qi Gong, Shiatsu, Thai Massage and Tui Na. The major organizations for practitioners of these modalities are:

American Association of
Oriental Medicine
909 22nd St.
Sacramento, CA 95816
(919) 443-4770 or (866) 455-7999
**www.aaom.org**

American Organization for Bodywork
Therapies of Asia
1010 Haddonfield-Berlin Rd., Ste. 408
Voorhees, NJ 08043
(856) 782-1616
**www.aobta.org**

## Aston-Patterning® www.astonenterprises.com

Aston-Patterning aims to increase the body's grace, resiliency and ease of movement by releasing layers of tension throughout the body. It uses movement education, bodywork, environmental design and fitness training. For information about trainings and certification, contact:

**Aston-Patterning**
P.O. Box 3568
Incline Village, NV 89450
(775) 831-8228

## Bindegewebsmassage

Bindegewebsmassage is a type of connective tissue massage originated in Germany. It is an adjunctive therapy in the treatment of organic and musculo-skeletal disorders.

## Bioenergetics   www.bioenergetic-therapy.com

Bioenergetics was created by Alexander Lowen, M.D., an outgrowth of his work with Wilhelm Reich, M.D. Bioenergetics is a way of understanding personality in terms of the body and its energetic processes. Bioenergetics therapy works with the mind and the body to release chronic stresses and chronic muscular tensions.

Dr. Lowen has written 14 books. An excellent introduction to bioenergetics is *Bioenergetics*, available at most bookstores and libraries.

For a brochure listing centers, workshops and books on bioenergetics, contact:

**International Institute for Bioenergetic Analysis**
Stenackestrasse 10, CH - 8902
Urdorf - Zurich, Switzerland  ++41 43 455 9152

## Biokinetics/Hanna Somatics

www.somatics.com
www.somaticsed.com
www.hannasomatics.com

Biokinetics uses a composite of techniques for rehabilitation through neuromuscular retraining. It is designed to release chronic muscular contraction and restore voluntary control of the muscular system. For further information about Biokinetics and training, contact:

**Association for Hanna Somatics**
925 Golden Gate Dr.
Napa, CA 94558
(707) 255-2473

**Novato Institute**
1516 Grant Ave., Ste. 212
Novato, CA 94945
(415) 897-0336

**Workshops: Lawrence Gold**
605 Calle de Valdes
Santa Fe, NM 87505
(505) 699-8284

## Body-Mind (also see Somatics)

"Body-mind" is a term used to acknowledge the intimate connection between the state of the mind and the state of the body. This is an awareness that is present in most forms of massage and bodywork, and many massage schools teach massage from a "body-mind" perspective. However, some forms make it the focus of the work. The programs listed below are designed as advanced programs for massage therapists, and focus on the body-mind connection.

**Body Synergy Institute, Inc.**
305 Bangor Rd.
Bala Cynwyd, PA
(610) 667-3070   www.bodysynergyinstitute.com

Curriculum includes deep tissue bodywork, body reading, using a floor-length mirror as an educational tool, working with postural history and attitudes, and using your body with awareness and ease.

**School for Body-Mind Centering**
189 Pond View Dr.
Amherst, MA 01002
(413) 256-8615   www.bodymindcentering.com

The school, founded by Bonnie Bainbridge Cohen, offers introductory and certification training programs in many locations. The course includes study of the body systems and how they support and initiate movement, as well as movement re-education to correct problems at their root level.

## Body Rolling<sup>SM</sup>

Body Rolling is a system of bodywork developed by Yamuna Zake. It involves rolling on balls to achieve the benefits of massage and stretching.

**Yamuna**
132 Perry Street
New York, NY 10014
(212) 633-2143   www.yamunabodyrolling.com

## Bowen Technique

This technique was developed in Australia by Thomas Bowen. It combines energy work with gentle soft tissue manipulation.  For further information, you can explore:

www.bowtech.com
www.boweninfo.com
www.bowendirectory.com
www.bowen-technique.co.uk

## Breema    www.breema.com

Breema takes its name from the Kurdish mountain village of Breemava where it originated and was passed down from generation to generation. It is a comprehensive system of bodywork, done on the floor, with a variety of techniques ranging from simple holding points on the body to techniques requiring flexibility and dexterity. This work is taught at:

**The Breema Center**
6076 Claremont Ave.
Oakland, CA 94618
(510) 428-0937

## Canadian Deep Muscle Massage

This work was created by Will Green, founder of the International Massage Association (IMA Group) and owner of Georgetown Bodyworks in Washington, DC. It is derived from a system of cross-fiber massage that began in northern Canada in the 1940s. Will added insights gained from the works of Therese Pfrimmer, Joseph Pilates, Ida Rolf, Dr. Samuel West, and Debra Smith.

For more information on Canadian Massage, visit **www.learnmassage.com**.

**Chair Massage** (or on-site or seated massage)

This refers to a brief bodywork session, usually a shiatsu-based routine, done in a special chair in which the client sits facing toward the cushions, exposing the scalp, shoulders, neck, back and hips. Sessions may last between five and thirty minutes.

Originally pioneered as "on-site massage", a modality for the workplace, it has expanded into many other environments. Chair massage is now offered in storefronts, health food stores, airports, airplanes, health fairs, grand openings, sporting events, and other locations. It has therefore come to be called "chair massage" or "seated massage" instead of "on-site."

Because of the relatively low cost of a brief session, it is more affordable than the usual full-body massage. Because it is done fully clothed, it attracts some clients who would be too uncomfortable for table massage. Because it is done in locations where the client is already present, it is more convenient than table massage. For all these reasons, the practice of chair massage has grown so fast that many of the massage table companies report they are selling more on-site chairs than massage tables. The large number of massage schools including chair massage in their curriculum is another indication of the popularity and wide-spread acceptance of this branch of the profession. Instructional videos on chair massage are widely available.

U.S. workshops on chair massage technique and marketing are offered by:

**TouchPro Chair Massage Seminars**
1-800-999-5026   **www.touchpro.org**
Instructors certified and supervised by David Palmer

A Canadian company offers 2-week residential trainings in Ontario:

Relax to the Max
251 Davenport Road
Toronto, Ontario M5R 1J9, CANADA
(416) 962-7441 or (877) 222-5782   **www.chairmassagetraining.com**

**Chi Kung/Chi Gong**

See Qi gong

**Colon Hydrotherapy** (also called colonics or high colonics or colonic irrigation)

A cleansing procedure for the colon, using purified water at controlled temperature and controlled pressure, providing a gentle, deep cleansing of the colon. Practitioners often use massage, reflexology or visceral manipulation skills during a session. Of the 50 states, only Florida licenses colon hydrotherapy. Certification is available through:

**International Association of Colon Hydrotherapy**
P.O. Box 461285
San Antonio, TX 78246
(210) 366-2888   **www.i-act.org**

**Cranio-Sacral Therapy** (also called cranial-sacral)

A technique for finding and correcting cerebral and spinal imbalances or blockages that may cause sensory, motor or intellectual dysfunction. Practitioners work with the subtle articulations of skull sutures, and the flow of cerebro-spinal fluid.

In addition, Cranio-sacral techniques are taught by the following institutions:

**Colorado Cranial Institute**
1080 Hawthorne Ave.
Boulder, CO 80304
(303) 443-6415
**www.cranialinstitute.com**

Craniosacral Therapy Association of North America
**www.craniosacraltherpy.org**
**info@craniosacraltherapy.org**

**The Upledger Institute**
11211 Prosperity Farms Road
Palm Beach Gardens, FL 33410
(561) 622-4334
www.upledger.com
www.craniosacral.com

**Equine Sports Massage**

Massage or other bodywork can adapted to horses for the purpose of enhancing performance and preventing injuries. This field has recently been developed and shows signs of gaining rapidly in popularity, as breeders are interested in any techniques that can give them a competitive edge. The Rolf Institute (see Rolfing, below) also refers rolfers who practice on horses.

According to Jack Meagher, author of *Beating Muscle Injuries for Horses* (available at **www.MyHorseStable.com/product21.html**), an equine sports massage practitioner applies techniques of human massage, especially sports massage, to horses. A pioneer in the fields of sports massage and equine sports massage, Jack Meagher turned to working with horses as a way of proving the value of sports massage techniques for athletes. By using the techniques on horses and achieving demonstrable results, he was able to rebut the contention that results with humans were due to psychological factors.

Equine sports massage is taught at the following locations:

**Don Doran's Equine Sports Massage Program**
9791 NW 160th St.
Reddick, FL 32686
(352) 591-4735
**www.equinesportsmassage.com**

**Equine Massage College**
16007 NCR 7, Wellington, CO 80549
(970) 568-3986
**www.equinemassagecollege.com**

**Equissage School**
P.O. Box 447
Round Hill, VA 20142
(800) 843-0224 or (540) 338-1917
**www.equissage.com**

**Equinology, Inc.**
P.O. Box 1192
Gualala, CA 95445
(707) 884-9963
**www.equinology.com**

**EquiTouch Systems**
Loveland, CO
(800) 483-0577
**www.equitouch.net**

**Integrated Touch Therapy**
P.O. Box 652, Circleville, OH 43113
(800) 251-0007
**www.integratedtouchtherapy.com**

**TT.E.A.M.**<sup>SM</sup> **Training International**
(Tellington-Touch Equine Awareness Method)
P.O. Box 3793
Santa Fe., NM 87501
(800) 854-8326   www.lindatellintonjones.com

## Esalen® massage   www.esalen.org

Esalen is a variant of Swedish massage pioneered at Esalen Institute in Big Sur, California. Esalen is the place where many therapies were tested or launched in the '60s and '70s, including gestalt therapy and Rolfing. The unique brand of massage practiced there typically involves total nudity and long flowing stokes. Esalen is known for its original, honest, nurturing and probing atmosphere. Esalen massage tends to be nurturing, trance-like and meditative, allowing the greatest possible unfoldment to take place in the client. For information contact:

**Esalen Institute**
55000 Hwy. 1
Big Sur, CA 93920
(831) 667-3005

## Feldenkrais®

Moshe Feldenkrais was an Israeli physicist who began developing this system in mid-life. Feldenkrais work emphasizes having a coherent body image and thinking a movement through. It also uses micro-movements for neuromuscular re-education. The system is most effective for pain relief, and also promotes grace and ease of movement. For further information contact:

**The Feldenkrais Guild of North America**
3611 SW Hood Ave., Ste. 100
Portland, OR 97201
(866) 333-6248   www.feldendrais.com

For information on trainings, refer to:

www.feldenkraisinstitute.org
www.feldenkrais-resources.com

## Geriatric Massage

Working with the elderly and the ill, often in a long-term care setting. A therapist doing geriatric massage should understand the physical and psychological characteristics of aging, and should also be familiar with the diseases that commonly afflict the elderly.

For more information on geriatric massage, contact:

**Daybreak Geriatric Massage Project**
(954) 578-5055   www.daybreak-massage.com

## Hakomi bodywork

Hakomi bodywork regards body, mind and spirit as one, and blends bodywork and psychotherapy into a simultaneous process. The work serves to lead a person to an awareness of limitations in his physical and psychological patterns, bringing the possibility of new openness and freedom.

> www.hakomi.com
> www.hakomiinstitute.com
> www.ronkurtz.com

## Healing Touch   www.healingtouch.net

Healing touch is an energy-based, hands-on technique done to balance and align the human energy field. The technique is approved by the American Holistic Nurses Association. Information about the technique, trainings, and organization membership can be obtained from:

> **Healing Touch International, Inc.**
> 445 Union Blvd., Ste. 105
> Lakewood, Colorado 80228
> (303) 989-7982

## Hellerwork®   www.hellerwork.com

Hellerwork is an outgrowth of Rolfing (see below), created by Joseph Heller. It integrates movement and verbal communication with connective tissue work. Information about Hellerwork can be obtained from:

> **Hellerwork, Inc.**
> info@hellerwork.com
> (800) 392-3900

## Horse Massage

See Equine Sports Massage

## Hot Stone Massage

Heated Stones are placed on the body in conjunction with Swedish massage to achieve a very effective relaxation massage. This modality, introduced to the massage world around 2002, has become tremendously popular in spas and salons. In 2005, searches on Google.com and Yahoo.com found 138,000 and 282,000 results, respectively, for "hot stone massage". Workshops are taught in many massage schools, and stand-alone trainings and videos are also available.

## Hydrotherapy

See Spa Treatments

## Infant Massage

Infant massage instructors teach parents the art of infant massage. Trainings are offered to certify people as infant massage instructors. For information, contact:

> **International Association of**
> **Infant Massage**
> 1891 Goodyear Ave., Ste. 622
> Ventura, CA 93003
> (805) 644-8524   www.iaim-us.com

> **International Loving Touch**
> **Foundation, Inc.**
> 4133 SE Divisions St.
> Portland, OR 97202
> (503) 253-8482   www.lovingtouch.com

Also offering information and contacts:

www.infantmassage.com
www.lastingi.com

## Jin Shin Do®

Jin Shin Do is a synthesis of acupressure theory, psychology, Taoist philosophy, and breathing methods, which helps release physical and emotional tensions and armoring. The Jin Shin Do Foundation has information about trainings and practitioners, as well as books, charts, videos and audiotapes.

**Jin Shin Do Foundation for Bodymind Acupressure**
P.O. Box 416, Idyllwild, CA 92549
(951) 659-5707   **www.jinshindo.org**
(for Canadian trainings visit **www.jinshindo.com**)

## Jin Shin Jyutsu®   www.jinshinjyutsu.com

This is an ancient art promoting harmony of life energy and the body. It was revived and systematized in the early 1900s by Master Jiro Murai. It was brought to the US in the 1950s by Mary Burmeister. It is an energy technique done with a light touch, and is often used as a self-treatment. For further information contact:

**Jin Shin Jyutsu, Inc.**
8719 E. San Alberto
Scottsdale, AZ 85258
(480) 998-9331

## Lomilomi

The traditional massage of Hawaii, it is taught at massage schools in Hawaii and some schools on the mainland. The Hawaiian Lomilomi Association maintains a directory of practitioners and teachers and links to informational websites about lomilomi.

Hawaiian Lomilomi Association
P.O. Box 2507
Kealakekua, HI 96750
(808) 322-3767   **www.lomilomi.org**

## Lymphatic drainage (manual lymphatic drainage^SM or MLD®)

The lymphatic system is a vital part of the immune system in the body. Lymphatic drainage massage assists the operation of the lymphatic system. The system was devised in the 1930s by a Danish massage therapist, Dr. Emil Vodder, and is popular and well established as a health modality in Germany and Austria.

## Medical Massage (clinical massage)

Working with injuries, pathologies and rehabilitation; working by physician's prescription. A program of instruction in medical massage is very desirable for a therapist interested in working in the health care system and obtaining insurance reimbursement for massage services. See chapter 21 for further information.

Founded in 1999, the American Manual Medicine Association is designed for the advancement of medical massage as a specialization within the practice of massage. In 2005, the Association adopted minimum standards for medical massage certification consisting of 600 hours of education with a specified curriculum, with a stated goal of an increased amount of required training in the future. The association has hired a lobbying firm to support the creation of medical massage regulation by state governments

As of 2005, the AMMA had selected three "model" schools: Blue Heron Academy, Grand Rapids, Michigan; Galen Institute, Wethersfield, Connecticut; and American Institute of Clinical Massage, Ltd., Post Falls, Idaho. On its website, the Association also maintains a list of approved CEU providers.

> **American Manual Medicine Association**
> 1845 Lakeshore Dr.,, Ste. 7
> Muskegon, MI 49441
> (888) 375-7245   www.americanmedicalmassage.com

## Myofascial Release

Myofascial release (MFR) is a technique for working with fascia as a means of achieving pain relief, restoring function and reducing stress. The system is taught in a series of seminars in various locations. It is designed to be used by massage therapists and physical therapists. For information about trainings contact:

> **John F. Barnes' MFR Seminars**
> (800) 327-2425   www.myofascialrelease.com

## Myopractic®   www.myopractic.com

This is a system of posture balancing and deep relaxation developed and taught by Robert Petteway. The three basic techniques are 1. releasing tension and holding patterns; 2. clearing scar tissue, trigger points and other obstructions in soft tissue; and 3. separating to release myofascial adhesions and balance muscles. The practitioner does deep muscle therapy while keeping her own body and hands relaxed, and the system relieves chronic pain and postural imbalances. Trainings are offered through:

> **The Myopractic Institute**
> Huntsville, Texas
> (936) 295-7799 or (888) 696-9898

## Myotherapy^SM

See Trigger Point Therapies

## Neuromuscular Therapy

See Trigger Point Therapies

## Oncology Massage

Comfort-oriented touch for cancer patients. Resources for studying this work include:

**www.medicinehands.com**, coordinated by Gayle Mac Donald, author of *Medicine Hands and Massage for the Hospital Patient and the Medically Frail Client*, beginning and advanced workshops are offered in various locations, including the Scherer Institute in Santa Fe, New Mexico (**www.shcererinstitute.com**)

Hospital Based Oncology Massage Training (40 credit hours) taught at Phillips School of Massage, Nevada City, California (**www.handsinharmony.com**)

Tracy Walton, (**www.tracywalton.com**), author of upcoming text *Caring for Clients With Cancer* and creator of a 24-hour workshop of the same name, offered at massage schools and other locations nationally.

**Memorial Sloan Kettering Hospital**
New York, NY
(212) 639-8629

**Cheryl Chapman**
touch2rn@aol.com

## On-Site Massage

See Chair Massage

## Ortho-Bionomy™

This system seeks to remind the body of its ability to find balance. The work involves positioning the client, working with points of tension in the body, and using movement. Results can include relieving pain, promoting emotional release, and improving structural alignment. For information, contact:

**Society of
Ortho-Bionomy International**
5335 N. Tacoma St., Ste. 21G
Indianapolis, IN 46220
(800) 809-3747 or (317) 536-0064
www.ortho-bionomy.org

**New Mexico Academy of Healing Arts**
(888) 808-5188 or (505) 982-6271
www.nmhealingarts.org

**AKS Massage School (Virginia)**
(877) 306-3422 or (703) 464-0333
www.aksmassageschool.com

**Maui Center for Ortho-Bionomy**
(808) 242-9162
www.zoee.biz

## Orthopedic Massage   www.omeri.com

This term is used by Whitney W. Lowe and Benny Vaughn to describe their work. Ten modalities are combined to create a comprehensive approach to the treatment of soft-tissue pain and injury conditions. The work shares some elements of sports massage and some elements of medical massage. The Institute offers a 100-hour certification program several times each year at various locations, and also publishes a newsletter "Orthopedic & Sports Massage Reviews". For further information, contact:

**Orthopedic Massage Education & Research Institute**
P.O. Box 1119
Sisters, OR 97759
(541) 549-2700 or (888) 340-1614

## Pfrimmer Deep Muscle Therapy® www.pfrimmer.com

Pfrimmer Deep Muscle Therapy is a system of corrective treatment to aid in the restoration of damaged muscles and soft tissue. It is intended to be used as one aspect of treatment for a wide range of muscular and soft-tissue conditions.

For more information, contact **Therese C. Pfrimmer International Association of Deep Muscle Therapists, (800) 484-7773**, or one of the two following Pfrimmer Institutes:

**Pfrimmer Institute of Indiana, Inc.**
809 South Harrison St., P.O. Box 287
Alexandria, IN 46001
(765) 724-9152 or (800) 622-8756
www.assti.com

**Pfrimmer Institute for Corrective Muscle Therapy**
1173 Egypt Road, P.O. Box 400
Oaks, PA 14456
(888) 355-2698   www.piforcmt.com

## Polarity www.PolarityTherapy.org

Developed by Dr. Randolph Stone, polarity focuses on the energy currents that exist in all life. The polarity therapist uses her hands as conductors of energy. The intention is to balance the electromagnetic energy in the body, toward the ultimate goal of uniting the body, emotions, mind and soul.

Polarity is commonly taught in massage schools, but programs also exist to teach polarity that have no connection to massage schools. Although many massage schools offer an introduction to polarity as part of their training, few offer a substantial amount of training.

The American Polarity Therapy Association (APTA) is a non-profit organization that distributes educational material, registers practitioners, hosts educational conferences and publishes a regular newsletter. The APTA also certifies schools as meeting their educational standards, and keeps a list of certified schools at **www.polaritytherapy.org**. For further information contact:

**American Polarity Therapy Association**
P.O. Box 19858
Boulder, CO 80308
(303) 545-2080

## Postural Integration

See Structural Integration

## Pregnancy Massage (or prenatal massage)

This is an adaptation of Swedish massage for the needs of pregnant women. It is sometimes called prenatal or perinatal massage, or massage for the child-bearing year. For further information, you can explore:

www.massagedoula.com
www.bodytherapyassociates.com

## Qi Gong (or Chi Kung)

This may be the most commonly practiced modality in the world. It is routinely used in Chinese hospitals as a healing modality. It involves a system of exercises designed to induce a state of mindfulness that can be used to generate Qi (or chi)—life energy. The name literally means "skill with life energy" and it evolved over two thousand years ago in Tibet and China.

Qi gong is related to Tui Na (below).

For further information, you can explore the following websites:

> **www.nqa.org** (National Qi gong association)
> **www.qi.org**
> **www.chilel-qigong.com**
> **www.qigonginstitute.org**

## Radiance Technique   www.authenticreiki.org

The Radiance Technique was formerly called The Official Reiki Program. For further information, contact:

> **The Radiance Technique International Assn.**
> P.O. Box 40570
> St. Petersburg Fl 33743
> (727) 347-2106   **www.trtia.org**

## Reflexology

> **www.reflexology.org**
> **www.reflexolgy-usa.org**

Reflexology is a system of massaging the feet, or feet and hands, with the intention of affecting other parts of the body. The feet and hands are regarded much like maps of the body, with points on the feet and hands corresponding to organs and tissues in the body. It is thought that sensitivity or tenderness in the feet or hands indicates imbalances in the corresponding body part, and by working with the point on the foot or hand, beneficial results can be achieved in the corresponding body part.

While many reflexologists spend an entire therapy session working only on the hands and feet (and sometimes ears), some spend approximately half of their time on the feet, and half on Swedish massage. Reflexology is taught at more US massage schools than any other form of bodywork.

Independent certification in reflexology is offered by:

> **American Reflexology Certification Board (ARCB)**
> P.O. Box 740879
> Arvada, CO 80006
> (303) 933-6921   **www.ARCB.net**

## Reiki   www.reiki.org

Reiki is an energy process for restoring and balancing life energy and promoting healing and personal transformation. The approach is thousands of years old, and was systematized in the 1800s by Dr. Mikao Usui. The practitioner attunes to and transmits reiki energy. Further information can be obtained from:

**International Association
of Reiki Professionals**
P.O. Box 6182, Nashua, NH 03063
(603) 881-8838   **www.IARP.org**

**The Reiki Alliance**
204 N. Chestnut. St., Kellogg, ID 83837
(208) 783-3535   **www.reikialliance.org**

**Reiki Council**
799 Roosevelt Rd., Bldg. 6, Ste. 321
Glen Elyn, IL 60137
(630) 926-5891   **www.reikicouncil.com**

## Rolfing®   www.rolf.org

Ida Rolf was the first to create, practice and teach a system of bodywork aimed toward working with the connective tissue of the body to achieve structural changes in the client. She originally called her system Structural Integration, but it came to be called Rolfing and is taught by:

**The Rolf Institute**
5055 Chaparral Ct., Ste. 103
Boulder, CO 80301
(800) 530-8875 or (303) 449-5903

## Rosen Method Bodywork®

**www.rosenmethod.org**
**www.rosenmethod.com**

Developed by Marion Rosen, this work emphasizes simplicity. The practitioner contacts contracted muscles and matches the muscle tension. The practitioner follows changes in the client's breathing as a means of guiding the client's inner process. The work can bring up buried feelings and memories, and can be a tool for pain relief and personal growth.

Below are the current contacts for Rosen Method Bodywork. They can give you information about trainings and practitioners in their areas:

| | |
|---|---|
| California: | **The Berkeley Center**<br>(510) 845-6606 |
| Florida: | **Rosen Center Florida**<br>(941) 541-0558 |
| Minnesota: | **Rosen Method Minnesota**<br>www.rosenmethodmn.org |
| New Mexico: | **Rosen Method Center Southwest**<br>(505) 982-7149 |
| New York: | **Rosen Method New York**<br>(860) 859-0574 |
| North Carolina: | **Rosen Method Bodywork Carolina Center**<br>(510) 525-3805 |

## Rubenfeld Synergy™   www.rubenfeldsynergy.com

This method integrates elements of Alexander, Feldenkrais, gestalt and hypno-therapy into a body-mind therapy that helps clients contact and release energy blocks, tensions and imbalances. Rather than treating illnesses, the practitioner treats the psychophysical problems people carry with them. By dealing with the emotional body, the practitioner can often abate physical symptoms. For information, contact:

**National Association of Rubenfeld Synergists**
7 Kendall Road, Kendall Park, NJ 08824
(877) RSM-2468 code 8516

## Seated Massage

See Chair Massage

## Shiatsu or acupressure

Shiatsu is a Japanese bodywork which uses pressure to points on acupuncture meridians. Practice of shiatsu is usually accompanied by study of Chinese five-element theory and meridians, and it involves a way of looking at the body that is completely different from the "muscles, bones and blood" view of Western science, focusing instead on the flow of life energy through meridians.

The name "Acupressure" is sometimes used to mean shiatsu, and is sometimes used to describe a finger-pressure technique similar to shiatsu but not identical.

## Somatics (Somatics Psychology or Somatic Therapy)    www.somatics.com

"Somatic" literally means "of or pertaining to the body." In the context of Somatics Psychology, it refers to the mind-body connection and makes use of techniques to bring awareness of the mind and the body to each other. It is therefore related to the form "Body-Mind" which is described above. For further information, you may wish to obtain "Somatics Magazine":

**Somatics Magazine and Novato Institute**
1516 Grant Ave., Ste. 212
Novato, CA 94945
(415) 892-0617   www.somaticsed.com

**United States Association for Body Psychotherapy (USABP)**
7831 Woodmont Ave., Ste. 294
Bethesda, Maryland 20814
(202) 466-1619   www.usabp.org

## Spa Treatments

Spa, or Health Spa, refers to an establishment that provides rejuvenating treatments in a residential setting (or non-residential at a day spa). Often at a resort and often luxurious in setting, spas aim for relaxation, therapeutic treatments, and beautification treatments. Modalities such as herbal wraps, seaweed wraps, mud baths, loofa scrubs and salt glows are designed to detoxify and refresh the system.

Related to spa treatments is Hydrotherapy, meaning "water therapy." It includes treatments like contrast baths (alternating hot and cold water), and wet sheet wraps. Hydrotherapy is a required course for massage licensure in Texas and Florida.

## Sports Massage

Sports massage is an adaptation of Swedish massage. Its purpose is to prepare athletes for sporting activity and help them recover from the exertion of sporting activity.

Sports massage trainings vary widely in length, and there is no standard training length, although the American Massage Therapy Association and the United States Sports Massage Federation both have standards for approving trainings.

**U.S. Sports Massage Federation**
2156 Newport Blvd.
Costa Mesa, CA 92627
(949) 642-0735

## Structural Integration (or Postural Integration)

This is a generic term for therapies that are related to Rolfing, in that they aim to improve the structure or posture of the client. See also Hellerwork.

The Guild For Structural Integration can be contacted at:

P.O. Box 1559, Boulder, CO 80306
(303) 447-0122 or (800) 447-0150
**www.rolfguild.org**

## Thai Massage

The traditional massage of Thailand includes passive stretching as well as stroking. Information and a state-by-state trainings directory are available from:

**International Thai Therapists Association, Inc.**
P.O. Box 1048, Palm Springs, CA 92263
(760) 6410756
**www.thaimassage.com**

Following is a sampling of trainings in Thai Massage:

Florida and New Jersey, **The Institute of Thai Massage**   www.thai-massage.org

Illinois   **www.thaibodywork.com**

Northern California, **Spirit Winds School of Thai Massage**   www.spiritwinds.net

San Rafael, CA, **The Center for Thai Massage**   www.thaimassagecenter.com

Hawaii, **Valerie Passion Flower**   www.thaimassagetherapy.com

Kathmandu, **The Healing Hands Center**   www.ancientmassage.com

## Therapeutic Touch (TT)

TT is a means of attuning to and directing the universal life energy. The goal is to release congestion and balance areas where the flow of life energy has become disordered. Removal of these blockages facilitates the person's intrinsic healing powers.

TT is most commonly taught to, and used by nurses. However, some massage therapists study TT and incorporate it into their work.

Several books are available on TT, including *Therapeutic Touch: A Practical Guide* by J. Macrae, Knopf, 1988; *The Therapeutic Touch* by D. Krieger, Prentice-Hall 1979; *Therapeutic Touch* by Borelli and Heidt, Springer Co., 1981.

The Nurse-Healers Association maintains a website that has useful information about TT, at:

> www.therapeutic-touch.org

## Touch For Health (see also Applied Kinesiology)

This is a system for using applied kinesiology to aid the bodyworker. Applied kinesiology makes use of the fact that certain conditions result in weakening of specific muscles. Through muscle testing, the bodyworker gains information about the specifics of the client's condition. Further information is available from:

> Touch For Health® Kinesiology Association
> PO Box 392
> New Carlisle, Oh 45344-0392
> (800) 466-8342 or (937) 845-3404   **www.tfhka.org**

## Trager®   www.trager.com

Dr. Milton Trager, M.D., had a gift for bodywork from a young age, and developed his own system of bodywork which emphasizes gentle rocking of the client, and rolling body parts to encourage release and loosening and softening.

Some massage schools offer brief introductory trainings in Trager bodywork, giving the massage therapist a glimpse into the system. Massage therapists with introductory training often integrate a bit of the Trager awareness into their massage work. However, Trager practitioners practice only Trager, at least during a Trager session. Information about becoming a Trager practitioner can be obtained from:

> Trager Association
> 13801 W. Center St., Ste. C; P.O. Box 1009
> Burton, OH 44021
> (440) 834-0308   **www.trager-us.org**

## Trigger Point Therapies (Myotherapy℠ or neuromuscular therapy)

This refers to any of several systems of working with trigger points. Trigger points are tender congested spots in muscle tissue, which may radiate pain to other areas. Significant relief results when the trigger point is treated.

The techniques used in trigger point therapies are similar to those used in Shiatsu or acupressure, but trigger point therapies are based on western anatomy and physiology. Many schools listed in the State-by-State directory offer training in trigger-point therapies. Several institutions have refined the art of trigger point therapy into a self-contained modality, and teach their therapy in a non-massage context. These schools are:

**Bonnie Prudden™ School of Physical
Fitness and Myotherapy**
P.O. Box 65240
Tucson, AZ 85728
(520) 529-3979 or (800) 221-4634
**www.bonnieprudden.com**

**The Academy For Myofascial Trigger
Point Therapy**
1312 East Carson St.
Pittsburgh, PA 15203
(412) 481-2553

**Neuromuscular Therapy Center**
900 14th Ave N.
St. Petersburg, FL 33705
(727) 821-7167
**www.nmtcenter.com**

**St. John Neuromuscular Therapy Seminars**
6565 Park Blvd.
Pinellas Park, FL 33781
1-888-NMT-HEAL(668-4325)
**www.stjohnnmtseminars.com**

## Tui Na

Tui Na is an Oriental bodywork related to Qi Gong. It is sometimes called Chinese
medical massage.

## Watsu™ (aquatic shiatsu)

Watsu (from "water" and "shiatsu") began when Harold Dull started floating people, applying the moves and stretches of the zen shiatsu he had studied in Japan.
Physical and emotional blocks are removed by the work, which can be done even
by small individuals since the client's body in water is buoyant. It is done in chest-
high, 94-degree water.

    Certification and information about classes in the United States and worldwide
can be obtained from the new Watsu Center at Harbin Hot Springs. Contact (707)
987-3801 or (800) 693-3296 or visit **www.waba.edu.**

## Yoga therapy

In this method, yoga asanas are used to facilitate healing. For further information,
explore:

    www.yogatherapy.org
    www.iytyogatherapy.com
    www.pryt.com
    www.yogatherapycenter.org

## Zero-Balancing

Developed by Fritz Smith, MD, osteopath, Rolfer and acupuncturist, zero balancing works with the relationship between a person's physical structure and their
energy. The practitioner works with fulcrums, points where structure and energy
can be accessed together, to bring about change.

    For fuller information about zero-balancing, trainings or practitioners,
contact:

**The Zero Balancing Health Association**
8640 Guildord Rd., Columbia, MD 21046
(410) 381-8956
www.zerobalancing.com

# VII

## Finding and Choosing a Massage School

# Finding a School

In the first four editions of this book, I published a state-by-state directory of United States massage schools. This fifth edition is the first to omit that directory. The reason for this change can be summed up in two words: The Internet.

The first edition of this book was published in 1992. It may be hard to imagine, especially if you are under 30 years old, but there was no Internet or email then. In order to create the initial directory of massage schools, I had to subscribe to massage and yoga magazines, clip ads for massage schools, and write to all 50 state governments to obtain lists of schools maintained by government agencies. Once I compiled a master list, I had to contact each school individually by mail or phone to request a catalogue. I extracted information from the catalogues to create each school's listings, and mailed or faxed a copy to the school for proofreading.

The task of creating the state-by-state directory became easier as the years passed, and more and more schools created an electronic presence on the web. Google was invented by the time I researched the fourth edition, which further simplified the task. However, creating a comprehensive directory of massage schools was still a tremendous undertaking, as by that time there were over 800 massage schools in the U.S.

Now there are over 1,000 massage schools, but searching for a school on the Internet has become so simple that it no longer makes sense to spend the time, energy, and paper resources to print a directory of massage schools.

In locating massage schools, your first stop should be NaturalHealers.com. That site maintains a searchable index of massage schools, organized by state. Their "featured schools" appear first, but you can click on "show all schools" to obtain a list of all the massage schools in a given state or states.

Other excellent lists of massage schools are maintained at AboutMassage. com, Massagetherapy.com and MassageRegister.com. In addition, searchable lists of massage schools can be fond at **www.365fitness.com, www.amtamassage.org, www.holisticjunction.com**, and **www.massagecolleges.com**.

If you consult several of these sites, you are sure to find all the schools in a given location, often with clickable links to the respective schools' websites. You can then narrow your search to a short list of schools that you will want to investigate personally.

If your search is not geographically based, but based instead on a preference for a type of massage, or a special emphasis of a massage program, it will be a bit more complicated. You will need to visit individual school websites to investigate their compatibility with your specific goals and interests. However, doing a Google search for "massage" plus the key words for your area of interest should provide you with a good starting point for your research.

# About Financial Aid

Federal funds become available to a school once it is accredited (or provisionally accredited) by an accrediting agencies recognized by the Secretary of Education.

Seven recognized accrediting agencies provide accreditation for massage schools. Six of the seven maintain websites with searchable databases making it easy to learn which schools are accredited by which agency. Once you locate a school (or schools) of interest by use of the eight websites listed above (or others you may find on your own), you can then check with the accrediting agencies to find out if the schools are accredited. If the answer is yes, you may be eligible for federal financial aid for massage school.

The agencies, along with the number of massage programs they accredited as of 2005, appear below:

ABHES (Accrediting Bureau of Health Education Schools)—72 schools
(703) 917-9503
**www.abhes.org**

ACCSCT (Accrediting Commission for Career Schools and Colleges of Technology)—181 schools
(703) 247-4212
**www.accsct.org**

ACCET (Accrediting Council for Continuing Education and Training)—24 schools
(202) 955-1113
**www.accet.org**

ACICS (Accrediting Council of Independent Colleges and Schools)—12 schools
(202) 336-6780
**www.acics.org**

COMTA (Commission on Massage Therapy Accreditation)—73 schools
(847-869-5039
**www.comta.org**

NACCS (National Accrediting Commission of Cosmetology Arts & Sciences)—67 schools
(703) 600-9503
**www.naccas.org**

Council on Occupational Education
(770) 396-3898
**www.council.org**

## Choosing a School

If you plan to work in a state that regulates massage, you should choose a program that meets the requirements for licensure in that state, typically an in-state massage school. If you plan to work in an unregulated state, you can choose any school.

The primary issues to consider in choosing a school are:

- cost
- quality of education
- emphasis of the curriculum
- atmosphere at the school

Cost—The school should not make it difficult to find out what their cost is. Find out whether there are extra charges added to the stated tuition. For example, are books included or are they extra? Are there lab fees? Are you required to purchase uniforms or professional massages from instructors? What is the school's policy concerning refunds?

If cost is an overriding factor for you, investigate whether there are any community colleges in your area that have massage programs. These will almost always be less costly than a privately owned and operated school. However, you may find a trade-off in having reduced personal attention and a narrower focus of the curriculum.

Quality of Education—What is the background of the instructors? Are they experienced, successful practitioners? Do they have experience as teachers? Is the facility well-equipped, spacious enough, and operated in an organized way? An increasing number of schools now offer an Associate's Degree in massage. Does this appeal to you?

Emphasis of the Curriculum—Some schools emphasize pathology and medical massage. Some emphasize career development and employability. Some emphasize relaxation massage or a more transformative approach to bodywork. Some lean toward oriental therapies, some toward sports massage, some toward rehabilitative skills. Some schools have a spiritual emphasis. You may find a blend of any of these at a given school. At this point, you may not know which emphasis you would prefer, but being aware of the differences will help you sort out your thoughts and feelings as you go about choosing a school.

Atmosphere at the School—This is a personal matter. Try to spend time at the school so you get the feeling of the place. You should be comfortable there. You are going to be asked to learn a new skill, give and receive massages, partially or completely disrobe, and go through a number of new experiences. Start from the position of feeling good about the place based on your personal experience there. Keep in mind that massage has a psycho-emotional effect, and massage students frequently experience emotional changes during their training. Is this a place that you think would be safe and supportive if that were going on?

Some suggestions for your process of choosing a school:

- Take a short workshop at 2 or 3 schools you are serious about

- Be wary of a school that puts pressure on you to sign up right away. It takes time to reach a decision about choosing a school.

- Get a referral from a massage practitioner or a friend.

- Check out whether the school is affiliated with an association, such as AMTA or ABMP. If so, are the politics and intentions toward the massage profession congruent with your own?

- Don't be afraid to meet with and interview instructors and administrative staff—as you get to know people at the school, your impression of the place will become clearer and more accurate.

- Does the program include instruction in how to start your own business, ethics, and "real world" issues. Some programs do, some do not.

- Does the school promote itself by talking disparagingly about other schools?

- During the interview process, is there a discussion of the psycho-emotional issues that may come up for you as you give and receive massages during your training? Do they seem supportive in this regard?

- Do they have a job placement program? If so, how is it run? How active is it? How successful is it?

There is a wide spectrum of massage schools to choose from, and a wide spectrum of types of practice. The best school for you is one that you will enjoy, where you will respect the teachers and other students, and receive a solid foundation in manual techniques, anatomy, and business practices.

The time you spend searching out the best school for you will pay dividends for years to come, so give this project the time and attention it deserves, and have a great time.

# Index